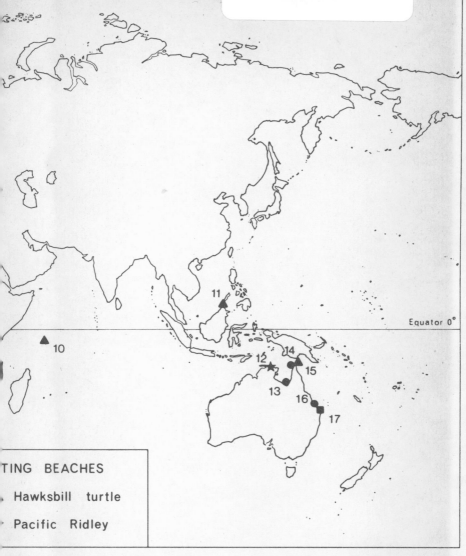

Equator 0°

TING BEACHES

Hawksbill turtle

Pacific Ridley

AL	13. BOUNTIFUL ISLAND	16. FACING & CURTIS ISLANDS,
CHELLES	14. CRAB ISLAND	NEAR GLADSTONE
	15. EASTERN TORRES	17. BUNDABERG &
	STRAIT	CAPRICORN–BUNKER CAYS

SEA TURTLES

Robert Bustard

SEA TURTLES

*

NATURAL HISTORY AND CONSERVATION

TAPLINGER PUBLISHING COMPANY
NEW YORK

First published in the United States in 1973 by
TAPLINGER PUBLISHING CO., INC.
New York, New York

Copyright © 1972 by Robert Bustard
All rights reserved.
Printed in Great Britain

Library of Congress Catalog Card Number: 72-2197

ISBN 0-8008-7018-2

Preface

Sir William Collins visited our turtle research headquarters on Heron Island in February 1967 to see nesting turtles. He was fascinated by the turtles and our work with them and suggested that I write a book on the subject. The account which follows has developed from this idea.

Our Queensland work has had a most important conservation impact. In July 1968, following our advice, the Government of Queensland passed legislation protecting all species of sea turtle and their eggs throughout the whole of the State. The purpose of this book is to give an account of sea turtles, current research on them, and to highlight the conservation problems of sea turtles world-wide. I thought that our approach and success in Queensland, together with our plans for the future, would reach a much wider audience in book form than is ever possible in scientific papers. A book on sea turtles might, therefore, provide much needed impetus for their conservation.

I am indebted to many people who helped me in my researches on sea turtles, and without whose help this book would never have been attempted. I am particularly indebted to Dr Alan Weatherley and Dr W. L. Nicholas of the Australian National University, who enabled me to initiate the long-term research programme in 1964, and to Dr R. D. Hughes, at that time a member of the Zoology Department staff, for his help, advice and interest throughout the work. In Queensland I owe an outstanding debt to Mr O. L. Tanis of Green-slopes, Brisbane. Without help and advice from Les Tanis over the years I doubt if the programme would have been continued. Quite apart from this I am most grateful to Les and Dorothy Tanis for rearing so many baby turtles as part of our programme, and for hospitality, Queensland style, on countless occasions.

During six seasons field work, many assistants, too numerous to name individually, have contributed to the programme by collecting routine data or carrying out experiments. However, I would like to single out Peter Greenham for special thanks.

On Heron Island I am grateful to Mr. Robert Poulson, until recently Manager of Heron Island Pty. Ltd. Under his management the resort co-operated closely with us and in addition made an annual grant towards the costs of our growth studies. The departure of Bob Poulson from Heron has been a real loss.

At the start of the work, the green turtle was entirely protected

PREFACE

south of 17°S. Annual permits to carry out this work have been
provided by the Queenland Government, and I am grateful to Mr G.
T. T. Harrison, Chief Inspector of Fisheries, and Mr E. Grant,
Senior Fisheries Biologist, for their help and understanding.

I am indebted to Mr Herbert H. Mills, Executive Director of the
United States National Appeal of the World Wildlife Fund, for his
interest in the work, and the U.S. National Appeal for supporting
the sea turtle resources study in Queensland, and to the Fauna Preserva-
tion Society of London for supporting an investigation into the status
of sea turtles in Fiji.

Virtually all the photographs in this book are my own. However,
several were kindly made available to me by Mr Colin Limpus and
Dr Peter Pritchard, and these are credited to them in each instance.
I am most grateful to Mr Barry Parr, Photographer at the Research
School of Biological Sciences, under whose guidance all the prints
for the book have been prepared, often from my original kodachromes.
I am indebted to Mrs Joan Goodrun for preparing the figures.

In the distribution maps I have given only the most important
rookeries for each species in an attempt to highlight key nesting areas.
I am indebted to Professor Archie Carr and Dr Peter Pritchard for
information concerning nesting by the loggerhead, Pacific ridley and
hawkesbill in the Americas. Clearly one has to draw a line somewhere
and make an arbitrary decision whether or not to list certain rookeries.
I appreciate that differences of opinion are bound to occur about this
and accept full responsibility myself for the maps as published.

I am grateful to Mr Les Tanis and Mr John Harris for most kindly
reading the whole text to reduce stylistic errors and ambiguities. I
am greatly indebted to Professor L. D. Brongersma for scientific
criticism of the book in manuscript.

The work on which this book is based was initiated while I was in
the Zoology Department, Australian National University. It was
continued while I was a Queen Elizabeth II Fellow of the Commonwealth of Australia. I am grateful for the Commonwealth Government
for their support during two key years of the programme. The basic
Heron Island work has continued, albeit on a smaller scale, since I
joined the Research School of Biological Sciences in 1968. The University has provided considerable financial and logistic support for the
programme over the years, although the work could never have been
carried through without outside support.

H. Robert Bustard

AUSTRALIAN NATIONAL UNIVERSITY
Canberra, A.C.T.

Contents

Diagrams and Drawings

Photographs

Introduction

Turtles have always fascinated people, partly because of the enormous size attained, partly because of their appearance – they are literally enclosed by a box or armoured shell – but mainly, I suspect, because they are living dinosaurs. Turtles such as *Archelon*, which reached a length of eleven feet, swam in Cretaceous seas 90 million years ago where they were contemporaries of the mosasaurs (giant marine lizards, reaching a length of up to forty feet), while other gigantic dinosaurs stalked the land. *Archelon* had already disposed of the heavy armour of its land-dwelling ancestors and appeared little different from the turtles that we see to-day. It is this direct link with the distant past – the Age of Reptiles – which makes turtles of extreme interest for scientist and layman alike.

Information on sea turtles is widely scattered through the scientific, anthropological and travel literature. Very little has been written in book form. James Parsons published a fascinating account entitled, 'The Green Turtle and Man' in 1962 and Professor Archie Carr wrote 'So excellent a fishe', published in 1967. These are the only books on sea turtles. Parsons' book, as indicated by the title, is restricted to certain aspects of one turtle species, and Carr's book is basically an account of his own turtle research based on Costa Rica, although he included a stimulating chapter 'Sea turtles and the future'. In my account I have tried to broaden the scope, firstly by including all seven species, and, more important, by considering the situation on a world basis. Naturally I have written from my own experience as far as possible, hence our work on the Great Barrier Reef plays a central part in the book. Since little has been published about our programme it remains little known either inside or outside Australia except to a few specialists. For this reason, and because Queensland is guardian of some of the world's most important remaining sea turtle populations, I consider this Australian bias desirable.

The main theme of the book is given in the sub-title 'Natural history and Conservation' and has world-wide relevance. I have tried to provide an account of the world's seven species of sea turtle, their present and future status, and what can be done to ensure that these enormous, shy, and completely harmless relics of a bygone age, are allowed to survive in a world dominated by a single species – man.

The book is divided into four parts. Part I provides background information about turtles so that the reader can place them in proper perspective. Part II – 'The lives of Turtles' – is an account of their behaviour and biology. Part III – 'Turtle Research' – gives an up-to-date account of some of the research being carried out on turtles. Part IV – 'Turtles and Man' – deals with conservation problems for turtles. Part IV contains a section on turtle farming since large-scale farming, in which the crop is produced from eggs laid in the farm by a captive breeding stock, could be a powerful tool in turtle conservation. When farms can meet the demand for raw turtle products the intense pressure on wild populations, which is responsible for their rapid and accelerating decline in numbers almost everywhere, will be greatly reduced.

'Turtles' contains very many unpublished observations of my own. I dislike the practice of continually interrupting the text by writing 'personal observations' or 'unpublished data' in such instances in order to attribute the statements to oneself. Wherever information is not attributed to a published source the reader can be certain that this is original information based on my own research.

PART ONE

The Turtle

TURTLES have a long evolutionary history as sea-dwelling reptiles extending back about 90 million years to the Age of Reptiles. Reptiles were the first true land-dwelling backboned or vertebrate animals to evolve. Amphibians, which were the first backboned animals to conquer the land – frogs, toads, newts and salamanders are modern representatives – remained tied to water for reproductive purposes and to maintain their body fluids. Amphibians evolved from fish which have remained aquatic to this day, although several species can leave the water for short periods of time. The reptiles developed an egg that could be deposited on land, and their way of life allowed them to live completely divorced from the watery environment. It was from the reptiles that the birds and mammals evolved to complete the vertebrate series as we know it to-day. In evolutionary sequence the vertebrates consist of fish, amphibians, reptiles, and birds and mammals – both of which evolved independently from reptile ancestors.

At a later period some reptiles returned to exploit the aquatic environment. Their limbs became modified into paddles and certain forms showed a remarkable degree of marine adaptation such as we associate with the whales and porpoises among modern mammals. All of these marine reptiles became extinct with the exception of the turtles of which seven living species are recognised.

Turtles, like whales, have not redeveloped the gills of their fishy ancestors and still breathe air using lungs like our own. Furthermore, turtles still lay eggs which can only develop on land. This involves them in lengthy migrations to suitable nesting sites and laborious nesting activities (described in Part Two).

Turtles belong to the order Testudines or Chelonia which is one of the four or five orders of living reptiles (opinions differ about the arrangement at order level). The first name is to be preferred as *Chelonia* written thus is the generic name for two species of sea turtle, hence resulting in possible confusion. The order Testudines includes the typical land tortoises, and amphibious or swamp-

9

dwelling species together with several freshwater forms that are as aquatic as the sea turtles.

Part One is arranged in three chapters. The first, Turtle Biology, provides a brief background to Testudine classification and then describes typical reptile features in more detail. Turtle evolution is then discussed and the second half of the chapter deals with adaptations to the marine environment.

Chapter 2 gives an up-to-date survey of the seven living species of sea turtles including their current status. A key to aid species identification is given in Appendix I. In Chapter 3 coral cays are described to provide a picture of favoured turtle nesting beaches.

The aim of Part One is to set the stage for an account of the Lives of Turtles in Part Two, Turtle Research in Part Three and Man and Turtles in Part Four.

CHAPTER I

Turtle Biology

TURTLES are reptiles. The living reptiles comprise about 6000 species and belong to one of four orders:

Order Squamata   – the lizards and snakes.
Order Testudines (Chelonia) – the tortoises, terrapins and turtles.
Order Crocodilia   – the crocodiles, alligators, caiman and gharial.
Order Rhynchocephalia   – of which the only living representative is the New Zealand Tuatara (*Sphenodon punctatus*).

The order Squamata contains the vast majority of modern reptiles. The order Testudines (Chelonia) consists of about 210 living species. It is an ancient order, the members of which have undergone little morphological change since the late Triassic about 200 million years ago. The order Testudines is usually divided into three sub-orders:

Sub-Order Amphichelydia   – This group included terrestrial forms like *Triassochelys* and amphibious species, most of which became extinct in the Mesozoic. This group, which existed from the Triassic to the Pleistocene, is now extinct.
Sub-Order Pleurodira   – There are now only a small number of living representatives grouped in two families, Pelomedusidae and Chelidae. The group originated in the Upper Cretaceous.
Sub-Order Cryptodira   – This sub-order includes the sea turtles and more than three-quarters of modern testudinates. The first fossils are from the Jurassic.

The Pleurodira and Cryptodira, which represent natural groupings, can be distinguished by the manner in which the head is retracted into the shell. In Pleurodires this is achieved by a sideways movement of the neck, hence its members are often known as 'side-necked' terrapins. In the Cryptodira the head is withdrawn by vertical movement of the neck vertebrae. As well as containing most species, the Cryptodira contains the most advanced members of the order and has the widest geographical distribution. Its representatives may be entirely terrestrial, semi-aquatic or entirely aquatic. In Britain these are referred to as tortoises, terrapins and turtles respectively. However, in the United States all are often called turtles, and in Australia, which is the only Continent without any terrestrial representatives, the terrapins are called tortoises. In addition to the sea turtles, the members of the Trionychidae and the sole representative of the Carettochelyidae, both fresh water groups, are entirely aquatic.

Sea turtles have been present in the seas since the Upper Cretaceous (about 90 million years ago). Their cryptodire ancestors have a fossil record extending back about 180 million years to the Jurassic.

Turtles like other reptiles are vertebrate animals. The vertebrate series, ascending the evolutionary ladder, comprises fish, amphibia and reptiles, from which the birds and mammals evolved. There are several characteristic reptilian features:

1. With few exceptions (e.g. soft-shelled turtles and the leathery turtle (*Dermochelys*)), reptiles have a body covered by scales and granules (compare the naked skin of Amphibia). The scales are obvious on the head and flippers of sea turtles other than *Dermochelys*.

2. Reptiles, like fish and amphibians, are exothermic (poikilothermic). This means that they obtain their body warmth almost entirely from an external source – the environment. This does not mean that reptiles are 'cold-blooded' since many terrestrial species have preferred temperature levels near our own and they are able to regulate their body temperature to some extent by behavioural means – choosing suitable surroundings. This does not apply to species which are aquatic (see below). In birds and mammals regulation of their internal body temperature is brought about by a series of complex physiological adjustments which maintain it within a narrow range.

3. Reptiles, unlike amphibians, do not go through a metamorphosis. They are true land-dwelling animals. All reptiles have lungs and breathe air, although some groups, the sea turtles being a prime example, have reverted secondarily to life in the water.

4. Reptiles either lay eggs or produce live young. The latter can result merely from the retention of yolky eggs in the oviducts until they are ready to hatch without provision of additional nourishment by the mother, or the developing young may receive nourishment by means of a placenta. Eggs may have well calcified shells like those of birds or the shells may be parchment-like (weakly calcified). All testudinates lay eggs. Although both shell types occur in the order Testudines, all sea turtles lay parchment-shelled eggs. The eggs develop extra embryonic membranes like the embryos of birds and mammals, these being an essential adaptation to a terrestrial environment. (Eggs were, of course, originally designed to develop in water and terrestrial animals have had to overcome the problem of desiccation during incubation on land.)

5. Reptiles other than crocodiles possess a three-chambered heart, the ventricle being incompletely divided by a septum (in the Crocodilia the septum is complete and the heart is, therefore, four-chambered). The incomplete division of the ventricle results in some mixing of the arterial and venous blood (compare birds and mammals on the one hand where the ventricle is completely divided into right and left parts, and fish on the other hand which possess a single auricle and ventricle). Fish possess what is called a single circulation; in amphibians (where there are two auricles and one ventricle) and reptiles, the circulation is known as incompletely double. In birds and mammals there exists a true double circulation – the blood passing twice through the heart in each complete circuit round the body; once as deoxygenated blood through the right side of the heart on its way to the lungs, and once as oxygenated blood through the left side of the heart on its way to the tissues.

6. Most reptiles have a squatting appearance, the limbs passing out sideways from the body so that the body lies on the ground except when the animal is moving; even then in most species the body is seldom raised much above the ground. (In sea turtles the body is dragged along the ground when the animals are ashore.)

7. There is a single bone in the middle ear to conduct vibrations from the ear drum across the middle ear to the inner ear. This arrangement is similar to that of amphibians and birds, and is to be contrasted with the arrangement of three bones – the stapeus, malleus and incus – in the middle ear of mammals.

8. The lower jaw of reptiles is composed of several bones (a single bone, the dentary, occurs in mammals) and articulates with the cranium by the quadrate.

It follows from (2) that reptiles avoid extremes of temperature. They do this by retiring to cooler retreats when it is very hot and by staying in safe retreats throughout the winter months in cold climates (hibernation). The distribution of sea turtles, which are mainly restricted to the tropics and subtropics, makes hibernation unnecessary. Unless they get far off course, or are carried on water currents to colder regions, the water never becomes too cold for them. Furthermore, the sea provides a relatively constant environment and they are never subjected to overheating effects.

As a result of the somewhat inefficient circulatory system (5) reptiles cannot sustain rapid activity for long. Short bursts of activity characterise many reptiles but these are often sufficient to enable them to escape from a predator. Most testudinates are slow-moving, at least on land, the expression 'as slow as a tortoise' being well known.

Like other reptiles many testudinates are long-lived and well able to survive long periods without food.

The most obvious characteristic of testudinates is the bony shell which encircles the body. This consists of an upper shell or carapace and a lower shell or plastron. These are usually joined at the mid-region of each side by the 'bridge'. There is an aperture at the front through which the head and front limbs emerge and a similar aperture for the hind limbs and tail at the rear. The basic function of the shell is undoubtedly protection from enemies. It is a considerable disadvantage in many forms, especially where it is heavy (land tortoises) and in most species limits movement considerably. Presumably it has been retained because its protective advantages greatly outweigh these disadvantages. Romer (1933) has pointed out that because they are commonplace objects we fail to marvel at chelonians. Were they extinct he says, their shells, the most remarkable armour ever assumed by a land animal, would be a cause for wonder.

The shell consists of two distinct materials, an inner layer of bony plates which is typically thick and an outer thin layer of horny scutes. The scutes do not conform with the position of the underlying bones and their number is also different. Both are characterised by a single row down the middle of the back. A row wider than the above occurs down each side, and a series round the perimeter of the upper shell.

The development of the carapace prevents flexibility of the back region which has led to the virtual disappearance of the dorsal musculature. Presumably the ventral musculature has been retained because of its important role in respiration. Similarly much of the skeleton has become incorporated into the shell.

The skull is characterised in most forms by the absence of openings (apses) in the temporal region, hence the chelonians are grouped with the Cotylosaur ancestors in the sub-class Anapsida.

All recent testudinates lack teeth which have been replaced by a horny beak forming a most effective cutting edge. Palatal teeth were present in one fossil chelonian.

The limbs are widely spaced transversely and project outwards at the sides. It seems likely that the method of locomotion antedates the development of the shell as it characterised the Cotylosaurs. On this view the shape of the shell is necessitated by the position of the limbs. The limbs and the skull are further points strengthening the relationship with the Cotylosaurs and suggesting a land ancestry. The oldest testudinate fossil known, *Triassochelys* from the Keuper of Germany, was a terrestrial form possessing a well-developed shell. This is also the only testudinate known to possess teeth which were no longer present on the jaws, being restricted to the palate.

The early history of the testudinates is obscure. As mentioned above, the encasing bony shell was already well developed by the Triassic. These forms also have the distinctive skull characters of the order. With one possible exception there are no known intermediates between early chelonians and any other reptile order. *Eunotosaurus*, discovered in the Middle Permian levels of South Africa, shows a number of features which may have characterised ancestral turtles. The ribs are expanded and leaf like, the number of dorsal vertebrae has been reduced to ten as in all chelonians, and the shoulder girdle has been moved inside the shell. *Eunotosaurus* can be taken to represent the way in which a Procolophonid Cotylosaur could have developed into a primitive turtle. Unfortunately, the similarities can also be explained as the result of parallel development. Hence, one cannot say conclusively that *Eunotosaurus* was an ancestral turtle. Whether or not *Eunotosaurus* is the link between Cotylosaurs and testudinates most authorities are to-day agreed that turtles are truly anapsid and developed directly from some Cotylosaur stock. The diadectomorph group of the Cotylosaurs is favoured with possible descent from pareiasaurs (Gregory, 1946; 1951) or diadectids (Olson, 1947).

The testudinate group has had a very long evolutionary history during which time it has remained remarkably similar in appearance. In sea turtles the reduction of the underlying bony shell, an adaptation to aquatic life, must have begun very early in their history. Turtles of Cretaceous seas had already disposed of the heavy armour. Sea turtles such as *Archelon* which reached a length of eleven feet, were contemporaries of the mosasaurs (giant marine lizards, reaching a length of thirty to forty feet, which swam by means of a long laterally flattened tail).

The sea turtles we know to-day provide a direct link with the Age of Reptiles. Not only have they remained virtually unchanged, but, were it not for man, would still abound in large numbers in all suitable tropical and sub-tropical seas. Clearly, theirs is a most successful way of life.

Romer (1956) points out that many modern testudinates are amphibious and that it is highly probable that this way of life has been the central one in testudinate history. It could have been inherited from presumed similar life habits in their ancestors (including diadectomorphs). Some testudinates (the tortoises) have become completely terrestrial, but the major trend has been the other way – towards a purely aquatic or even marine way of life. Apart from sea snakes, sea turtles are the only modern group of reptiles which successfully exploit the marine environment. Some crocodiles are estuarine and may travel some distances to sea but none are truly marine. In addition, one lizard, the so-called marine iguana (*Amblyrhynchus cristatus*), feeds on algae which it gathers on the sea-bed offshore.

SEA TURTLES

Adaptations to the Marine Environment

The main differences between sea turtles and their terrestrial relations (the tortoises) are in the shell and limbs. The highly domed carapace of tortoises would be difficult to propel through the water; in turtles this has become streamlined, with the result that the maximum height has been greatly reduced. Furthermore, in order to reduce weight, since it is advantageous for marine creatures to have a specific gravity similar to that of sea water, the bony elements in the shell have been greatly reduced. Below the overlying scutes there is only a fairly thin layer of bone in most species. The plastron is reduced and less well protected by bone than the carapace.

In the leathery turtle (*Dermochelys coriacea*) the horny outer layer and the normal bony shell have almost completely disappeared and have been replaced by superficial platelets which occur in the leathery skin. The leathery turtle is the only truly pelagic species of turtle, and as was to be expected, this mode of life led to the greatest possible reduction in the weight/volume ratio.

The stubby cylindrical limbs of tortoises have been converted into broad, flattened and strong, but thin, flippers, which offer a large area of resistance to the water when oriented broad side on as in the active swimming stroke. The front flippers are the important swimming organs, the rear flippers acting as rudders. The flipper area results from extension of the phalanges (finger bones), and this is most noticeable in the front flippers where each of the finger bones has been greatly lengthened. Turtles have five fingers and toes but these are all incorporated into the flipper.

The swimming action of sea turtles is most graceful to watch. The front flippers perform upward-backward and forward-downward movements reminiscent of the action of a bird's wings. As in birds, the angle of the organ of propulsion is altered between the active and passive strokes. Both front flippers work in unison. The action is quite different from that of most terrapins which swim by synchronous movements of diagonally opposed limbs. The limbs of terrapins are still adapted for terrestrial movement but possess webbed feet.

The aquatic adaptation of the limbs of sea turtles results in their being clumsy when moving on land. Unlike tortoises the body is not normally lifted clear of the ground during locomotion. There are two types of terrestrial locomotion in sea turtles. One consists of a series of pull-pushes in which all four limbs work simultaneously (e.g. the green turtle). The other, which appears much more efficient, comprises the usual series of limb movements of terrestrial animals in which alternate limbs move together – the left front limb moving with the right rear limb and vice versa. This type of locomotion is shown by the loggerhead, ridleys and hawksbill turtle. When badly frightened the green turtle may move for short distances using alternate limb movements. This 'gallop' results in the front of the plastron being raised from the ground and the rear slewed from side to side. It is interesting to note that hatchling green turtles move on land by the normal quadrupedal method, the change to the adult pattern taking place when they are about one year old.

Turtles obtain very large amounts of salt both directly from their food and when feeding. Like other sea creatures they need a method of excreting the excess salt which cannot be disposed of in their urine. Special salt-excreting glands open beside the tear duct of the eye. This gives rise to the popular story that nesting turtles are crying, either because of the pain (work) involved in nesting or to keep their eyes free of sand. In actual fact they are excreting salt all the time but this only becomes noticeable when the turtles are out of the water. The eye has become adapted for under water vision and is, therefore, markedly short-sighted on land.

Hearing

Hearing is not well developed in sea turtles. As with all reptiles there is no external ear to collect auditory stimuli. However, in sea turtles the eardrum is covered by ordinary skin which greatly reduces sensitivity. Low notes are heard best. Turtles are sensitive to ground borne vibrations and, presumably, to similar stimuli in the water.

The Sense of Touch

Turtles are sensitive to touch particularly on the soft parts of the flippers, but also on the carapace.

The Sense of Smell

Although I know of no work conducted specifically on sea turtles, and little is known about the testudinate group as a whole, they are assumed to have a keen sense of smell on the basis of the well developed olfactory areas of the brain. These are relatively larger in testudinates than in other reptiles.

Respiration

Since sea turtles breathe air like terrestrial animals they need to be able to hold their breath for considerable periods of time when under water. This requires that they be able to fully ventilate their lungs during respiration and extract a maximum of the contained oxygen. The ability to go into oxygen debt over short periods is also important. When oxygen supplies are irregular it is necessary to have a progressive shut-down in the supply of oxygen to the tissues so that only the essential tissues receive a normal oxygen quota when this is in short supply. In this way one series of respirations can be made to last much longer.

Reproduction

Fertilisation is internal and all species lay eggs. Copulation occurs mostly at the water surface in sea turtles, and a female is often seen surrounded by two or more males. In order to maintain his position (this is rather difficult as a somewhat domed carapace and smooth plastron have come together) the male hooks the thumb claw on each front flipper over the front of the female's carapace on to the soft parts between the neck and shoulder. Females which nest shortly after mating may show signs of minor bleeding in this region, and the area is frequently slightly raw in appearance.

It is not known if sea turtles mate between producing each clutch of eggs. It is known that a number of other testudinates are able to maintain viable spermatozoa in the female reproductive tract for periods of up to several years (Oliver, 1955). Whether or not sea turtles have this faculty is not known. However, the greatest mating activity always precedes the nesting season and spills over into the early part of nesting. Later in the season, when many females have still to lay several clutches of eggs, mating activity is not observed and females with fresh mating wounds are rarely seen ashore.

Although many lizards and snakes produce live young, all testudinates like the other archaic reptile groups (crocodiles and the tuatara), lay eggs. Due to the high juvenile mortality sea turtles need to produce large numbers of eggs. In a nesting season many species lay between five hundred and a thousand eggs. As in the dinosaurs (Colbert, 1962), there is a tremendous discrepancy between the size and weight of the young at hatching and these statistics in the adult. A sea turtle weighing 400 lb. produces a hatchling which on emerging from the egg weighs about three-quarters of an ounce. During its growth a 400 pound turtle has, therefore, to increase its weight at hatching by about 8,500 times! By way of comparison, a human only goes through approximately a fourteen to twenty-fold weight increase during growth.

Watching the laborious nesting process and taking into account the lengthy oceanic migrations which accompany it, one realises the great changes which would have resulted had sea turtles evolved viviparity. Not only would the animals never need to come ashore, but the lengthy migrations to suitable nesting beaches would also be unnecessary. Furthermore, the enormous production of eggs could be replaced by a small number of relatively large progeny.

Temperature Relationships

Most reptiles like to bask in the sun in the early morning in order to raise their body temperature to preferred levels. They then maintain their temperatures at these levels throughout the day by alternative basking and retreating to shade. The sea turtles do not have the same scope to alter their body temperatures which usually closely approximate that of the water. However, some species, such as the flatback (*Chelonia depressa*), spend hours floating, apparently asleep, at the water's surface. Similar behaviour also characterises at least some sea snakes. This behaviour in both reptiles is undoubtedly connected with temperature requirements, although sunshine effects, such as vitamin D production, may also be important. Heat gain from the sun during basking will raise the body temperature well above that of the surrounding water. Furthermore, the surface layer of the sea is much warmer than deeper down so heat loss to the surrounding water is also decreased at the surface.

Many reptiles have preferred temperature levels near our own body temperature. Temperatures in the sea are very much less than this, resulting in a need to be able to operate at much lower temperatures much or most of the time. However, after feeding it would appear to be advantageous to raise one's body temperature (by basking at the surface) so that digestion can proceed more swiftly thereby making room for the next meal. In this way more

1. (a) View of Heron Island from the edge of the reef at extreme low tide. At such times one can walk from the island to this point.

(b) Aerial view of Crab Island, N.W. Cape York extreme northern Queensland. Crab, an uninhabited cay designated as an Aboriginal Reserve, is a key rookery for the green turtle and also an important flatback nesting site.

2/3. (a) Barrier Reef hawksbill turtle (*Eretmochelys imbricata*).
C. LIMPUS.

(b) Leathery turtle (*Dermochelys coriacea*) a pelagic species with large flippers. The well-defined longitudinal ridges on the carapace do not occur in adults of any other species.

(c) Olive ridley (*Lepidochelys kempi*) ashore in Surinam, South America. P. C. H. PRITCHARD.

(d) Kemp's ridley (*Lepidochelys kempi*) on beach at Rancho Nuevo, Tamaulipas, Mexico. P. C. H. PRITCHARD.

(e) Loggerhead (*Caretta caretta*). The head is large, the beak parrot-like and the flippers are proportionately small.

(f) Green turtle (*Chelonia mydas*). Note the domed carapace, large scales on the front flippers and four postocular scales immediately behind the eye.

(g) Flatback (*Chelonia depressa*). This species is characterised by the greatly depressed carapace and numerous small scales between the fingers of the front flippers.

4. (a) Erosion of the *Casuarina* stand on the south-east corner of Heron Island. Nesting turtles hasten the erosive process.

(b) South beach, Heron Island, showing vegetation and beach rock. From left to right *Messerschmidia argentea, Pandanus tectorius, Casuarina equisetifolia.* Below *Casuarina* and on extreme right are *Scaevola frutescens.*

food can be assimilated than is needed for just keeping alive and moving about. These extra resources can be used to increase the growth rate of immature turtles or to build up reserves for long migrations across the open sea where food may be scarce, or for production of eggs in adults.

Even in only 20–30 feet of water, the water temperature is much lower at the bottom than near the surface. This results in a drop in body temperature when the turtles sink to the bottom to sleep which they usually do under rocky ledges where predation hazard is reduced. The fall in body temperature results in an overall drop in metabolic activity and hence a reduced need for oxygen.

Defensive Behaviour

Sea turtles possess no special defensive devices apart from their shell which is present in all species other than the leathery turtle. As mentioned above, adaptations which the shell has undergone to fit it for a fully aquatic existence have reduced its protective value. Sea turtles, unlike tortoises for instance, are unable to completely withdraw their heads and limbs within the shell.

Probably the greatest defence which sea turtles possess against enemies is their large size – they outgrow most potential enemies. Whereas many carnivorous fish can and do devour hatchling turtles, there are few fish (some sharks are an exception) which are large enough to attack an adult turtle. To what extent large turtles actively avoid sharks is unknown. It seems likely that they recognise them and keep as far away as possible. It must be remembered that in the water turtles are strong swimmers. When at rest they usually take up a position in which the head and anterior of the body face under, and is partly protected by, an overhanging ledge. (These comments do not apply to the leathery turtle.) This may explain why damage usually affects the posterior of the body and rear flippers. However, this could also result from attacks from the rear when the turtle is swimming away. It could also result from the fact that most anterior attacks being directed at the head would prove fatal. There is so little known about the lives of turtles at sea that it is fruitless to speculate.

Even the largest turtle – the leathery – is not immune from predation at sea. Caldwell and Caldwell (1969) recorded remains of a leathery turtle in the stomachs of three killer whales (*Orcinus orca*) taken from a single pack off the island of St Vincent in the lesser Antilles (West Indies). There are several eyewitness accounts of shark attacks on large turtles. A Queensland fisheries inspector told me about an attack on a large loggerhead, which he estimated to have a shell length of about 42 inches, by a tiger shark and a hammerhead shark. The attack occurred while the turtle was at the surface of the sea near his patrol boat. In less than a minute the only trace of the turtle remaining was an area of blood-stained water.

Longevity

Testudinates are among the longest living of the reptiles. Many are renowned for their longevity. Most longevity records for testudinates, however, refer to tortoises. Flower (1925; 1938), who made exhaustive studies on the longevity of animals in zoological gardens, found no impressive longevities among captive sea turtles. The longest recorded were as follows: green turtle 15 years, hawksbill 15⅔ years (and still alive) and loggerhead 23 years (and still living). Apparently loggerheads were kept in the aquarium at Lisbon for 33 years. These unimpressive longevities may in part reflect unsuitable conditions, in particular absence of sunshine or substitute artificial illumination of suitable wavelength, a criticism equally applicable to conditions in which most sea turtles are kept to-day.

CHAPTER 2

The World's Sea Turtles

THE seven species of sea turtles recognised are grouped in two families and five genera. With the exception of the flatback (*Chelonia depressa*) and Kemp's ridley (*Lepidochelys kempi*), both of which have a restricted distribution, they occur circumglobally in tropical and sub-tropical seas. Over this extensive distributional range they show little morphological variation. The green, loggerhead, hawksbill and leathery turtle have each been split into two subspecies, one for the Atlantic and Mediterranean and one for the Pacific and Indian Oceans. However, there is very considerable doubt if these are valid. A land bridge has existed between North and South America for approximately one million years, yet there is little difference between green turtles on the two sides of the Americas. This information strongly suggests that sea turtles have not been evolving rapidly in recent geological time, a hardly surprising finding since the group has changed so slowly throughout its very long evolutionary history (Chapter 1).

The family Cheloniidae contains four of the five modern genera and all but one species. The genera *Caretta* and *Eretmochelys* each contain only a single species, whereas *Chelonia* and *Lepidochelys* both have two species. The members of the Cheloniidae are the loggerhead (*Caretta caretta*), the hawksbill (*Eretmochelys imbricata*), the green turtle (*Chelonia mydas*), the flatback (*Chelonia depressa*), the olive or Pacific ridley (*Lepidochelys olivacea*) and Kemp's ridley (*Lepidochelys kempi*).

The family Dermochelyidae contains the monospecific genus *Dermochelys* erected for the leathery turtle (*Dermochelys coriacea*).

Six of the seven sea turtle species occur in Queensland waters (Kemp's ridley is the exception) and apart from the leathery turtle all are known to nest within the State.

Species identification is fairly straightforward. A key to all seven species is given in Appendix I.

During the species by species account which follows the present status of each species worldwide is discussed.

THE GREEN TURTLE

The general appearance of the green turtle is shown in plate 2/3. There are marked variations in the size of the head, which is, however, always small in relation to the size of the turtle, compared to the flatback or loggerhead. The degree of curvature of the carapace also shows considerable geographic variation but the whole range may be seen within a single population. The horny scutes on the carapace are well marked. Coloration is extremely variable even within a single population so that it would be extremely tedious to give an all-inclusive description. The ground colour is usually greeny-brown to brown with darker markings. In turtles where the darker markings are relatively pale and the ground colour dark the contrast between them is slight. The darker markings may take the form of spots or blotches or streaks. Where they are numerous the turtle may appear to have a predominantly black carapace. Some individuals have a pale greenish-olive ground colour and virtually lack darker markings. The above range is shown by the Heron Island nesting female population. The flippers and head are olive coloured.

The largest individual I have seen on the Great Barrier Reef had a shell length measured over the curve of 50 inches and I estimate weighed about 400 lb. Carr (1952) refers to former American records of up to 850 lb. He records a maximum of 600 lb for the Pacific race.

The green turtle is predominantly vegetarian except in the first year or so of life when it is carnivorous. The diet consists of marine algae and angiosperms including representatives of the genera *Zostera*, *Thallassina*, *Enhalus*, *Posidonia* and *Halodule*. In certain areas, such as the Galapagos Islands, they are reported to feed extensively on mangrove leaves. Green turtles will also take any animal food they can catch and on the Great Barrier Reef there are numerous records of their eating jellyfish.

As a result of their diet, green turtles occur in shallow seas where there is sufficient light on the sea-bed to ensure an abundant growth of marine grasses. Areas of continental shelf are, therefore, extensively used, particularly where the water is less than 4 fathoms deep. When they want to retire to sleep they seek out a location which provides some degree of safety from large predators such as sharks. On coral reefs they move under an overhanging ledge and face inwards. Duncan (1943) noted that in the Caribbean they seek out small, deep, rocky potholes for sleeping quarters. Carr (1952) reported a diurnal migration from sleeping to feeding areas in the population in the Gulf of Mexico and Florida Bay. Carr pointed out that in the Caribbean green turtles are most readily found in places in which eel-grass (*Zostera*) flats are pitted with frequent rocky holes, and that such situations are available over a wide territory in Gulf and Caribbean shore waters, as well as about oceanic islands.

The green turtle is the best known species since its flesh is most highly esteemed by people everywhere and is the basis of turtle soup. In certain areas of the world the species has been grossly over-exploited for several hundred years. Like the giant tortoises of the Galapagos the green turtle provided fresh meat for seamen and was much sought after by the early navigators. It first became depleted in numbers where colonial naval activities were high.

Furthermore, the usual European method of taking turtle was disastrous. Females were turned on their backs when they came out of the water without even being given the chance to lay their eggs. This resulted in only one sex – the egg layers – being exploited while the much less biologically valuable males remained unused.

The situation facing the green turtle varies greatly in different parts of the world. This is well illustrated by the fact that the Bermuda Assembly of 1620 passed an act forbidding killing of turtles below eighteen inches in shell size. Clearly the green turtles of the Caribbean region were over-exploited at a very early date, long before the discovery of Australia by Cook.

In American waters population numbers are now very low compared to former times. The most important nesting grounds to-day are at Tortuguero in Costa Rica (the headquarters of Professor Archie Carr's research team) and uninhabited Aves Island in the Eastern Caribbean. The latter rookery seems to have survived due to its remoteness. It is little more than a sandbank and its small size and low elevation make it hard for turtle fishermen to find. Trinidad and Surinam are also important nesting grounds for the green turtle in the Americas. Ascension Island, South Atlantic, is a major rookery for the populations which feed on the South American coast.

Little is known about nesting by this species on the African mainland.

Important breeding colonies have recently been reported in

South Yemen, Arabia, by Hirth and Carr (1970) and a very large green turtle rookery has lately been discovered in Turkey. Green turtles were once extremely numerous in the Seychelles and Mascarene islands in the western Indian Ocean. Aldabra, approximately 600 miles north-east of Dar-es-salaam, was long an important rookery on a world basis. Recent reports provide tragic reading because indications are that the Aldabra populations have been virtually wiped out. The same is true for Assumption Island. Aldabra green turtles have recently been totally protected but this legislation may have come too late to save this previously enormous rookery from extinction. As in so many parts of the world the Seychelles story makes depressing reading. Some years ago I advised the British Government on conservation of the green turtle in the Seychelles. It was particularly distressing to know that similar advice tendered in a detailed report almost forty years ago (Hornell, 1927) had gone unheeded.

In the Seychelles to-day only Astove and Cosmoledo (Wizard Island) seem to support significant green turtle populations. Many rookeries which once supported large populations of green turtles have been completely exterminated. In the Americas these include the Bahamas, Florida, the Dry Tortugas, and the Cayman Islands.

Three small islands off Sarawak (Malaysian Borneo) form one of the largest green turtle rookeries in the world. However, even there, where the adult turtles are never slaughtered and only the eggs are collected due to Moslem custom, Professor Harrisson has recently reported a sharp decline in numbers.

The green turtle is still abundant in Australian waters along the Great Barrier Reef, in Torres Strait, the Gulf of Carpentaria, Northern Territory waters and in Western Australia. The only commercial fishery is in Western Australia where the species is fished under strict control and a careful watch is maintained on the populations. In view of its depletion and near extinction in many other parts of its range Australia has a worldwide obligation to see that its present sizeable populations are maintained. How this is being brought about in Queensland is the subject of Chapter 10.

The localised feeding grounds and extremely localised rookeries of the green turtle made it an easy victim for man. Traditional local uses of meat, oil and shell have expanded as the result of both population growth and commercial demand. Turtle oil is now sought for the cosmetics industry, the skin for the leather trade, and the meat for the tourist gourmet trade. Add these to calipee requirement (for soup), and it is easy to see why the species has been heavily over-exploited.

To summarise, the green turtle was once very numerous in all suitable areas (shallow seas where the algae and sea grasses which form its major food grow) in the tropics and subtropics where water temperature exceeds 20°C. In most of these areas it has become greatly depleted and in some virtually extinct. However, there is no threat to the future of the species at the present time since in some areas, such as Australia, it is still present in substantial numbers. This is not to suggest that every effort should not be taken to prevent the extinction of populations elsewhere. These deserve careful conservation as a valuable material resource and because of their scientific interest (turtle zoogeography is still in its infancy).

THE FLATBACK

The flatback is shown in plates 2/3 and 16. It is readily distinguished from the green turtle by the much flatter carapace, by scalation differences and by coloration. As a result of its much flatter form it is much lighter than the green turtle and, of course, our length measurements, which are made over the curve of the shell, are correspondingly lower. A series of 180 individuals measured in North Queensland averaged 35 inches in carapace length and the mean weight of 10 nesting females was 160 lb.

Like Kemp's ridley, the flatback has a very limited geographical distribution and remained virtually unknown until very recently. Its very existence as a species in its own right has only won international recognition in the last five years (Chapter 6).

The flatback was first reported from northern Australian waters and is now known to be present across the north of the Continent from the north of Western Australia, through the Northern Territory to Queensland. Recently we have shown that this tropical species also comes ashore to nest in south-central Queensland, near Bundaberg, and Mr C. Limpus has discovered other, much larger, nesting aggregations of the species near Gladstone, central Queensland.

Unlike all the other species of sea turtles there is no reason to suspect that its numbers have decreased in recent times since its favoured habitat has been little affected by European colonisation of the Continent. However, it remains potentially vulnerable due to its restricted range, and developments now getting under way in the north are bound to pose a threat to at least parts of its range in the not too distant future. Clearly Australia will have to accept ultimate responsibility for the continued survival of this particularly interesting species of sea turtle.

I have summarised all available information on the flatback turtle in Chapter 6.

THE LOGGERHEAD

The loggerhead, shown in plate 2/3, has a large head which is extremely broad posteriorly, with large dark brown eyes. The carapace and flippers are reddish-brown. The head is similarly coloured excepting the region of the jaws where it is a yellowish colour. The plastron is yellow.

Carr (1952) says that there are records of individuals of the Atlantic race weighing between 700 and 900 lb but emphasises that a loggerhead of more than 300 lb is a rarity to-day. In Australia, where the large (old) individuals certainly have not been taken by humans, the species is very much smaller. The average size and weights of nesting females are considerably lower than for green turtles. Indeed, few of our tagged loggerheads are heavier than the lower end of the green turtle nesting population, with a weight of about 150 lb. Carr considers that the loggerhead may be next in size only to the leathery turtle and considers that the Pacific race may be even larger than that of the Atlantic. He says that the world's record for head width is held by an Australian specimen in the Bell Collection at Cambridge University with the incredible width of 285 mm (11.2 inches).

The loggerhead is almost entirely carnivorous feeding on crabs and other crustaceans, shellfish, sponges, jellyfish, fish and sometimes algae. The jaws are extremely powerful. An individual on the reef at Heron Island was seen to bite clean through a clam shell with a thickness of 8 mm ($\frac{1}{3}$ inch).

The loggerhead is an adaptable animal much given to wandering. It occurs on the continental shelf, ascends creeks, and often occurs in the open sea where it spends long periods of time floating, apparently asleep, on the surface, basking in the sun.

Much less is known about this species than the edible green turtle. Documentation is best for the United States where there is no doubt that the species is declining fast. This is due to a number of factors among which seaside development ranks high. The combination of bright lights and human activity has frightened turtles away from beaches which once formed important rookeries. Furthermore, bright lights confuse the sea-finding mechanism of the newly-hatched young and result in huge losses of baby turtles which never reach the sea. For this reason it is important that main roads should not be rooted near rookeries. In the United States, Professor Archie Carr says that in some areas hatchlings are being crushed by the thousands on coastal highways.

In the south-eastern United States egg predation also seems to be a key factor. Raccoons (*Procyon lotor*), which are an important egg predator, have increased rapidly recently and are destroying a disturbingly large proportion of turtle nests on mainland beaches.

A sanctuary has recently been created for the loggerhead in Natal following the extensive work of George Hughes. This most gratifying news will protect an important loggerhead population.

In Australia loggerheads are still numerous. However, Australia has yet to face the development which has occurred in the United States and unless action is taken now to protect key rookeries these will be lost with increasing coastal development.

Loggerheads nest extensively on the mainland in Australia, as elsewhere, which increases their vulnerability both to predation and alienation of beaches. On the Australian mainland monitor lizards (goannas), including *Varanus varius*, patrol the beaches and detect eggs by smell. Pigs and foxes introduced to Australia since European settlement have both gone wild and become numerous. Both eat any turtle eggs they find and detect the presence of nests by smell. Fox destruction of a loggerhead nest at Mon Repos in south-east Queensland is shown in plate 12. Attacks seem to be most frequent when the embryos are near full-term. A fox does not usually eat more than about one-third of a clutch but the nest is exposed and the heat of the sun and seagulls complete the destruction. I have counted four nests destroyed by foxes in one night on about half a mile of beach.

In some areas of north Queensland pigs are very numerous and I have seen up to 15 in one group on a beach.

Although loggerheads are seldom eaten, their eggs are relished by coastal people everywhere. As a result of the population explosion together with the general availability of power boats, this threat has increased greatly for all species of sea turtle. Uninhabited rookeries formerly never visited by people can now be visited regularly in order to collect eggs. To summarise: The loggerhead is fast becoming a depleted species. Its mainland rookeries are often adversely affected by human encroachment. Hunting pressure on its eggs – both by humans and introduced predators – is showing a marked increase.

THE HAWKSBILL

The hawksbill is one of the smaller turtles. Carr (1952) states that the heaviest specimen on record weighed 280 lb and was taken at Great Sound, Grand Cayman (British West Indies). However, a hundred pound specimen is rare there to-day. The largest specimen seen by Carr was a male from Florida with a carapace length of 33 inches. Carr noted that a good-sized female from Barbados had a carapace length of 23 inches. Data on the Pacific populations are much sparser.

At birth the carapace scutes do not overlap. At several weeks or months of age the imbricate scutes, characteristic of the species, develop. However, in old turtles the overlap becomes progressively less until the scutes may lack any overlap like the green turtle. Overlapping scutes, therefore, is an unreliable diagnostic feature since it does not occur in very small young or in many of the larger (older) individuals. The tortoiseshell coloration may not be very apparent in the living individual but in some individuals the carapace may show the colourings seen in polished tortoiseshell – radiating markings of reddish, yellow, shades of brown and black. The head is brown often with a reddish tint and the jaws are yellowish. The upper surfaces of the flippers are darkish brown and the lower surfaces, like the underside of the head and the plastron, are yellow. The hawksbill is shown in plates 2/3 and 24.

Like other turtles the hawksbill starts life as a carnivore but as an adult it becomes omnivorous. It feeds largely on molluscs, crustaceans, ascidians, jellyfish and marine algae, according to Carr (1952). The hooked jaws are well adapted to prising molluscs and crabs out of crevices in or around coral. The hawksbill is the most restrictedly tropical of the sea turtles but occurs circumglobally in tropical seas. It is now rare throughout much of its former range. Further details on the hawksbill are given in Chapter 7.

Professor Carr commented that the present distribution of the species 'is a ghostly outline of the primitive range, except perhaps in parts of the Mediterranean from which it appears to have been completely extirpated'.

The hawksbill nests in small numbers in several areas throughout the Caribbean and the south Gulf of Mexico. The species is also known to nest on Rolas and Sao Thomé Islands in the Gulf of Guinea, West Africa. The hawksbill used to be numerous in the Seychelle Islands in the western Indian Ocean but has been heavily over-exploited there. Nesting also occurs on very small islands in the South China Sea. In Australia until 1970 we knew of no important breeding ground for the species although isolated nestings were recorded as far south as Brisbane. Absence of a recorded rookery was puzzling, as the species is by no means uncommon in northern Australian waters where it has probably been exploited much less than in other parts of its range. However, we now know that the hawksbill nests extensively on several small islands in parts of Torres Strait (see Chapter 7). The hawksbill is well known in the Fiji Islands where it has been the subject of gross over-exploitation and is greatly depleted in numbers. This has occurred despite excellent legislation on paper, which protects adult turtles of all species from November to February inclusive (the main breeding time) and the eggs of all species at all times. Poaching is rife, the adult turtles are taken for food and the eggs collected whenever possible (Bustard, 1970).

The hawksbill is known to people around the world as the tortoiseshell turtle as the scutes of the carapace provide the tortoiseshell of commerce. This has been the species' undoing for centuries, and countless books describing travels to remote coastal areas record the removal of the scutes by heating the living turtle over a fire. Some people eat hawksbills and, as with other sea turtles, the eggs are eaten whenever located.

A large part of the hawksbill fishery occurs at sea due to the difficulty of securing nesting individuals. The hawksbill comes ashore, often in small numbers, on countless nesting grounds and its rapid nesting often results in the turtle returning safely to the sea even though people subsequently locate the nest and take the eggs. However, like the green turtle, it is easily taken at sea, foraging around its favoured reefs and rocky areas.

The advent of plastics in the 1940s seemed to indicate a more secure future for the species. However, tortoiseshell has recently come back into vogue and skins are now also in demand. Furthermore, the calipee is being used successfully in the manufacture of 'green turtle' soup. Added to the commercial activities is the constant raiding of nests by coastal people for food. It is not difficult, therefore, to understand why the future of the hawksbill turtle is in great jeopardy (Chapter 10).

THE PACIFIC RIDLEY

Comparatively little is known about the Pacific or olive ridley. Carr (1952) cites the maximum size seen by him as twenty-seven inches in shell length. In appearance (plate 2/3) the olive ridley has an almost circular carapace, very nearly as broad as long. The carapace is high, particularly near the mid-line. The coloration is fairly uniform olive without any distinctive markings. Little is known about the feeding habits of this species which is probably largely vegetarian although it is also recorded as having taken shellfish and sea urchins.

The Pacific ridley occurs in parts of the Indian Ocean, in the Pacific and parts of the Atlantic Ocean. This range does not appear to be the result of depredations. Its confusion with the loggerhead has resulted in its going unrecognised in many areas. For instance, the first published record of the species in Australia occurred in 1970.

The Pacific ridley is undergoing a very high rate of exploitation along the Pacific coast of Mexico due to the demand for leather and oil. In the Guianas the eggs are considered a delicacy and egg collecting at Eilanti beach (Surinam) and Organabo beach (French Guiana) was nearly 100 percent for many years according to Dr J. P. Schulz. Without doubt this species must be considered as depleted and the rapidly increasing rate of exploitation gives reason for serious alarm at least in parts of the species' range. In Queensland, like all other species of sea turtle, it is completely protected. Unfortunately we still do not know how important the Queensland rookeries are.

Reserves have been set up at Wia Wia in Surinam and Shell Beach in Guyana. At Eilanti beach in Surinam 300,000 eggs were bought from egg collectors in 1967 and reburied for natural incubation. Mexico has operated widespread tagging studies and hatchery efforts on a gigantic scale.

KEMP'S RIDLEY

Kemp's ridley, not found in the Pacific, differs from the Pacific ridley in its grey coloration, as well as differences in lateral counts (see key) and in skull characters. Like the Pacific ridley it is a small species.

Kemp's ridley is known from 'the Gulf of Mexico, mostly in the northern portion, northward along the Atlantic coast to Massachusetts, whence it is carried with some frequency to England, Ireland, the Scilly Isles, and the Azores' (Carr, 1952). For many years nothing was known about its reproduction. Indeed the first description of the species' main breeding rookery at Rancho Nuevo in Tamaulipas, Mexico, was given by Hildebrand (1963). Hildebrand estimated that at least 40,000 came ashore to lay on a single day on one mile of beach!

Nesting occurs during daylight mainly between 9 a.m. and 1 p.m. Hildebrand suggested that diurnal nesting could be a defence against the nocturnal coyote which is the main local egg predator. The species lays three clutches of eggs in a nesting season. The first clutch comprises up to 180 eggs, and the third only 80 to 110. There is no regular interval between nestings, which reputedly coincide with strong winds. The fact that nesting is so highly aggregated both temporally and spatially and that it occurs on windy days, which quickly wipe out the tracks, explains why the rookery was not described previously.

Hildebrand reported that considerable nesting by individuals and small groups extends from Sotloa Murina to Punta Jeref, and that scattered nesting occurs from Port Aransas, Texas, to the Tuxtlas in Veracruz.

The future of Kemp's ridley is quite obscure. The species is extremely vulnerable because its entire breeding range appears to be restricted to a section of almost uninhabited coast of the State of Tamaulipas, Mexico. For three years the Government of Mexico each season posted soldiers to patrol the nesting beaches. Hatcheries were also used to protect eggs from predators (both human and non-human). The Government of Mexico re-opened the species to exploitation by a large Company in 1970 while still preventing the local peasants from taking any eggs. Following this announcement Mexico was deluged with complaints by conservationists in the hope that the President of Mexico could be encouraged to rescind the order re-opening the species. The Company failed to

33

make contact with populations of Kemp's ridley, and it appears unlikely that the species will be opened again next year.

LEATHERY TURTLE

The leathery turtle, shown in plates 2/3 and 17, is the most distinctive of the sea turtles being placed in a separate family, the Dermochelidae, of which it is the sole living representative. It is also by far the largest living species. The carapace length may exceed sixfeet, and weights of up to at least 1,200 lb would appear to be authentic, although few probably exceed a weight of about 800 lb.

This species is readily distinguishable from all other sea turtles by its smooth relatively scale-less skin which is black, spotted with white.

The food of the leathery turtle consists largely of jellyfish (Brongersma, 1969).

The leathery turtle is a truly pelagic species much given to wandering great distances at sea. Carr has described the species as having a temperate range with tropical nesting habits and this gives some idea of its enormous distribution.

The leathery turtle, in my opinion, is one of the most, if not the most, threatened sea turtle world wide. Its only rival for this unenviable status is the very restricted Kemp's ridley. Important nesting grounds have only been known to science for a few years. The most important of these outside of the Americas is in Trengganu in eastern Malaya. Unfortunately, the eggs are harvested as food in Trengganu and, due to very efficient marketing, virtually every nest is located and the eggs removed. To date conservation effort has not been able to secure nearly sufficient eggs for hatchery incubation to offset the tremendous drain imposed by human consumption of virtually the total egg lay. It seems certain that the Trengganu rookery is being seriously over-exploited but it has not yet proved possible to reduce the level of exploitation.

The most important nesting ground for the leathery turtle in the Western Hemisphere is in French Guiana near the Marowijne River. In June and early July 1969 it was estimated that up to 300 leathery turtles were nesting on a good night. Pritchard (1971) considers that this rookery is substantially larger than the one at Trengganu, and all possible steps are being taken to safeguard the future of this important discovery.

The leathery turtle also nests in considerable numbers in Costa

Rica, and in much smaller numbers in Trinidad, Surinam, Ceylon and on the Tongaland coast of Natal. However, none of these rookeries appear important compared to the nesting beach in French Guiana and Trengganu. The latter is thought to have between 850 and 1600 nesting females each season.

Nesting by the leathery turtle has recently been reported in Fiji where legislation is being drafted to apply total protection to the species (Bustard, 1970). To date no Australian rookery has been discovered although the possibility that one exists somewhere in northern Australia cannot be discounted.

The leathery turtle requires a substantial breeding area in a stable country, where protein from the turtle is not important, so that the rookery can enjoy effective total protection. Until this situation exists the fact that the species is circumglobal in distribution in warm or warm-temperature seas must not be allowed to obscure the basic insecurity of its breeding beaches.

The current situation of the seven species of sea turtle may be summarised as follows:

Green turtle: depleted world-wide, critically endangered in some parts of the world (such as the Caribbean) but still abundant in other areas (for instance, Australia).

Flatback: numerous in its restricted geographical range.

Loggerhead: becoming depleted, seriously in some areas, less seriously in others.

Kemp's Ridley: situation currently critical.

Pacific Ridley: similar to the loggerhead.

Hawksbill: clearly a seriously depleted species in many or most parts of its range.

Leathery turtle: world numbers very low, in urgent need of effective protection at several world rookeries.

The leathery turtle is the only species of sea turtle given star listing in the *1970 Reptile Red Data Book*, published by the International Union for the Conservation of Nature and Natural Resources, which indicates that the species is critically endangered.

CHAPTER 3

Coral Cays

LIKE a huge bumble bee the Queensland Airlines D.C.3 droned slowly northwards. It was December 1964, and I was on my way to have a first look at the Great Barrier Reef. However, my mind was not on the reef but on a proposed future research project on the population ecology of the giant tortoises of the South American Galapagos Islands. I envisaged this study as playing an integral part in the desperately needed conservation of these magnificent creatures and also providing a marked contrast to my work during the last two years on geckos. I needed now to look at another reptile, preferably with a completely different population structure. Although I had followed sea turtle research closely over the years, particularly through the papers of Professor Archie Carr and Mr Tom Harrisson, I had never thought of carrying out research on sea turtles myself. The thought did not cross my mind even now, and I continued to ponder logistic and priority problems for Galapagos work.

Suddenly as the plane swung away from the coast a fascinating panorama opened up below and this absorbed all my attention. In these days the Saturday scheduled flight from Brisbane to Gladstone flew out over the reef so that the occupants, mostly tourists, could have a look at the Reef from the air. This morning the tide was low and the reefs were exposed. The greatest attraction to me in flying over reefs is the range of water colours resulting from the varying depths. Looking down from several thousand feet one is provided with a practical lesson in physical geography in which one can see just how the reefs have developed and compare their protected side with that open to the weather. Soon we saw a cay, as islands formed from coral sand are called, and then another and another. The islands were idyllic, with their beaches of clean white coral sand and small waves quietly breaking on their shores. Each cay was surrounded by a reef platform of variable dimensions, which was mostly exposed at this stage of the tide, and at the perimeter the deep blue colour of the water indicated that the coral fell away almost vertically providing deep water round the reef edge. The central parts of the islands above the high tide mark consisted of an apparently solid mass of pale green vegetation. I recall looking for coconut palms along the beaches and being disappointed at not detecting any. Later I was to learn that coconuts are restricted to the far north of Queensland.

After examining several islands and their associated reefs, I noticed that instead of being placed in the middle of the reef, the islands were usually markedly off-centre. Clearly they had built up towards one end of the elevated reef platform as a result of wind and wave action.

Soon we were starting our descent to Gladstone airport and the two and a half hour flight was coming to an end. The air terminal turned out to be one of these quaint Queensland ones totally without pretension of any sort. The strip was unsealed then and the scrub grew right up to the edge of the strip. The waiting room-ticket office consisted of a tiny wooden structure raised well off the ground in the typical Queensland fashion to allow good air circulation and to provide protection from termites. It was extremely hot, and, of course, not even a fan was provided. The 'hut' possessed a wooden bench along two walls. There were no other furnishings.

From Gladstone I travelled by launch to Heron Island in the Capricorn Group. The launch trip took between four and five hours during which there was little to do or see. The first cay became visible about half way. This was Masthead Island, a cay lacking tall trees. Somewhat later much smaller Erskine Island came into view. The fringing casuarinas gave Masthead a Robinson Crusoe atmosphere. It certainly looked most inviting. However, like tiny Erskine, it was uninhabited.

After a further hour we caught our first sight of Heron Island. All we could see initially was a smudge of green on the horizon, but as we approached we saw a small expanse of white surmounted by the green. The overall lowness of these cays makes them difficult to see at a distance particularly if there is a substantial swell.

We arrived at Heron at about five o'clock and made our way across the soft powdery coral sand to the Research Station. Only two hours later I was watching my first nesting turtles and in several days knew that I simply had no choice but to start a research programme on sea turtles! This project prevented the initiation of the proposed Galapagos giant tortoise work.

The cays of the Capricorn–Bunker group, like all true cays, are built up entirely from coral sand and pieces of coral. Cays tend to be small and these are no exception. The largest in the group, North-West Island, is about two hundred and twenty acres and almost a mile long. However, many are very small with a total acreage of ten acres or less and the longer dimension only several hundred yards. Most are extremely low, so low in fact that a tidal wave of about six feet would inundate most of the island. The highest point on Heron Island, which occurs part way along south beach, is only 12 feet above mean tide level and most of the island is very much lower than this. Wreck Island is unusual in that although very narrow it rises to a height of 20/30 feet above mean tide level.

Usually the beaches are gently sloping terminating at a more or less well marked bank, of variable height and slope, which encircles the island. On Heron Island this bank averages about three feet in height on the north and eastern beaches and reaches a maximum of about 12 feet on part of south beach. The banks play an important role in turtle nesting (see Chapters 5 and 6).

Coral sand is extremely porous so provides excellent drainage for incubating eggs. Except in the older parts of the island where the vegetation consists of *Pisonia* forest there is little humus content. On exposed beaches a superficial layer of broken shell and coral fragments is often present after storms.

Beach rock is present in variable quantities on most of the Capricorn–Bunker cays. There has been much speculation about how this is formed. It consists of fragments of coral and/or coral sand which have become cemented together. Frequently, once the surface layer is broken, it readily disintegrates. Beach rock, where extensive areas are present, provides a considerable barrier to turtles attempting to emerge from the sea except when it is completely covered by the tide. The extensive beach rock greatly reduces utilisation of this beach area for nesting by green turtles. A view of part of the beach-rock present on south beach, Heron Island, is given in plate 1. Loggerheads very rarely cross any areas of extensive beach rock. Even where it is much less extensive as on areas of north beach, Heron Island, it may form a low 'wall' and thus hinder turtle progress up or down the beach.

On some islands, Wilson and Wreck for example, large slabs of beach rock have been cast up on the beach by cyclonic storms effectively preventing turtle access to these parts of the island. The beach rock may also prove a serious obstacle to hatchling turtles making their way to the sea (Chapter 8).

Cay vegetation shows marked similarities throughout the whole Indo–Pacific region. Typically the central part of Capricon–Bunker islands is dominated by a dense forest of *Pisonia* trees (*Pisonia grandis*) which may reach a height of over one hundred feet. *Pisonia* has large, soft, pale-green leaves and forms a canopy so that there is no bush, shrub layer or annuals in the *Pisonia* forest. The branches are fibrous and readily break off when stressed. During cyclonic storms, falling *Pisonia* branches are a serious hazard. At such times the leaves are shed or become wind-scorched with the result that the wind resistance of the tree is greatly reduced.

The *Pisonia* forest demarcates the oldest existing part of the island. Typically the *Pisonia* forest is surrounded by a fringing forest of *Casuarina equisitifolia* and to a lesser extent *Pandanus* palms (*Pandanus tectorius*, and others). Hence areas where *Pisonia* forest reaches down to the beach are undergoing serious erosion.

The area of high beach platform immediately above the bank has shorter but rounded and spreading trees (*Messerschmidia argentea*) which reach a height of about twenty feet, and somewhat lower bushes of *Scaevola frutescens*. These may be interspersed with the *Pandanus* and *Casuarina*. All four may be found growing on the bank slope (plate 4). *Messerschmidia* and *Scaevola* both have branches growing horizontally close to the ground and provide nesting cover attractive to green turtles. *Messerschmidia* has a gnarled trunk and the leaves are soft, non-shiny, dark green and covered with tiny hair-like processes which give them a silvery sheen, hence '*argentea*'. *Scaevola frutescens* has a smooth trunk and branches, and the pale green leaves are shiny. At least two species of grasses, *Stenotaphrum subulatum* and *Sporobolus virginicus*, are important in stabilising the bank and newly-formed dunes which do not yet possess bush or shrub cover.

Examination of the vegetation provides extensive insight into the history of the cay. These small cays are dynamic entities which undergo considerable changes in shape and size as a result of sand deposition or erosion. The limits of the *Pisonia* forest represent the boundaries of the island at the height of a previous erosive period. The other vegetational zones represent younger sections of the island which have been added during subsequent building-up periods which then underwent successive plant colonisation. One of the interesting aspects of coral cays is that this process can be seen in action to-day. Since turtles play an important role in erosion, the whole problem deserves discussion.

If one examines the outer fringing vegetation of a cay, which is also an important turtle rookery during the summer, one is immediately struck by the absence of young *Scaevola* and *Messerschmidia* bushes, *Pandanus* and *Casuarina* trees. Quite clearly no regeneration is taking place. If one examines the same cay in early summer prior to the arrival of the turtles numerous seedlings will be seen. These will be particularly prominent on new areas of high beach platform. However, after several weeks of turtle activity all will have been destroyed. The turtles prevent seedlings 'getting away' and hence halt regeneration in the fringing zone of the island above the bank where they nest. Since the vegetation plays an important role in consolidating the perimeter of the island, the turtles help the erosive process. However, their influence is much greater than this.

When erosion results in tree roots becoming exposed at the edge of the bank, turtles hasten the loss of these trees, since they tend to become entangled in the roots and nest below them rather than climbing the bank. This results in further undermining of the trees. An example of this as it affects *Casuarina* on Heron Island is shown in plate 4. At the northern end of Shark's Bay, where the photograph was taken, two rows of *Casuarina* have been lost in the last four years. While it is true that erosive factors are currently at work at that part of the island and would continue in the absence of turtles, it is equally certain that the turtles cause the erosion to proceed much more rapidly than would occur in their absence.

There is a third situation in which the turtles play an important role in erosion. The fortnightly spring high tides come right up to the bank, and, where this is pronounced, result in a cliffing effect – the bank is sheer to a height of several feet. The first turtles arriving after these tides are unable to climb the sheer bank so are compelled to nest at the foot. In the process they dig into the bank (throwing sand seawards) and undermine it. The combination of moving sand seawards and bank cave-ins result in the bank being moved back in the direction of the interior of the island. Subsequent turtles are able to climb the bank which has now reverted to an inclined plane. They nest either on the bank slope or on top of the bank and, consequently, tend to move further areas of sand seawards. Provided there is a tendency for erosion to occur, this sand is removed by the sea during the next spring tide cycle and the newly-formed 'cliffs' result in the whole process commencing again. The sequence is shown diagrammatically in figure 1.

Whereas, in the absence of turtles, trees, bushes and grasses consolidate the dunes and the bank slope, tending to minimise erosion effects, the presence of turtles actively potentiates erosion. This is a result of interfering with vegetation regeneration, preventing grass colonisation of the bank and by actively moving sand seawards. If a small area of high beach platform is enclosed to prevent turtle access, the result is most startling – regeneration takes place rapidly.

One might be excused for wondering how vegetation ever colonises these cays under such conditions. This process can be seen, nevertheless, on some Capricorn cay beaches at present. It must be remembered that turtles only occupy a fairly narrow zone around the perimeter of the island and beyond this have no effect on the vegetation. On islands with beaches showing a substantial net gain of sand, once the build-up reaches a certain stage the area of unconsolidated dune becomes broader than most turtles penetrate. The absence of vegetation will tend to make green turtles avoid the area and loggerheads will nest on the seaward edge of the dune. Under such circumstances we have seen the grass *Stenotaphrum subulatum* successfully cover large areas over a period of four or five years. In the early years its growth was seriously affected by turtle activity. However, as it became established turtles posed only a slight problem since they tend to avoid digging in areas of grass, finding it difficult to commence a body pit. Over a shorter period we have watched a new layer of *Scaevola* become established, and these small bushes will now attain full size unless the additive process on this beach is reversed. Hence, the bushes and trees which now fringe the island did not develop in their present position. Due to turtle activity, we know they must have made their key growth further inland and, since they cannot move, the bank must have moved and encroached upon them.

The fortnightly spring high tides come right up to the bank in the day-time (the day tides being higher than those at night) as is shown in plate 4. Where erosion has been occurring the vegetation suffers inundation by salt-water at root level; but most species appear fairly resistant to salt.

There is yet another relationship between the vegetation–cay

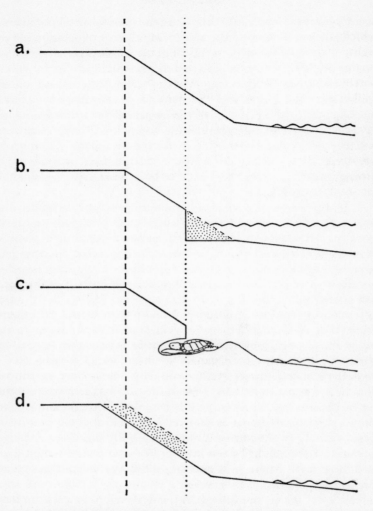

FIG. I A diagrammatic representation of the role of the green turtle in bank erosion on nesting cays. In each section of the figure the high beach platform, the bank (inclined slope) and beach (very shallow slope) and the sea are indicated. Sand just displaced is dotted. (a) situation at the start of an erosive cycle, (b) cliffing of bank by fortnightly high tides, (c) turtle, unable to climb bank, digs into base, and (d) undermines it, resulting in the top of the bank being shifted backwards towards the centre of the island, and the slope of the bank being restored to (a).

accretion/erosion cycle and the size of the nesting turtle population which the cay supports. On a cay where dense vegetation comes right down to the spring high-tide mark there is nowhere for turtles to nest. As noted previously they do not dig in grassy patches and where these occur in any small open areas or a dense wall of *Scaevola* is present at the spring high-tide mark there is no place for the turtles to dig. Given access to some suitable areas the turtles can in time enlarge these, as a result of their interaction with the vegetation. However, this requires abundant utilisation by nesting turtles, and on cays where nesting sites are extremely limited, and the nesting population is therefore small, it is difficult for the process to get started. On such cays, the building-up process, by providing new areas of high beach platform, above spring high tide, often provides the first opportunity in the long-term cycle for turtle colonisation. It then becomes a question of whether or not sufficient turtles utilise the area to prevent its complete colonisation by dense vegetation. I have seen early stages in this process in the Fiji Islands, for instance at Nanuku Levu in the Eastern Group.

Before leaving the vegetation I would like to stress that despite the overall similarity between widely distant cays – for instance in the Fijian cays *Messerschmidia argentea*, *Scaevola frutescens* and *Pandanus* are equally conspicuous as on the Great Barrier Reef – there may be marked differences between the dominant vegetation of cays only a few miles apart. These differences usually reflect the age of the cay, or its previous history. For instance, on Wilson Island the *Pisonia* forest is poorly developed and the dominant tree on most of the island is *Pandanus*. On Erskine Island *Pisonia* is extremely stunted and *Messerschmidia* occupies the dominant bush/tree niche. Many younger cays only have a cover of grass and other low vegetation.

The water table is often close to the surface but its position may vary greatly over distances of only ten yards. Hence turtles in certain spots will succeed in nesting despite prolonged periods without rain, whereas others only a few yards away will be unsuccessful. Surprisingly this water is often fresh. On One-Tree Island there is a pond in the middle of the cay filled with somewhat brackish water which rises and falls with the tide. Bores have been sunk on several islands and have struck fresh water reserves although these were not adequate for commercial purposes.

The Capricorn–Bunker cays possess no indigenous terrestrial

vertebrate animals other than birds. They are important nesting grounds for the white-capped noddy tern (*Anous minutus*) where the *Pisonia* forest is well developed, and many also support very large populations of mutton birds (*Puffinus pacificus*). Populations of reef herons (*Egretta sacra*), from which Heron Island derives its name, also occur on many of the older cays. A pair of white-fronted sea eagles (*Haliaetus leucogaster*) also nest on each tree-covered cay.

It is the absence of other vertebrates which makes the cays such ideal nesting places for turtles since the eggs cannot be destroyed by monitor lizards, dingoes, foxes and pigs which patrol many mainland beaches.

Cyclones can do tremendous damage to cays, and as a result of their lack of elevation, considerable areas of them may be swept over by cyclonic waves. During cyclone Dinah in February 1967, we estimated that the bank was eroded back eight feet on south beach Heron Island. Naturally these cyclones destroy huge numbers of incubating turtle eggs.

The major rainfall pattern results from cyclonic activity towards the end of the summer. The wettest month is March in which there is an average of about 1500 mm of rain, based on data for the years 1959 to 1965 inclusive. Onset of wet weather varies from year to year but the months December to February and April and May average around 1000 mm based on rainfall information over the same period. The dry season starts in August and lasts until November or, exceptionally, December. Rainfall for November and December is highly variable; for instance November 1961 was exceptionally wet (1710 mm), the average for the remaining six years being about 600 mm.

Rainfall patterns in November and December greatly affect turtle nesting success since nesting commences immediately following the driest part of the year. When little rain falls in November (and this may extend into at least part of December), it is extremely difficult for turtles to excavate an egg chamber and many attempts are usually necessary before success is achieved (see Chapter 4).

The Capricorn–Bunker cays have an oceanic climate and summer temperatures show little variation throughout the twenty-four hour period. Temperatures measured in a standard Stevenson screen one metre from the ground over the period November to February inclusive varied from 21–30°C (70–86°F). The variation over a twenty-four hour period seldom exceeded 5°C (9°F). Rainfall and temperature were measured on Heron Island but are similar throughout the group.

Although the detail presented in this chapter is based on cays in the Capricorn Group at the southern end of the Barrier Reef, the general information is of wide applicability.

PART TWO

The Lives of Turtles

THE chapters which follow deal almost exclusively with the small but vitally important segment of the turtles' lives spent ashore. This is because we know virtually nothing about the day to day lives of turtles at sea.

In Chapter 4 a detailed account of the nesting behaviour of the green turtle is provided. The green turtle is chosen for this account as in most parts of the world it is the species most likely to be encountered. There are no marked differences in nesting behaviour between green turtle populations in different areas of the world. Furthermore, the account can be taken as providing a typical outline of nesting for any species of sea turtle since differences between species are relatively minor. A brief account of loggerhead nesting appears in Chapter 5 in order to point out the degree to which other species may diverge from the green turtle.

A whole chapter (6) has been devoted to the flatback turtle, since this is by far the least known of the world's sea turtles and one with which we have considerable experience. The chapter provides a summary of current information on the species.

Chapter 7 provides Australian information on three other species of sea turtle.

CHAPTER 4

Nesting Behaviour of the Green Turtle

THE calm water in the moonlight is like a pool of mercury. The noise of the waves breaking against the reef's edge reaches our ears. As we watch the moon's reflection on the water, a silvery shape becomes visible about three yards from the beach. The object, or the part that is visible, is smooth and somewhat rounded. The silvery sheen is due to the moonlight striking the wet smooth surface. Suddenly the object heads beachward with three sudden, jerky movements and as the gentle swell recedes, the shape of a turtle is unmistakable. It remains stationary for several minutes, the water lapping against its shell. It appears very large. Periodically it raises its head, then starts to move up the beach. The movement is laboured and the animal clearly has some difficulty in hauling its weight across the soft sand. Soon it stops to rest.

After about a minute the head is raised and the creature makes several throaty noises, then movement up the beach recommences. The reptile progresses by advancing both its front flippers together and literally dragging itself forward. Later we see that by acting in unison with the front limbs, the rear flippers also help to push it forward. Hence the body is never raised clear of the ground but moved forward a few inches at a time by simultaneous pulling and pushing of both pairs of limbs. The turtle makes a series of these movements and then rests. As it progresses farther up the beach we notice that the rest periods decrease until they average under a minute's duration.

Now the turtle is almost upon us. She, for the turtle is a female which has come ashore to lay her eggs, had emerged from the water only a few yards to our left and appears to be making for a clump of what we learned later was called *Messerschmidia*, situated immediately behind us. We are sitting – motionless as instructed – on the sand above the spring high-tide mark close to the vegetation. The turtle is now no more than two turtle lengths from our feet and for a moment it appears that it will actually walk over us.

49

When it first dragged itself out of the water it appeared enormous and beside us in the shadows we are again impressed by its size. It must measure between three and a half and four feet in shell length and over three feet in breadth. The head is small, and the front flippers, now so close to our feet, are large and powerful. As we sit, scarcely daring to breathe, it raises its head and we learn that the noise we heard on the beach at the end of rests was made by it exhaling air from its lungs. It takes a breath and then laboriously pull-pushes its great weight abreast of us, stops, and then moves just past us. The incline has increased as it is nearing the edge of the 'bank' of sand which runs round the island. The increased slope together with a change in the resistance of the sand to pressure – the sand above the high-tide mark being dry and soft – causes it to make very little progress with each forward movement. It rests.

We are on a small cay on Australia's Great Barrier Reef where one of the prime attractions after dark is turtle watching. This is our first turtle and now that it is safely up the beach we feel we can relax a little. Looking down the beach we can count eleven other tracks and see four other turtles making their way across the sand and one returning to the water. Before going turtling we carefully re-read a brochure we had been given on arrival at the island. This outlined how to watch turtles digging their nests and laying their eggs without frightening them. The brochure stressed the importance of keeping out of sight of beaching turtles and those making their way up the beach to the vegetation zone. We were told to avoid using torches wherever possible, at least until the turtle was laying its eggs.

We decided to move in among the bushes to continue watching our turtle . . .

The turtle has now moved about six yards over the bank and is close to a *Scaevola* bush. As we watch her, she makes several sweeping movements with her front flippers rather like swimming into the sand, and then moves forward. At the rear of the bush she stops again and makes a similar series of front flipper movements after which she rests. The front flipper movements are continued with increasing force. The flippers are angled slightly so that they dig into the sand and each backward stroke showers sand vigorously behind the turtle. After a few minutes the rear flippers move. The front flipper action has resulted in piles of sand collecting at each side of the turtle where the front flipper stroke ceases. As the turtle moves slightly forward by digging into the sand, the rear flippers are able to reach this sand. Working independently they push it backwards. By now there is quite a depression around the turtle. The head is just below the level of the sand surface and the turtle is digging vigorously with the front flippers. Interruptions by rest periods are frequent. The digging continues for a total of about twenty minutes when suddenly the action of the rear flippers changes. Instead of pushing sand backwards by a lateral action the flippers dig downwards, curve and become almost like hands. They seem to be trying to scoop sand. The body of the turtle, which has been resting stationary on the sand throughout the preceding twenty minutes, now moves slightly at the rear so that each scooping flipper is in turn placed directly over the same spot.

The depression in which the turtle is resting is approximately oval but somewhat larger than the turtle. The bottom is almost horizontal; if anything the turtle is angled slightly downwards posteriorly. The depth of the depression, which is known as the body pit, is about fifteen inches. The domed region of the centre of the turtle's carapace is on a level with the sand surrounding the pit.

The rear flippers continue to work away in the soft sand. They seem to be making very little progress. As each 'handful' of sand is removed, surrounding sand falls in almost negating the digging effort. However, after a further five minutes a definite depression forms. The flippers go through a scooping process which culminates in a flipperful of sand being lifted out of the hole in the cupped flipper and deposited on the ground beside the hole. The flippers are now decidedly hand-like in their action and are seen to be remarkably flexible.

A definite and regular series of actions takes place between which the turtle rests. The left rear flipper hangs down the hole. The right rear flipper is resting flat on the sand adjacent to the hole. The turtle breathes, then the left flipper reaches down the hole and scoops sand. The sand is deposited on the left hand side of the hole and then the right rear flipper flicks sand laterally. By pressing down firmly with the left rear flipper the posterior of the body is raised clear of the hole. It is then rotated to position the right flipper directly above the hole. The flipper is then curved so as to enter the hole without damaging the walls and scoops sand which is deposited on the right of the hole. The left rear flipper flicks sand away, the body is rotated once more and the left flipper positioned over the hole. This flipper is curved and enters the hole. It reaches down and activity ceases. The rest periods invariably occur with the same flipper, but it can be either one, resting in the hole. Digging may involve one series of flipper movements but more usually two or three cycles are completed between rests. The lateral flicking action of the flippers prior to their insertion into the hole reduces the piles of extracted sand. If not removed these piles would become so large that sand would fall back into the hole.

Each rest period is terminated by the turtle elevating its head and exhaling noisily. It then gulps air into its lungs by a pumping action of the throat. When on land, turtles have considerable difficulty in breathing. At sea the water provides support for their bodies but when ashore their weight presses down on their lungs making inhalation difficult. In turtles the problem is overcome during the several hours involved in nesting by elevating the head as described above.

The hole dug by the rear flippers, called the egg chamber, is now almost as deep as their reach. As digging progresses the turtle achieves greater digging depth by raising the front of the body slightly with the front flippers and so angling the rear downwards. During the next ten minutes little progress is made. Sand slipping into the hole, particularly when the rear of the turtle is moved to position the next digging flipper, seems to just keep pace with that removed by the digging action. As we watch, a small avalanche of sand enters the hole from a cave-in of the wall at the left of the egg chamber. Digging action ceases. After several minutes the turtle moves forwards and then clambers out of the body pit. As a result of the sand slippage it has abandoned the hole and will move off to try again somewhere else. The whole laborious process has to be carried out again from the commencement of digging the body pit.

Clearly, sand moisture is the major factor in determining success or failure in digging the egg chamber. After prolonged periods without rain, when the sand is very dry even at the level of the floor of the body pit, digging the egg chamber is extremely difficult. Other factors which affect digging success are discussed below. When the sand is very dry few turtles are successful at their first attempt. In fact, many fail even after digging for the greater part of a night during which five or more egg chambers may be attempted. These turtles, and others which give up after two or three attempts,

5. (a) Female green turtle lying in shallows to escape attention of promiscuous males, Bountiful Island, Gulf of Carpentaria, Australia.

(b) Female green turtle stranded on the beach by receding tide after having swum to the water's edge to avoid male attentions. Bountiful Island. Note barnacles on head.

6/7. (a) Male green turtle back to camera (note the greatly elongated tail) courting female.

(b) First stage of courtship — nuzzling — in the green turtle. The male is facing the camera. Bountiful Island.

(c) Subsequent stage in courtship. Male green turtle (facing camera) is making a 'bite' near the female's shoulder. The thumb claw, which the male uses to hook onto the female during copulation, is clearly visible on the left flipper.

(d) A pair of copulating green turtles, Bountiful Island.

8. (a) Rocky Island, N.W. of Mornington Island, Gulf of Carpentaria, north Queensland, from the air. The craters on the beaches result from turtle nesting.

(b) Aerial photograph of an aggregation of courting green turtles in the shallows, Rocky Island, N.W. Mornington Island, Gulf of Carpentaria, Australia.

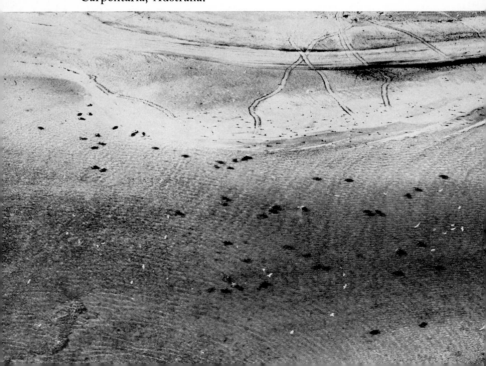

return to try again the following night and/or the night thereafter. We have records of a number of turtles which have tried for up to five nights before succeeding. During this time they may dig up to twenty egg chambers. Fortunately for the turtles the vast majority are successful long before this!

Our turtle has now moved about eight yards further inland and has commenced digging a body pit partly underneath an old *Messerschmidia*. The area adjacent to the site, and between the first nesting attempt and the present location, is clearly popular with turtles as the sand is 'cratered' with old diggings. The second location selected is a crater. As is often the case, the head down posture, resulting from entering the old pit, released the digging urge, and front flipper digging activity commenced. The depressions result mainly from the leaving pit, which we will see later, although signs of egg chamber activity indicate that some were the sites of unsuccessful nesting attempts.

After about fifteen minutes, front flipper activity ceased and the rear flippers changed their action to digging instead of pushing sand away. After the initial difficulty in digging the hole, progress is fairly rapid until the hole is almost half dug and the turtle strikes an obstruction. The turtle attempts the downward scooping action with the digging rear flipper and is rewarded. The obstruction gives way and the flipper brings up three broken turtle eggs. Digging continues. The turtle has by chance dug its egg chamber in the site previously used by another turtle. Hence in digging its own egg chamber it is destroying the earlier eggs. Each flipperful of sand includes eggs. Many are broken but some are intact. The broken eggs contain well-developed turtles almost ready to hatch. They are fully pigmented and try to move on the sand. However, a considerable amount of yolk is still present and the baby turtles have a fold across the middle of the plastron. All will die. With the coming of dawn one sharp sighted silver gull (*Larus novaehollandiae*) will detect the carnage and soon a flock of gulls will descend on the baby turtles and rip open the undamaged eggs to get at their contents. Even if the gulls do not detect the undamaged eggs the baby turtles therein will be killed in a few hours by the heat of the sun.

The egg chamber has now reached the full depth – the maximum reach of the rear flippers even with the added assistance given by angling the rear of the shell downwards. The turtle is engaged in widening the foot of the chamber. Near the surface the egg chamber is approximately square – slightly wider from left to right than from front to back and the sides descend almost vertically. The breadth (left to right) is eight inches. Enlarging the foot of the egg chamber by sideways scooping movements of the flippers occupies about ten minutes. The digging action has altered. Each flipper makes several scooping movements before being withdrawn with its load of sand. This results from the difficulty in obtaining sand now that the chamber is nearing completion. Shortly thereafter, the left flipper is placed half-way into the hole but instead of digging is positioned against the posterior surface of the hole diagonally from left to right. The egg chamber is now complete and ready to receive the eggs. In shape it is rather like a pear with a definite neck-region and a much wider chamber below, which will house most of the eggs. The egg chamber is sixteen inches deep, and since the body pit has a depth of fifteen inches the foot of the chamber is approximately thirty-one inches below the level of the surrounding sand. A diagrammatic representation is given in Figs 2 and 3.

The right rear flipper is brought backwards to cover part of the hole and the cloacal region, which opens on the underside of the short thick tail, contracts several times. This is followed by exudation of about a tablespoon of viscous mucus which falls into the egg chamber. After a couple of minutes an egg is extruded and falls into the hole, soon to be followed by another and then another. The eggs are white, almost circular, slightly larger than a ping-pong ball and covered with mucus. The shell is soft and parchment-like similar to that of most snakes and lizards. The shell can be dented as the egg is not quite turgid. There are now eight or nine eggs in the egg chamber and this time the turtle expels two eggs together. As egg laying progresses eggs come out in

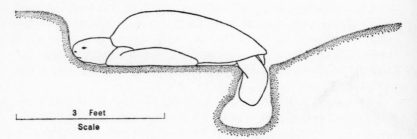

3   Feet
Scale

FIG. 2 Green turtle in body pit with completed egg chamber.

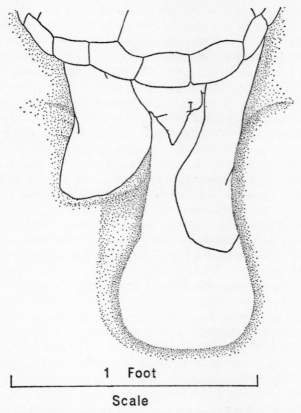

1 Foot

Scale

FIG. 3 Rear view of green turtle and almost completed egg chamber.

twos, occasionally in threes or even fours. Between each laying there are contractions of the cloacal region, and preceding laying muscular contraction in which intra-abdominal pressure is increased by slight limb retraction. This probably helps to eject the eggs.

The turtle has now laid 134 eggs and the rate of egg laying has decreased markedly. Eggs are being laid singly or in twos. After expelling its 140th egg the turtle rests. The mucus which dripped from the cloaca periodically during laying, and which coated each egg, is still extruded each time the cloaca contracts but now no further eggs are laid. After a couple of minutes the rear flipper in the neck of the egg chamber is removed and reaching out to one

55

side drags sand across to the edge of the egg chamber. The flipper stops just short of the egg chamber. The right rear flipper then performs a similar action. These movements show a remarkable degree of sensitivity quite unexpected in a heavy animal which appears clumsy on land. At no time do the flippers touch the eggs nor do they make any strong sweeping action close to the eggs until these have been covered by a substantial layer of sand. After a few minutes a mound of sand builds up over the site of the egg chamber as a result of the action of the rear flippers which is now more vigorous and involves a vertical patting action as well as horizontal movement of sand. Digging the egg chamber and covering the eggs is one of the remarkable feats of turtle behaviour since it is carried out so precisely without any visual cues.

Without warning the front flippers now make several sweeping movements sending a shower of sand backwards. The rear flippers then continue to pile sand on the mound. The tail seems to serve as a location point in this behaviour as sand is dragged in by the rear flipper until the flipper or the sand it is guiding touches the tail. Periodically, the rear flippers consolidate the sand on top of the eggs by a kneading process using the sides of the curved flippers. The front flippers move again and gradually their action becomes more vigorous. At the same time, rear flipper activity decreases and eventually ceases altogether. The front flippers may act in unison or individually. The action of the rear flippers during the covering action, as when excavating, is always an alternate movement.

After half an hour the turtle does not appear to have filled in the body pit to any extent. The powerful action of the front flippers has been directed at the low wall of sand in front of the head and as this caved in the turtle has slowly moved forwards. The result of its activity, therefore, has been to dig out in front and fill in behind. Its tail is now almost a yard in front of the position where we think the eggs were laid. I say 'think' since it is impossible to be certain about this as the whole area has been disturbed by the filling-in activity and the front flipper action has spread sand to both sides as well as tailwards.

The action continues with the front flippers now often acting together and performing such a vigorous breast stroke that at the end of each stroke both flippers strike the shell making a loud noise. We can hear similar noises coming from several areas down the beach, so presumably a number of other turtles have also reached this stage of the filling-in process.

After a further half hour the turtle has moved at least three yards farther forward and we notice that the body pit is becoming shallower. The 'wall' of sand in front of the head is now noticeably lower. In the last hour the turtle appears to have moved appreciably more sand in the filling-in process – we estimate about a third of a ton – than it did in digging the body pit and egg chamber. The turtle has stopped and raises its head to breathe. Without warning it then climbs out of the egg chamber and turns to face the sea. It rests again, before moving on. On reaching the bank it makes one strong series of flipper movements and toboggans down the bank coming to rest partly under a *Messerschmidia* branch at the foot. It recommences forward pull-push movements but despite its strength is unable to displace the branch and it is obvious that it will not be able to pass underneath. After some minutes it makes a clumsy attempt to back out. It stops to breathe. The head is lifted above the branch and after breathing comes to rest on top of it. When the turtle next moves it lifts its front flippers in an attempt to climb over the branch. The left front flipper, which is on slightly higher ground, easily clears the obstruction but the right flipper, despite numerous attempts, cannot do more than come to rest partly on the branch with the weight on the wrong side. After a pause lasting four minutes the turtle now attempts to back out but is unable to lift the left front flipper back over the branch which is partly under the shoulder of the left flipper. Rotation of the flipper is handicapped by the trunk of the bush which comes into contact with the distal part of the flipper at each attempt to free it. We can see only one way in which the turtle can free itself. It must move forwards about six inches in order to secure freedom of movement to rotate the left flipper and hence bring it back across the branch. The turtle makes numerous movements all to no avail. After forty-five minutes it happens to be in a position where it can free itself, presumably as a result of chance. It brings the flipper back over the branch and turning sideways moves around it and proceeds on to the beach. The limb action is the same as when it came up the beach; however, the downward slope makes movement easier than when it was ascending, and a greater number of limb movements occur between rests.

The turtle beached shortly after high-tide and now the tide is almost out. A strip of low beach rock which it must have swum across on the way in is exposed near the foot of the beach. Beyond this there is an area of muddy sand stretching for about seventy-five yards, and farther out portions of the coral on the reef flat are exposed.

The turtle continues down the beach and reaches a low area of beach rock only six to eight inches in height. It could clear this with ease yet to our amazement it makes no attempt. Instead it turns sideways and moves along the sand parallel to the rock. The turtle turned left and in this direction the beach rock is increasing in height. Only two yards to the right there was a break in the beach rock which the turtle apparently did not see. After moving about thirty yards the turtle stops, approaches the beach rock, turns again and moves back in the direction in which it came. Half-way back to where it first struck the rock it makes another unsuccessful approach. It continues parallel to the beach rock until it strikes the break and moving through this continues down the beach. Soon the turtle is on the area of muddy sand. Progress across this is extremely slow with frequent lengthy stops. It takes twenty-five minutes to cross this region and eventually reaches the sea where it rests with its head just at the water's edge. Soon it crawls into the water. Due to the air in its lungs it is extremely buoyant and is able to swim despite the shallowness of the water. It heads directly towards the deep sea over the edge of the reef. There is still a mound of sand on the carapace. However, this is soon washed off as it reaches deeper water and exhales. The last we see of it is when it comes up for air about a hundred yards from the water's edge. We had spent six hours watching our first turtle which we later learned was about twice the average nesting time for a green turtle.

Having closely watched one turtle lay, one finds only minor variations with subsequent green turtles. I say this as one who has watched many hundreds of nesting green turtles. Variations almost all result from the special circumstances of that particular nest except for cases of damage to the turtle.

It is not uncommon for a turtle to lose part or all of one rear flipper as a result of shark attack. Naturally this is a handicap in the digging of the egg chamber. The greatest disadvantage often results from a damaged flipper. Even when the rear limb has been bitten off above the 'knee' the stump still goes through the normal sequence of digging actions in its turn. However, in these cases the stump does not affect the excavation. A less seriously damaged flipper may actually handicap the digging process by striking the wall of the egg chamber and so causing sand slippage. However, the usual result of damage to a rear flipper is merely to prolong the time necessary for the excavation of the egg chamber, since at best productive digging is only taking place for fifty percent of the time. When one rear flipper is damaged and cannot participate in digging the resultant egg chamber will be of an irregular shape. The chamber will only be little excavated on the damaged side (since the other flipper cannot reach far across) and frequently extremely well excavated on the undamaged side.

We have several turtles in our marked populations which have sustained damage to both rear flippers. Some of these are only able to dig shallow egg chambers so that many of the eggs roll about the floor of the body pit, and a few are quite unable to dig an egg chamber. However, all of these still respond to the biological urge to nest and come out night after night spending many hours in fruitless digging attempts. Those that are unable to dig an egg chamber may eventually perhaps drop the eggs at sea. Some return to the sea laying a series of eggs as they progress down the beach.

Loss of a front flipper is a much greater obstacle to a turtle's future life and one would expect such turtles to fall victim to a shark. Indeed, it is difficult to see how they escaped from the initial attack. Remarkably, they learn to swim using the remaining flipper and still come ashore to nest. One of our largest turtles (carapace length forty-six inches) has lost its left front flipper at the shoulder (plate 12). This turtle is so heavy that it would have some difficulty getting up a steep beach even undamaged yet it manages to haul itself ashore using only the right front flipper. Progress up even a narrow beach is extremely slow – it takes it half an hour to cover what a normal turtle would accomplish in about five minutes. Turtles lacking a front flipper are still able to make a body pit although this is shallower than usual. The egg-laying process, of course, is not handicapped. However, these turtles may have difficulty in clambering out of the body pit after covering over the eggs. A group of us twice removed the large damaged female shown in plate 12 after she had completed disguising the nest site and put her back in the sea.

Green turtles emerge to lay their eggs only under cover of darkness. They also show a strong tide-cycle response, coming ashore on or around the high tide. Although this saves them considerable travelling on land before nesting the converse is the case when they have to return to the water. Since the time of high water changes daily so does the nesting time of the turtles. On the Barrier Reef cays where we work it would not be possible for a turtle to come ashore on most low tides. Quite apart from the impossibility of crossing the reef platform, which extends for up to half a mile at low tide, negotiating the reef edge would be hazardous or impossible. There are usually breakers at the edge of the reef and except when the edge is covered by several feet of water, turtles presumably face a similar risk of being smashed against projecting coral, as would small boats. Since the turtle plastron is not nearly so protective as the carapace, this risk may be serious.

The green turtles we study mostly come ashore from about one hour before, to one to two hours after the time of high tide. Since there are the customary two tides a day there is always a night high tide. When this occurs in the evening around nightfall the turtle beaching times are distorted since they wait for twilight before emerging. This results in all emergence taking place after high tide on two or three nights in the fortnightly tide cycle. At these times turtles are influenced by both tides. The tide which has been the night tide reaches the stage when it is high around dawn. At such times the turtles come in earlier than one would anticipate and may all be up before high tide. This depends on the time of high tide in relation to dawn. The day high is now occurring in the late afternoon and some turtles respond to it by beaching on the falling tide as soon as it becomes dark. After several days this tide becomes the night tide and the early morning tide reaches its maximum height during the day.

Turtles which come ashore in the hour or two preceding dawn usually become nervous at daybreak and return to the water unless they have made substantial progress with their egg chamber or are laying. Successful turtles remain ashore, unless frightened by people, to complete the filling-in process in the usual way. They can still be nesting when the sun is high providing excellent opportunities for photography.

The relationship between high tide and beaching is so well established that we know exactly at what time one should go out each night in order to see turtles. Since we want to see all the turtles, our patrolling hours are considerably in excess of this but the times are invaluable for visitors to the rookery.

Often we see turtles swimming parallel to the beach in shallow

9. (a) Green turtle excavating body pit, Heron Island.

(b) Green turtle commencing excavation of egg chamber. Bountiful Island.

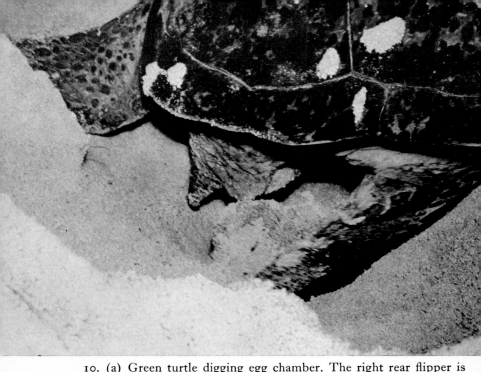

10. (a) Green turtle digging egg chamber. The right rear flipper is cupped like a hand and is removing sand.

(b) Green turtle with a neatly excavated egg chamber almost full of eggs.

water before they emerge. Whether they are looking for under-water cues before beaching is problematical. However, it seems likely that they have a good knowledge of the underwater geography of the area adjacent to their breeding ground.

Turtles are uniformly shy when just emerging from the water and there is a tendency to wheel round and shoot back into deep water if disturbed. As they progress farther up the beach they become more tolerant to disturbance although there is great indi-vidual variation. Some turtles when half-way up the beach will merely partly retract their head and front flippers should someone come close, and after a few minutes, if not disturbed further, will continue up the beach. Others partly turn round to subsequently continue up the beach. But some turn round and, even in the absence of further stimuli, continue quickly back to the water and swim out towards the reef edge. We have noticed that turtles are most nervous on nights when the moon is nearly full. This does not result merely from being able to see better, since, on nights when there is little or no moon, they are also more tolerant of torchlight.

Turtles are myopic when out of the water but even so their visual abilities must not be underestimated. At night, except when the object is completely stationary, their sight is better than man's. People walking on the white coral sand are easily detected at distances of several hundred yards.

During progression up the beach unusual objects are avoided. Often the turtle will turn aside to give a large log or object such as a rowing boat a wide berth.

The response of frightened turtles which return to the sea also shows much individual variation. Some swim round the island to beach somewhere else later the same evening, others return the following night but some may not return for two or more nights.

On all the islands we have examined, nesting is not uniform round the circumference of the island. Usually there are markedly favoured beaches. These lack bands of beach rock and usually have a deep water approach. Available nesting area above spring high-tide mark is also important. If the vegetation comes down as a solid wall to near the high-tide mark then little nesting can occur.

The nesting process is an arduous one for turtles. A number of turtles die ashore in situations where death must have occurred suddenly. On one occasion, I came up behind a turtle sitting in the laying position with a fully excavated egg chamber. When I carefully looked round the side to see if it was tagged, I found that it was dead. Clearly death had occurred almost instantaneously. The egg chamber had not been damaged and the turtle showed no external signs of damage. Not uncommonly, we find green turtles which have died above the high-tide mark within sight of the sea and are undamaged like the individual photographed on the high beach platform at Wreck Island. It seems probable that these turtles died as the result of a heart attack brought on by the heavy work involved in the nesting process.

Throughout nesting, turtles appear to cry. This has been described as a method of keeping the eyes free of sand. However, the behaviour is related to salt extraction (see Chapter 1).

One feature of the nesting process which requires further study is nest site selection. How does a turtle select a nesting site? We have done some work on this problem. In order for its eggs to incubate successfully on the cays with which we are familiar, it is essential that the turtles climb the bank before laying their eggs. This is because the fortnightly high tides come right up to the bank and will inundate any nests laid below it. The waterlogging effect, combined with salinity, kills the eggs. In practice ninety-five percent of the green turtles we have observed have nested above the bank.

Since the bank is ill-defined or even absent on some beaches, climbing the bank cannot be the whole answer. We have noted that green turtles show some tendency to nest close to substantial vegetation – large bushes or trees. Wreck Island provides a ready-made experimental situation in that it had a long sand-spit much of which is well above the spring high-tide mark. However, only two bushes are present on the whole area. We examined green turtle tracks in this region and noted that no matter where the turtle came out of the water it altered direction once it got up the beach and headed for one or other of the two *Messerschmidia*. This was convincing information that green turtles are strongly attracted to the vegetation zone for nesting and will not nest in the absence of trees. A surveyed map of this sand-spit and all the green turtle tracks which were fresh enough to survey on the day the work was carried out is shown in figure 4.

Finally, we needed to look at nesting sites where there were no trees whatsoever – where the climax vegetation was grasses or where vegetation was completely absent. As described in the next chapter, loggerhead turtles will nest on nascent cays which completely lack vegetation. We found that at the southern end of the Great Barrier Reef green turtles may emerge on these cays. However, the tracks indicate that these turtles crawl up the beach to the top of the cay and, in the absence of bushes or trees, soon crawl down the other side into the water without attempting to nest. It should be pointed out, however, that in north Queensland and elsewhere green turtles may nest on islands lacking tall vegetation.

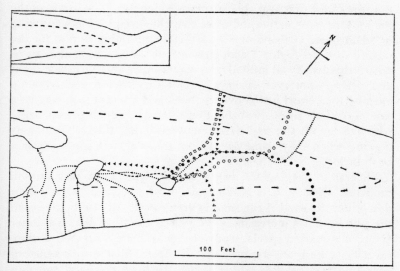

FIG. 4 Surveyed maps of Wreck Island sandspit in January 1968; inset showing low water mark and high water mark (dotted), enlarged detail shows vegetation and turtle tracks. Note that all tracks 'home in' on the vegetation.

All these pieces of information confirmed our previous feelings that our green turtles homed in on the vegetation zone. If they use bushes or trees as cues for nesting areas in combination with the sand characteristics described, then the eggs will clearly be laid above the spring high-tide mark. Trees, with the exception of mangroves, do not grow where they are liable to be inundated by the sea, and mangroves are associated with mud, not with sand suitable for turtle egg incubation.

It is worth noting that this observation could not have been

63

verified on an island which was uniformly well vegetated as one could not determine which of the available cues was attracting the turtles. Furthermore, green turtles do not necessarily lay beside vegetation but within the vegetated zone.

Selection of the actual site used for nesting is probably very complex. It has been mentioned above that a head-down inclination such as results from falling into an old pit is often sufficient to initiate the body pit digging behaviour. However, many turtles wander considerable distances before nesting and the majority do not nest in the first available location (which would be just over the bank). Our information indicates that this preliminary wandering or 'choosiness' is abandoned by a turtle attempting to nest for the second or third night. Although such turtles (the tags allow us to positively identify all individuals) may wander about the first night and perhaps not even attempt serious digging, on the following evening they crawl just above the bank and attempt to construct a nest at once. It seems probable that these individuals are not quite ready to lay on the first occasion. Wandering turtles often start digging when they come up against some obstruction such as a bush or log.

Success in digging the egg chamber depends in part on soil moisture. Clearly, it is much easier to dig a small hole straight down into the sand if the sand is very moist. All else being equal the task becomes increasingly difficult as the sand dries off. Peter Greenham made a special study of this problem with us and came up with some interesting results. He found that the presence of very fine tree rootlets which helped to bind the sand together resulted in digging success in areas where sand moisture alone would have resulted in failure. Since turtles tend to dig near vegetation this factor is important. Peter Greenham's work, combined with work of my own on controlled incubation of eggs under various regimes in the laboratory, resulted in an interesting general conclusion, namely, under average conditions of tree rootlets, if the sand was moist enough for the turtle to successfully dig a chamber it contained an adequate water content for incubation. This ensured that turtles were prevented from laying in areas where soil moisture would be too low for the eggs to survive. Clearly, the turtle has no control over the rainfall pattern and hence the water micro-environment of the nest, after egg laying. However, the mechanism described above will, on the average, increase incubation success, particularly in dry years. Full details of this and other physico-chemical features of the nest and eggs are given in Bustard and Greenham (1968) and Bustard and Greenham (1969).

Sometimes during the digging of the egg chamber the turtle comes across a large root. If this crosses the middle of the chamber the turtle may have to abandon the area and start again elsewhere. At such times it always chooses a new site and digs a fresh body pit. However, on a number of occasions we have watched turtles most adeptly remove sand round a root obstruction and so utilise the existing egg chamber.

As occurred in the nesting sequence described in this chapter, turtles quite often dig up nests laid previously by other turtles. This behaviour may be important in regulating population size and is discussed in Chapter 9.

Sometimes two turtles which are wandering about looking for a nesting site collide. Lack of manoeuvrability often leads to this when they are close to each other, and one is reminded of large ships at sea. Where both turtles are surprised – as when one descends an incline and bangs into another – both may return to the sea at once. Usually a turtle which is digging or filling in, and using its front flippers, is safe from disturbance. Nearly all turtles seem to detect the vibrations caused by the digging turtles and any which approach closely soon depart under a shower of sand. The one time that nesting turtles are vulnerable to disturbance by others is when they are quiet such as when digging the egg chamber or during laying eggs. I have seen many good egg chambers abandoned after another turtle slid into the body pit on to the occupant! In this case, the laying turtle will not move away and the attempts of the other turtle to climb out of the body pit may be ludicrous to watch. When two turtles are found nesting very close together this is usually the result of the second turtle commencing digging operations when the first has a well-formed egg chamber or is laying.

There are variations in the arrangement of the rear flippers during egg laying in the green turtle. They are either spread together over the nest or one or both flippers project posteriorly into and are pressed against the rear of the egg chamber. If only one flipper enters the egg chamber the other will serve to partly cover it during laying.

Clutch size averages about 110 eggs and is influenced by the size of the turtle (see Chapter 9). The largest clutch which I have observed consisted of 200 eggs. The smallest natural clutches consist of about sixty eggs. I say 'natural' as when turtles commence laying they can be easily disturbed and their reaction to disturbance depends on how severe this is. This sensitivity to disturbance is well marked until about thirty to forty eggs have been laid. If frightened before this they often stop laying, cover in the nest in the normal way and return to the sea. Evidence that the clutch was not a full complement is obtained when the same turtle emerges the following night and proceeds to lay the balance of a normal clutch of eggs. Touching the cloacal region early in the egg-laying process is often sufficient to cause the turtle to stop laying and fill in. When small clutches are laid without detectable disturbance examination of our records invariably shows that the turtle was disturbed previously and is now laying the balance of the clutch.

When the turtle is badly frightened it may leave the nest and, without making any attempt to even cover the egg chamber, return to the sea dropping eggs as it goes down the beach. After egg laying is well advanced, and when covering in, turtles are oblivious to all but the most severe disturbance. The only exception to this concerns turtles which are still filling in after daybreak. These are easily frightened.

The function of the very considerable task involved in continuing the body pit forwards after covering the egg chamber, is to disguise the actual site of the eggs. If this were not done then a predator could follow the tracks up the beach and know exactly where the eggs were located. A visual searcher is unable to detect the site of the eggs as a result of digging out and filling in this continuation of the body pit. Presumably, there is considerable survival value in the trait since the green turtle devotes a great deal of effort to it. On average, probably two-thirds of the total work involved in nesting takes place after egg laying. An example of a particularly well disguised nesting site of a green turtle is shown in plate 11. Unfortunately for the turtles, many egg predators have an acute sense of smell so the laborious work involved in disguising the nest site may be to no avail. In Australia there are no nest predators on the cays but on the mainland beaches large monitor lizards (*Varanus varius*) are a common predator. These lizards are particularly fond of eggs of all kinds and regularly patrol the beaches detecting nests by their smell, weeks after obvious visual signs have been obliterated. Other predators such as introduced fox and pigs, which are now numerous, also detect turtle eggs by smell.

Wind and heavy rain affect the nesting situation for turtles. When high winds are blowing, turtles tend to beach on the lee side of the island. They appear particularly affected by wind when on the beach and will turn so that their back faces into the wind and move parallel to the wind along the beach. Winds of about twenty knots or more cause dry surface sand particles to become airborne and cause a most unpleasant stinging sensation on bare arms and legs if one sits on the sand. The turtle is virtually at ground level and undoubtedly this effect on the eyes is the main problem.

Turtles do not object to nesting during heavy tropical storms, as my team know only too well. We may have a month or more of wet weather towards the end of the summer during which tropical downpours are an almost nightly occurrence. However, when the storm precedes turtle emergence it often causes a marked drop in nesting success. The turtles make their way up the beach as usual, but when they reach the vegetation zone the sand is wet instead of dry and soft. The latter seems to be an important releaser for starting digging because on very wet nights many turtles wander aimlessly for long distances returning to the sea without having made any digging attempts. Turtles are easily frightened by lightning and on nights when this is common beaching is impaired.

In concluding this chapter it is worth very briefly reviewing the main problems which nesting turtles face and how they overcome these. Basically they require to make a subterranean chamber large enough to contain the full egg complement and to place this so that none of the eggs suffer heat or drought effects due to being too close to the surface. Both the construction of the egg chamber and the environmental considerations necessitate a pre-liminary dig – the body pit. It would be a hopeless task, under average conditions, to attempt to dig a hole straight downwards commencing from the sand surface. Sand slippage would frustrate success and if this could be achieved it would result in a much wider hole being dug than is either necessary or ideal (see Chapter 8). Furthermore, the upper eggs would be only a few inches from the sand surface. Such eggs would be lost by overheating and the whole clutch would be likely to suffer from drying effects. Hence the body pit is an essential part of the nesting process.

CHAPTER 5

Nesting Behaviour of the Loggerhead Turtle

IT is four-thirty in the afternoon and although nightfall is still two and a half hours off, the heat of the day has passed and the shadows cast by the *Casuarina* trees fringing the beach are beginning to lengthen. The tide is in, high water was just before four.

Glancing out to sea from beneath a large *Casuarina*, where we spent the heat of the afternoon, we catch sight of a large head about fifty yards offshore. This disappears and soon we can pick out a turtle swimming lazily shorewards with slow powerful strokes of its front flippers. It reaches the shallows and stops. The head is raised and as well as taking a breath, the animal looks around. The large brown eyes are a conspicuous feature of the huge yellow-orange head. The jaws have a parrot-like beak. This is the turtle of 'Alice in Wonderland' – the loggerhead (*Caretta caretta*).

The turtle crawls a couple of yards forward and is now on the wet sand at the edge of the receding tide (plate 13). The massive head is lying flat on the ground. The turtle raises its head to breathe and then replaces it on the sand and moves forward up the beach. The head forms a furrow in the sand. Movement is rapid compared to the green turtle. Instead of the clumsy progression with all four flippers moving together, the loggerhead moves in the usual quadrupedal manner by means of alternate limb movements. It stops half-way up the beach and looks around. Unlike the green turtle it appears alert. However, this may result at least in part from the large head and conspicuous eyes. Once again the head is lowered and the turtle moves forward up the beach. Shortly after crossing the high-water mark the animal stops to take a breath. It then makes several swimming movements with the front flippers during which the head 'noses' into the sand. The flipper movements are clearly exploratory to test the sand. The turtle, apparently unsatisfied, moves forward a further four yards and repeats the process.

The turtle is now just over the top of the low bank and what

68

appears to be sniffing the sand is a prominent feature of its behaviour. It seems satisfied with a spot as it continues digging. The
digging action does not involve synchronous flipper movements
as in walking or swimming. Both front or rear flippers may act
together or separately. When both rear flippers are working at the
same time their motion alternates, so that as one starts pushing
posteriorly the other moves forward. The action of the front
flippers is weak resulting in a pile up of sand about half-way
towards the posterior of the body. At the commencement of the
front flipper stroke the flippers are brought together in front of the
turtle's head. They move through an arc of almost 180° ending up
against, or close to, the carapace. During the forward movement
they are lifted well clear of the ground. At the start of the rear
flipper action the flippers are about 180° apart, nearly at right
angles to the body. During the digging stroke each flipper moves
through an arc of between 70–80°. After no more than five minutes
of preliminary digging, excavation of the egg chamber commences.

The body pit is shallow (plate 13). The head and front of the
carapace are well above the level of the surrounding sand and the
body slopes downwards posteriorly.

The action of the rear flippers changes from pushing sand
posteriorly to a downward digging action comprising two distinct
sequences. First the flipper loosens sand by a rotating movement,
which may be repeated, then the flipper digs into the sand and
removes a 'handful'. The two distinct movements are best developed during the early stages of digging the egg chamber.
Throughout this process the front flippers serve to anchor the
turtle.

The digging action of the rear flippers is similar to that of the
green turtle but between each flipper entering the hole the whole
body is rotated from side to side so as to place the digging flipper
immediately above the hole. This movement is much more pronounced than in the green turtle. The right rear flipper reaches
down the hole and scoops sand. The sand is deposited on the right
hand side of the hole and the left rear flipper flicks sand laterally.
The turtle then presses down firmly with the right rear flipper to
raise the posterior of the body well clear of the hole. By means of a
swinging action at the shoulders with a minor contribution from
the right flipper, the body is rotated to position the left flipper
directly above the hole. This flipper is then curved so as to enter
the hole without damaging the walls and scoops sand which is

deposited on the left. The right flipper flicks sand away, the body is raised on the left flipper, rotated, and the right flipper positioned over the hole ready to repeat the cycle. Pronounced side to side rotation of the body is a characteristic feature of the loggerhead during construction of the egg chamber. Rest periods are few while digging the egg chamber. Indeed the whole behavioural sequence from first emerging from the water appears more purposeful, probably as a result of the virtually continuous action, than in the much slower green turtle.

As the egg chamber deepens the front flippers are used to raise the anterior of the turtle (plate 14) and so angle the posterior downwards to increase the reach of the rear limbs. When the flippers are unable to remove any more sand from the foot of the chamber the flipper action changes and sand is removed from the lower sides of the hole. This results in the completed chamber being much broader at the foot, similar to that of the green turtle.

The loggerhead's carapace is shaped differently from the green turtle's, extending farther backwards. This results in the egg chamber being dug below the rear of the carapace instead of behind. Whereas it is always possible to observe egg laying in the green turtle (except when both flippers cover the hole) it is never possible in the loggerhead. In female green turtles the tail protrudes from near the rear of the shell. In loggerheads the short stubby tail of females is housed well under the carapace.

Although the actual egg laying cannot be seen it is easy to determine when eggs are being expelled since the posterior edges of the rear flippers, which are placed flat on the sand at either side, are raised every time eggs are laid. Furthermore, it is only during egg laying that the turtle is still.

Suddenly the loggerhead starts filling in the egg chamber. The same initial careful movements occur as in the green turtle, but as covering in proceeds a different action becomes noticeable. Between bouts of sweeping sand over the egg chamber the turtle uses its 'knees,' supporting much of the weight of its body, like tamping irons to consolidate the sand. Each 'knee' is brought vertically downwards, one at a time, and the alternate limb movements cause the posterior of the turtle to rock from side to side. This action is a conspicuous part of the covering in process in the loggerhead and results in the sand being packed down firmly in the vicinity of the egg chamber.

It is now exactly fifty-five minutes since we saw this loggerhead emerging from the water. Farther down the beach another logger-head is returning to the sea. We can count a total of seven tracks on the stretch of beach within view. All belong to loggerhead turtles. No greens will appear until darkness is falling.

The loggerhead is now filling in with the front limbs and from time to time moves forward a little. The rear flippers push sand backwards. Sometimes alternate flippers work together as in walking or the flippers alternate in a quite unpredictable manner. As time progresses the turtle uses its front flippers more than the rear ones.

After about half an hour the turtle stops filling in, raises its head, looks around and starts walking down the beach to the sea. Return to the water is particularly rapid, the turtle covering thirty yards in forty seconds. There is a brief stop just over half-way and another at the water's edge. About thirty yards out to sea the head is raised well clear of the water and following an inhalation the turtle is seen no more. It is now six-thirty and darkness will fall in about half an hour. There is still no sign of any green turtles emerging.

An interesting feature of the nesting behaviour is the occurrence of loggerhead rookeries on some well-established cays and green turtle rookeries on others. For instance, on Wreck Island at least half the nesting turtles in most years are loggerheads. On Heron, loggerheads only average about fifteen percent of the population, and on North-West Island loggerheads are very rare. During the tagging of almost one thousand green turtles on North-West Island, only two loggerheads were encountered. So far we have seen no obvious differences between these cays which can explain their selection by one species or the other. These species' island preferences are continued over periods of many years. We do not know how long but in the seven years of our work no noticeable changing trend has been detected. We have never had any flatbacks (*Chelonia depressa*) nesting in the Capricorn cays although the flatback nests on the adjacent mainland.

As we saw from observing the loggerhead nesting, this species will come out to lay during daylight hours under the motivation of a high tide. However, since they seldom emerge before about four-thirty in the afternoon, suitable tides only occur for several days each fortnight. This results in the majority nesting at night. When high tide occurs around dawn some loggerheads beach in the early morning after it is light which is well after the last green turtles emerge. The numbers beaching after dawn, however, are very much smaller than those that come ashore in the late afternoon.

The usual quadruped locomotion used by this species allows it to make much better progress on land than the green turtle. Most observations describing the very laboured terrestrial locomotion of sea turtles when ashore are based on the green turtle. The loggerhead makes good progress across the sand as do the hawksbill and the ridleys.

A feature of the nesting behaviour of the loggerhead is the absence of wandering which often characterises the nesting of green turtles. Loggerheads usually climb the shallow sandbank, which encircles Capricorn cays, at the spring high-tide mark, and nest almost immediately. Where there is a steep bank they may nest at the foot but where the bank is high and can be climbed they frequently nest on the bank. This is often the case on sections of the beach at the Mon Repos loggerhead rookery near Bundaberg. Loggerheads do not select nesting sites adjacent to vegetation. Indeed, unlike the green turtles which we have studied in the Capricorn cays they will nest in the absence of trees and bushes. These are absent from most of the dunes at Mon Repos although some *Casuarina* have been replanted recently. This behavioural difference from green turtles means that loggerheads colonise younger cays – from the stage of bare sandbanks through to having grasses and other low vegetation but no trees or bushes. During this time the loggerheads do not have to compete with green turtles for nesting space (see Chapter 9).

At least twice as many loggerheads as green turtles nest below the bank where the eggs are inundated by the fortnightly spring high tides. These nests are not necessarily laid adjacent to the bank. It is not unusual to find a loggerhead nesting half-way up the beach. It seems likely that the greater percentage 'error' in this species results from failure to 'home-in' on vegetation before nesting as does the green turtle.

The body pit is usually poorly developed in loggerheads, often being only a very slight depression in the sand no larger than the turtle's body. Normally, it is much deeper at the rear than the front with fore-flippers and head often not below the level of the surrounding sand (plate 14). Even when the body pit is well developed, the carapace of the turtle (particularly the front portion) is usually well above the level of the surrounding sand. The pit is little wider than the carapace, and the front and rear, especially the front, are ill-defined.

Loggerheads spend much less time than green turtles covering and disguising their nesting site. In part, this reflects the much smaller body pit in the loggerhead. In filling in the body pit the green turtle commences with a definite wall of sand in front of it. During the filling in process the pit becomes shallower as a result of a slight change in the angling of the front flippers. The loggerhead, however, starts with little or no sand in front of the head. In shallow body pits the turtle will only throw sand around for a few minutes with the front flippers and then head back to the sea. Where the body pit is better developed anteriorly the filling in process takes rather longer but it never approaches the time or effort spent by green turtles.

The whole nesting cycle of the loggerhead is much faster than the green turtle, averaging about two hours. This is due to their more rapid locomotion, absence of wandering before selecting a nesting site, a shallow body pit, more rapid (continuous) digging of the egg chamber and much reduced disguising of the area after nesting.

As mentioned in the previous chapter, the function of the body pit is to remove the dry unconsolidated surface sand to expose moister sand in which the rear flippers can excavate an egg chamber. It also has the important result of locating the eggs at a greater depth where they are less liable to encounter environmental stress and predators. However, the loggerhead achieves both of these objectives by confining most of its digging effort to the rear of the body pit where the egg chamber will be dug. This is a much more efficient procedure since it greatly reduces the amount of sand to be shifted. Quite apart from the whole procedure being achieved in a very much shorter time, I have a distinct impression that loggerheads are able to excavate a successful egg chamber in conditions where, due to sand dryness and the absence of tree rootlets, green turtles would not succeed.

These detailed descriptions of the nesting behaviour of the green and loggerhead typify the overall similarity of the nesting behaviour of all sea turtles but also point out the sort of differences which occur between them.

CHAPTER 6

The Flatback

THE flatback is an excellent example of a large animal that was long denied complete scientific recognition even though it occurred in relatively large numbers in its preferred habitat, and could not be confused with related species. It did not finally obtain full recognition until the late nineteen sixties.

The story concerning the acceptance of the very existence of the flatback turtle (*Chelonia depressa*) by the international scientific community is an interesting one. As well as illustrating the caution necessary in a scientific approach to any problem it shows how papers tend to be overlooked or inadequately evaluated, and points out some of the difficulties associated with working on large animals like turtles.

In 1880 Samuel Garman described a new species of sea turtle in the Bulletin of the Museum of Comparative Zoology at Harvard. He named the turtle *Chelonia depressa* and listed one of his two specimens as coming from Penang (Malaya), and the other from northern Australia.

In 1889 G. A. Boulenger, the great reptile systematist at the British Museum, published his Catalogue of the Chelonians in the British Museum. In this he considered *Chelonia depressa* to be synonymous with the green turtle *Chelonia mydas*.

To appreciate what follows one must know something of the situation as it was at the end of the nineteenth century. Adult turtles were rare in museum collections because it is difficult to preserve and transport such cumbersome animals (this is still the situation to-day). Early taxonomists, who had to work on only a few specimens from any one region, which did not encompass the various age-classes (sizes), were not aware of the changes in shape undergone by the scutes during growth. As a result of this, specimens showing markedly different scute shapes, and often different colour patterns were believed to represent different species.

Clearly the easiest stage of the life history to collect, preserve and transport are the hatchlings. Anyone who has examined series of hatchlings will have been impressed by the great variability shown by these, especially in the number of scutes. This range of variation is not present in adult individuals, so one can only surmise that, although the variability in the scutes in itself may have no influence on the viability of the individuals, it is the expression of abnormal development which may also have affected other parts of the animal, and that this makes these hatchlings less viable. Quite apart from this, however, the great variability of hatchlings led herpetologists to believe that the species were extremely variable, and in consequence of this the number of recognised species was reduced to four (green turtle, hawksbill, loggerhead and leathery turtle). In this way the two ridley turtle species were included in the loggerhead and the flatback in the green turtle.

In view of the above, it is not surprising that Boulenger referred *depressa* to the green turtle. Furthermore, the fact that turtles are marine animals and that species like the green turtle, the hawksbill, the loggerhead and the leathery turtle have a world-wide distribution may also have influenced herpetologists. It was believed that there were no barriers that prevented marine animals crossing the oceans of the world, and one could just not understand that there could be species of turtles with only a very limited distribution.

In 1890 George Baur examined Garman's cotypes. In a paper published in the American Naturalist of that year, he concluded that not only was Dr Boulenger's action in synonymising *Chelonia depressa* with the green turtle incorrect, but that Garman's species belonged to a different genus from the green turtle.

In 1908 Mr A. R. McCulloch described a new genus and species of sea turtle which he named *Natator tessellatus* on the basis of a single juvenile specimen from Darwin. As was later demonstrated by Fry (see below) this individual belonged to the same species as the North Australian cotype of Garman (1880). However, since the young *depressa* possess distinctly areolated scutes for some months after hatching, McCulloch's specimen appeared very different from Garman's older specimen which lacked these. McCulloch does not refer to Garman's paper describing *Chelonia depressa* so that presumably he was not aware of its existence. If he had known about it he would either have identified his specimen with *depressa* or indicated the characters in which he believed it to differ. The fact that there is no difficulty in recognising *Natator tessellatus* as being identical with *Chelonia depressa*, as the last named is understood to-day, shows that McCulloch provided an adequate description and figures.

As we saw above, Baur believed *depressa* to belong to a distinct genus, although he did not name this. McCulloch, probably unaware of Baur's paper, believed the same and named the genus.

Moreover, Barbour (1914) showed that Garman's type series for *depressa* was composite (embraced two different species): he pointed out that the cotype from Malaya is a specimen of the green turtle (*Chelonia mydas*). One can understand that this discovery merely served to reinforce scepticism about the status of *depressa*. If the describer cannot himself separate the proposed new species from the species he states it is distinct from, then one must be excused for wondering if the differences are real!

In 1913 Dene Fry at the Australian Museum published a paper entitled 'On the status of *Chelonia depressa* Garman' in the Museum Records. This was the result of his own investigations. It was a major paper of twenty-seven pages plus four pages of plates and was important in a number of ways. Firstly it very clearly demonstrated that there was a most distinctive species of sea turtle in the area and showed in great detail how that species could be distinguished from the green turtle. Secondly it showed that McCulloch's type agreed with Garman's series except for the areolae and showed that these are only present in the juvenile condition, hence that both descriptions referred to the one species. In addition to an extensive morphological treatment in which he weakened his arguments by placing emphasis on skull characters that are subject to considerable variation, Fry quoted field descriptions which clearly refer to an otherwise unnamed species. As a result of Fry's paper Australian herpetologists interested in taxonomy, myself included, have never doubted the existence of a distinct species of sea turtle inhabiting northern Australian waters which was named *Chelonia depressa* by Garman in 1880. Although I had, of course, examined McCulloch's type and Fry's material, prior to 1968 I had never seen an adult or a living individual of the species. However, *Chelonia depressa* did not yet secure overseas recognition.

In 1961 Dr Wermuth and Professor Mertens published an illustrated checklist of the chelonians and crocodilians of the world. Since there are only some 210 species of living chelonians and about twenty crocodilians, most distinctive species were very fully illustrated in the four hundred and twenty-two pages of the check-list. However, amazing as it may seem, the only reference to *Chelonia depressa* appears under the list of synonyms for the

11. (a) Mass tracks showing very high density of nesting, mainly by loggerheads, at Wreck Island, Capricorn Group.

(b) Area of disturbed sand resulting from the nesting process of a single green turtle.

12. (a) Beaching female green turtle with the left front flipper missing from the shoulder region.

(b) A loggerhead turtle nest excavated by a fox (*Vulpes vulpes*), Mon Repos beach near Bundaberg, S.E. Queensland.

Pacific race of the green turtle! In rejecting the existence of a distinctive species of sea turtle in northern Australian waters Wermuth and Mertens follow Boulenger's action of 1889 exactly. However, there is an important difference. Fry's major paper had appeared in the interval.

It is only fair to point out, however, that in taking this action Wermuth and Mertens were following the action taken by previous reviewers. Garman's juvenile cotype from North Australia was considered to be an aberrant *mydas* by Loveridge (1934), Siebenrock (1909) and Malcolm Smith (1931). Thus these authors followed Boulenger's action of 1889. However, it is hard to believe that reviewers after 1913 could have studied Fry's important paper of that year.

Most readers must wonder why on-the-spot investigations were never carried out. The reason for this is simple – northern Australia is very sparsely populated and is a very long way from the south. Furthermore, there are very few people in Australia interested in sea turtles. An investigation, had this materialised, would have been much more likely to be carried out by an overseas visitor. Further evidence of lack of turtle data for northern Australia is given in Chapter 9. Hence *Chelonia depressa* remained virtually unknown in life to scientists (it was well known to aboriginal and island people) and very scarce in museum collections.

It is to be appreciated that Williams, Grandison and Carr decided to re-investigate *Chelonia depressa*. There was every reason for them to undertake this work since one had the opinion of Fry on the one hand (backed up by Baurr and McCulloch) that it was a distinct species, and on the other hand the opinion of Wermuth, Mertens and others, based on a study of the pertinent literature, that it was not. Williams, Grandison and Carr (1967) arrived at the conclusion that *depressa* was a distinct form. Referring to the genus *Chelonia* they wrote, 'one local population, however, is morphologically so distinct that it may be *tentatively regarded as a species*. . . . This sharply distinguished taxon is *Chelonia depressa* Garman . . .' Since they continue, 'The dearth of information on the distribution of breeding grounds of *Chelonia* in Australia makes it difficult to judge whether, and to what degree, *depressa* and *mydas* may nest sympatrically', they are obviously searching for information to clinch the distinctiveness of *depressa* from *mydas*. The knowledge that the two species nested side by side and were readily separable without the presence of intergrades would provide this information. That they were correct in believing it to be a distinct species was confirmed by further research (see below).

The paper by Williams, Grandison and Carr again highlighted the extreme paucity of information on the biology of the flatback. Accordingly we published our available biological information to clinch the fact that *Chelonia depressa* is a distinct species from the green turtle of the Great Barrier Reef (Bustard and Limpus, 1969). Cogger and Lindner (1969) also comment on the reticence of Williams, Grandison and Carr (1967) to recognise the flatback as a distinct species. They wrote, 'Subsequently Williams *et al.* (1967) have confirmed the reliability of most of the features on which Fry differentiated *depressa* from *mydas*, and have provided additional distinguishing characters. Nevertheless these authors have still only "tentatively" recognised *C. depressa* as a distinct species'.

It is only now, therefore, that the existence of the flatback as a species in its own right is being internationally accepted and the world's sea turtle count can be increased from six to seven species. It seems virtually certain that no more species of sea turtles as distinctive as the flatback remain to be discovered. Any future additions will result from splitting existing species, most likely the green turtle.

The story of how I came to see my first flatback is scarcely less remarkable. One night in mid-January 1968 I was returning 'home' at the end of a busy night's work on Heron Island. I took the short cut back to the Research Station as I had one green turtle near there still to tag. This individual had not finished laying when last checked. As I climbed wearily up the twelve-foot bank I wondered, as I had done on countless previous nights, how the turtles ever make their way up these steep slopes.

I had just tagged the green turtle, receiving a faceful of sand in the process. It was actively throwing sand backwards and was almost ready to return to the water. I was writing up the particulars of the individual and as I brushed the sand off the side of its face to check the postocular number a figure in the darkness asked why I was doing that. I am normally patient with 'tourists' but at the end of a tiring night one's patience is apt to reach a low ebb. However, in the course of a brief exchange, the voice, which belonged to Mr Colin Limpus of Bundaberg, informed me that there were flatbacks near his home in south-east Queensland. I was incredulous as the scant published information on the distribution of *depressa* always referred to the tropical north of Australia. The Capricorn–Bunker islands lie at the southern breeding limits for the green turtle and even the comparatively hardy loggerhead does not nest much further south. I had certainly not expected to hear of flatbacks nesting in south Queensland!

As a result of our discussion in the early hours of that morning I accompanied Mr Limpus when he returned home the following Saturday, having readily accepted his offer to take me to the beach where he had seen the flatbacks.

On arrival in Bundaberg we went down to Mon Repos beach in the afternoon so that I could examine the site.

That evening we returned to Mon Repos shortly before high tide in the hope of seeing a flatback, which Colin had explained to me were rare there compared to the loggerhead. It was a cool night, temperature shortly after midnight being 23°C (74°F), and due to a slight breeze it felt much cooler so that we were glad of our jerseys. A number of loggerheads were nesting. At forty-five minutes past midnight as we were walking along the beach we saw my first live flatback returning to the water. This individual is shown in plate 16. An examination showed that she had nested just over the top of the bank. The first attempt at digging an egg chamber had been abandoned for no obvious reason and egg laying had occurred in the second chamber dug.

Mon Repos, about eight miles east of Bundaberg, is situated approximately 25° south. It is the largest of eight sandy beaches interrupting the 14 miles of rocky coastline between the mouths of the Burnett and Elliot Rivers. The beach, which is exposed to the surf of the open sea, is just under one mile in length, flanked by rocks at both ends, has rocks near the low-tide mark on part of the beach and is backed by sand dunes varying from one to seven feet high. The beach is composed of fine mineral sands, with a fine covering of coarser material and broken shells. Following storms the coarse component is much more conspicuous.

The dunes slope upwards from the spring high-tide mark and consist entirely of fine mineral sands to a depth of over one yard. The slope of the beach varies from 3 to 8°. The natural dune cover consisted of *Casuarina equisitifolia* L. and *Pandanus tectorius* Park forest but has long been cleared by man. Apart from some *Casuarina* recently replanted there is no tall vegetation. The dominant cover consists of the grass *Spinifex hirsutus* and the convolvulus *Ipomoea pes-caprae*. Both of these grow down the dune towards the sea and are, therefore, important in dune stabilisation and reformation following erosion.

A view of part of the beach is given in plate 12.

As on the nearby Capricorn cays the wettest months are from December to March when rainfall at Bundaberg averages more than 150 mm per month. Maximum–minimum temperatures at Bundaberg from November to February approximate 30–16°C (86–61°F). Water temperature, measured one metre below the surface, about a hundred metres offshore averaged 26°C.

Despite the great reluctance with which the very existence of the flatback was accepted, this turtle is very different in appearance from the green turtle. Ways in which it can be separated readily from all other sea turtles are given in the key (Appendix I). A general description of the animal is given below.

The carapace is greatly depressed compared to the green turtle, hence *depressa*, and the scutes are very thin and oily. This feature alone provides ready separation from the green turtle which has an outer covering of hard, horny scutes. The rim of the carapace is curved upwards particularly towards the rear (plate 2/3). The front flippers are quite different in appearance and toughness from those of the green turtle. The scales covering the upper surfaces of the front flippers of the green turtle are comparatively few in number and all large. In the flatback the scales in the area of the flippers between the fingers are small and very numerous (fig. 16). Whereas the flippers of the green turtle are tough to the touch and extremely powerful, those of the flatback are soft and considerably less powerful. If a flatback is turned on its back it is relatively easy for the terminal region of a front flipper to be damaged or actually broken. I have never seen this happen in the green turtle.

As is shown in the plates, the head of the flatback is large compared to that of the green turtle. There are many other features which serve to distinguish between individuals of the flatback and the green turtle. These are not provided in the key (which is purposely kept as simple as possible consistent with providing reliable identification). For instance, the upper eyelid in the flatback possesses series of small scales whereas in the green turtle this area is covered by enlarged scales.

Coloration also provides ready identification. In the adult green turtle of the Great Barrier Reef, the head and flippers vary from grey-green to light tan, and the carapace is typically olive-green or olive-brown with pronounced chestnut-brown and/or black streaks and blotches. The head and flippers of the flatback are olive-grey, the anterior of the head is yellowish, and the cara-pace is a darker olive-grey than the flippers with indistinct darker markings (see frontispiece). I would be most surprised should anyone confuse the flatback with the green turtle once they have seen illustrations of both.

Virtually nothing had been written about the biology of the flatback. Fry (1913) quoted Mr H. W. Christie, Lighthousekeeper at Point Charles, near Darwin, Northern Territory, as follows:

'*C. depressa* lays its eggs on all the sandy beaches round here and on some of the islands, namely – Indian, Baresand, Quail and West Peron. On the last-mentioned island, possessing five miles of beach, I counted thirteen nests within a space of twenty yards. They come and lay on the beach near the lighthouse, usually at spring-tide. The next spring-tide they return and lay very near the same spot, and so on, for five or six months. They do not seem to have any particular breeding season, but towards the end of the dry season, in the months of August, September and October, there is, if anything, a little slacking off. The females usually lay at night time, and with the aid of a hurricane lamp, of which they take not the slightest notice, I have often watched them preparing their nests and laying their eggs. They twist about so as to harden the surface somewhat before commencing to dig. The hind flippers alone are used in excavating and are worked alternately, being turned outwards like a scoop, a sharp jerk throwing the sand a yard away. The hole made is eight or nine inches in diameter and one foot or more deep. She then moves her vent over the hole and fifty or sixty eggs are laid in about five minutes. The average number of eggs laid is fifty; the greatest number I have seen is seventy-eight, and the smallest twenty-four. The hole is then filled in and a large mound scraped over it, the front flippers being used for this – thus the eggs are eighteen to twenty-four inches from the surface. She then makes for the sea. The period of incubation is about six weeks. When leaving the nest the young do not run together but spread out and run fan-wise to the water, as I have counted fifty-two separate tracks. The eggs and meat are a great source of food to the blacks; I have eaten hundreds of the eggs but find the meat disagreeable and not nearly so good as that of *C. mydas*. I never saw these turtles basking in the sun. They are apparently nervous creatures in the water but when up on the beaches laying they take notice of nothing and will crawl over a sleeping black or through his camp fire. *C. depressa* is much flatter than *C. mydas* and is shell-less – that is, there are no hard plates, but a leathery skin only envelops the bony skeleton. *C. depressa* is known to the Larrakeyah tribe as 'Adymer', to the Bierly tribe as 'Ballan', and to the Wogite tribe as 'Ingering'.'

In view of the extreme paucity of information we have published our own knowledge (Bustard and Limpus, 1969, Bustard, Greenham and Limpus, 1971).

The nesting behaviour of the flatback is extremely interesting in that it shows features which we have come to associate with either green or loggerhead turtles.

After leaving the sea flatbacks ascend the beach rapidly with few rests. Locomotion is achieved by simultaneous action of all four flippers as in the green turtle but, due to the reduced weight of this species, is much less laborious. The appearance of the track is somewhat intermediate between that of green and loggerhead turtles. On reaching the bank, flatbacks rapidly climb it, resorting to quadrupedal locomotion on steep portions like green turtles. Having climbed the bank wandering does not usually occur in the flatback, nesting taking place immediately on top of the bank or on the bank itself. The body pit is very shallow and poorly developed. During its construction unequal front flipper action may cause the carapace to swivel from side to side. At the end of scooping out the body pit some of the flatbacks observed moved forward about two feet. The body pits were completed in an average of eleven minutes.

The movements during digging the egg chamber are closely similar to the loggerhead turtle. The side to side movement of the rear of the carapace to position each digging flipper directly over the hole, and the elevation with the front flippers so that the rear flippers can attain a greater digging depth (plate 14), are both well developed. During the latter action the anterior of the plastron is raised about six inches from the ground.

During egg laying one rear flipper hangs down into the hole and the other is placed on the sand to one side. The view of the completed egg chamber is obstructed by the carapace. Laying of the moderately small clutch of about fifty very large eggs (see Chapter 8) occupies approximately ten minutes.

During the process of filling in the body pit and disguising the nest site, the turtle moves slightly forwards. This distance averaged only thirty inches and filling in took about twenty minutes in five flatbacks which were observed closely. Turtles suddenly stopped filling in, raised their heads, looked around, and moved off towards the sea. The upturned edges of the carapace result in considerable quantities of sand remaining on the shell. Quadrupedal locomotion is used in descending the bank but once on the beach they use the usual green turtle method of forward pushes with all four flippers acting together. This provides fairly satisfactory locomotion in the flatback. One individual crossed fifty-four yards of beach in seven minutes and another took ten minutes to traverse forty-six yards.

The total time occupied by flatbacks in completing the nesting process, timed from leaving until returning to the ocean, averaged eighty-two minutes for five turtles. One flatback completed the cycle in exactly one hour. The longest time was ninety-five minutes.

The nesting behaviour of the flatback includes a number of features which we have come to associate with the loggerhead and which are not seen during nesting by Barrier Reef green turtles. However, the sequence also includes some distinctly green turtle traits. The flatback will lay in the absence of trees or bushes. In my experience the green turtle will not do this but the loggerhead frequently does. Absence of wandering over the bank and the poorly developed body pit are also features of loggerhead nesting. However, the method of locomotion and the positioning of rear flippers during laying are similar to the green turtle. Time taken for the nesting process was shorter than for either green or loggerhead turtles on the nearby coral cays. However, sand differences may have been in the flatback's favour.

The deep water approach to Mon Repos, compared to the encircling shallow reef platform on the cays, may have been responsible for the apparently much less well-defined relationship between time of high tide and beaching in the flatback.

At Mon Repos the nesting season is short, shorter even than that of the other turtles at that latitude, being largely restricted to the first half of the summer. However, in the far north flatbacks appear to nest throughout most of the year sometimes with local peaks in certain months.

An assistant, Mr Alvar Mould, and three Torres Strait Islander trainees spent about a month on Crab Island in November–December 1970 studying the flatback turtle. Crab Island (plate 1) is very close to the mainland but completely lacks mainland egg predators (monitors, pigs). On three-quarters of the island there is a high beach platform below the bank vegetated with convolvulus (*Ipomoea*) and tussock grass. During very high tides two-thirds of this area floods. On about ten percent of the island there is a gently sloping beach with no definite bank area and on the remaining ten percent there is a well pronounced, steep bank.

The party found that virtually all flatbacks beached to nest during daylight hours, the peak being about 3.00 p.m. although they could expect individuals at any time between 9.45 a.m. and 11.30 p.m. During the time of the Crab Island work the high tides occurred during the day but it was possible for turtles to come ashore at any state of the tide. The tide cycle in the Gulf of Carpentaria is extremely unusual, there being in general only one tide cycle in each twenty-four hour period instead of the usual two complete cycles. On some days there may be only half of a tide cycle in the twenty-four hour period. The difference between high and low tide, which is, of course, very variable, averaged about six feet according to Mr Mould. Under these circumstances it is somewhat difficult to state why virtually all of the 180 flatbacks tagged should have come ashore to nest during the day, an observation which disagrees with Christie quoted by Fry (1913). One can only draw the conclusion that the species is not averse to day nesting – even in mid-summer in the tropics – and that the turtles were presumably loosely correlating their nesting with higher states of the tide.

The team observed that on most of the island where the vegetated high beach platform occurred the turtles nested anywhere on this platform. Where a gradual slope was present with no bank, the flatbacks moved inland until they reached the *Casuarina* belt and nested among the most shoreward trees. Where a pronounced bank was present the turtles dug into the foot of the bank if it was steep, or laid just over the top if it was shallow and easily climbed. The third situation is similar to Mon Repos and at both locations the flatbacks behaved similarly. At Crab Island failure to climb the bank in most cases resulted in many nests being inundated by the highest tides with possible substantial loss of incubating eggs.

Mr Mould noted that the flatbacks were of a very nervous disposition. They reared up, swivelled round and tried to bite when tagged which never happens with green turtles and rarely with loggerheads. One individual which was closely observed took only forty minutes to lay its fifty-four eggs from the time it emerged to re-entering the sea.

From the large numbers of hatchlings emerging throughout the study it was clear that flatback nesting had been in progress for some considerable time. Mr Mould formed the opinion that the nesting season was tailing off towards the end of the year. Crab Island is also an important green turtle rookery, but during the time that the party was on Crab no green turtles nested nor were green turtle hatchlings observed. The only turtles seen, other than flatbacks, were two nesting hawksbills, which laid about mid-December.

The Crab Island party weighed ten flatbacks and since there is no published information on weights for this species their findings are of great interest. The turtles varied from $31\frac{1}{2}$ to $38''$ in shell length, measured over the low curve (average $35''$). The ten individuals weighed measured from $33\frac{1}{2}$ $''$to $35\frac{1}{2}''$ in carapace length and had a mean weight of 160 lb. The smallest weighed 152 lb and the largest 158 lb. Both the lightest (149 lb) and the heaviest (179 lb) measured $35''$. Four flatbacks with $34\frac{1}{2}''$ carapaces were weighed and all were either 157 lb or 158 lb. The weights of three which measured $35''$ long were recorded. These three had differing carapace breadths which showed a weight correlation. The breadths and weights were $28\frac{1}{2}''$, $29''$ and $30''$ and 149 lb, 160 lb and 179 lb respectively.

The flesh of the flatback is not generally relished by Europeans, aboriginals or islanders with the result that the species is little molested. However, the eggs are widely eaten by aboriginal people. Numerous attempts have been made to explain the difference in taste between the flesh of the flatback and green turtle on the basis of feeding differences. Even now little is known of the feeding habits of the flatback. Cogger and Lindner (1969) wrote, 'Older local natives who until 1939 had often been employed diving for trepang consider that *C. depressa* largely lives on trepang, having been frequently encountered where these were abundant. This view is supported by the fact that prawn trawlers frequently take *depressa* from the "clean" bottoms over which the trawlers usually work.'

Flatbacks spend much of the day floating on the surface basking in the sun. It is not uncommon to see birds resting on their backs. Beebe (1938) wrote about a different species, 'a large turtle passed (the boat) with two terns roosting on its shell. This is a common sight up and down the tropical west coast (of America) . . . perhaps there is something of mutual help in warning of approaching danger.' As suggested by Beebe, the birds undoubtedly serve to warn the turtle of human approach, while the birds receive a perch – always at a premium at sea.

It has long been known that the flatback lays much smaller clutches of eggs than, for instance, the green and loggerhead: Christie, quoted in Fry (1913), said an average clutch consisted of fifty eggs and gave a range from twenty-four to seventy-eight. Cogger and Lindner (1969) examined fourteen nests and found these contained from forty-one to seventy-four eggs, average fifty-three.

I have no information on the status of the flatback in Western Australia except that it occurs in the north-west of the state. Since the time of Fry (1913) it has been known from the Northern Territory and North Queensland. Cogger and Lindner in the paper cited above refer to it nesting in the Coburg Peninsula area and also on the Sir Edward Pellew Islands in the Northern Territory part of the Gulf of Carpentaria.

I have numerous nesting locality records for the flatback in northern Queensland. The flatback nests extensively on the outer islands associated with Mornington Island including the Pisonia and Bountiful Groups as well as on Crab Island described above.

Bountiful Island was so named by Matthew Flinders because of the abundance of turtles when he visited it in December 1802. His account of the visit, published in 1814, is interesting as it appears it may contain a very early reference to the flatback. A party of men had been sent ashore at night to turn turtles in order to provide fresh meat for the crew. Flinders wrote,

'Next morning, two boats went to bring off the officer and people with what had been caught; but their success had been so great, that it was necessary to hoist out the launch; and it took nearly the whole day to get on board what the decks and holds could contain, without impediment to the working of the ship. They were found by Mr Brown to be nearly similar to, but not exactly the true green turtle, and he thought might be an undescribed species. We contrived to stow away forty-six, the least of them weighing 250 lbs, and the average about 300; besides which, many were re-turned on shore, and suffered to go away.'

Flinders had been sent by the Admiralty to continue charting the east coast of Australia. His complement included botanists but no zoologists or perhaps the flatback might have been known

86

and accepted by the scientific world more than a century and a half ago. Flinders did not comment on the taste of the meat of the suspected undescribed turtle species. However, it seems certain that if these turtles were different from the green turtle that they were flatbacks. Australian green turtles are similar to those occurring elsewhere so that there is no reason to consider that the crew might have thought Australian green turtles a distinct species. A further piece of evidence that they may have been flatbacks is that Bountiful is now known to be an important rookery for the flatback as well as for the green turtle. However, one feature tends to suggest that the turtles were not flatbacks but green turtles. This is the weights recorded by Flinders which are greatly in excess of those we obtained for adult flatbacks in the Gulf of Carpentaria.

Flinders continued his account,

'This *Bountiful Island*, for so I termed it, is near three miles long, and generally low and sandy; the highest parts are ridges of sand, overspread with a long, creeping, coarse grass, which binds the sand together, and preserves it from being blown away; grass of the common kind grows in the lower parts, and in one place there were some bushes and small trees. The basis consists partly of a streaked, ochrous earth, and in part of sand, concreted with particles of iron ore. Nothing bespoke this island to have been ever before visited, whence it is probable that the natives of the neighbouring lands do not possess canoes; for with them, the distance of four leagues from Cape Van Diemen would not have been too great to be passed, though too far in a tide's way for such rafts as I saw at Horse-shoe Island.'

Were Flinders to re-visit Bountiful to-day I doubt if he would detect any important differences. The aborigines of nearby Mornington Island possessed only rafts so that passage to Bountiful was indeed impossible, and though to-day they possess some boats with outboard motors, they are all settled now at the south-western tip of Mornington far distant from Bountiful. Bountiful Island, although gazetted as an Aboriginal Reserve, is very seldom visited by anyone. It has been left to the turtles.

After leaving Bountiful, Flinders proceeded to Pisonia Island where he noted.

'More holes were scratched in the sand here by the turtle, than even upon the island last quitted; and several of the poor animals were lying dead on their backs. The isle is nothing more than a high sand bank upon a basis of coral rock, which has become thickly covered with wood, and much resembles several of the smaller isles in Torres Strait. There was no trace of former visitors, though it is not more than four miles from the island where Indians had been seen in the morning; the tides probably run too strong in a narrow-four-fathom channel close to Isle Pisonia, to be encountered by their rafts.'

On 31st November 1969, I surveyed Bountiful and Pisonia Islands for turtle tracks from the air. The survey was carried out in the early morning following a night high tide so that the tide was receding and the tracks of the previous night had not been destroyed by the sea. At the main Bountiful Island I counted about 500 tracks made over the two preceding nights, at Pisonia the tally was between 250 and 300. Pisonia, also an Aboriginal Reserve, is seldom visited by aborigines and together with Bountiful comprises two of the major turtle rookeries in northern Queensland (see Chapter 9). In June 1970 I landed at Bountiful to have a closer look at the turtles.

CHAPTER 7

Hawksbills, Ridleys and Leathery Turtles

GENERAL information on these turtles is given in Chapter 2 with emphasis on the worldwide conservation situation in Chapter 10. Very little is known about these turtles in many parts of the world. This chapter summarises Australian information on the three species – an area for which information is lacking and virtually nothing has been published. Large portions of the tropical north of the Australian continent have not been fully explored and it is certainly true to say that at a scientific level at least, the same holds good in many parts of the world. Turtle conservation depends *a priori* on knowledge of the whereabouts of turtles. Turtle workers are still in this preliminary phase since funds and personnel have not been available to speed up detailed survey work.

Of the three species, only the hawksbill is well known in Australia. Up to 1969 no nesting rookeries had been recorded for any of the species in Australian waters. The first scientific report of the Pacific ridley nesting in Australia was only published in 1969 (although it is by no means uncommon), and we have just had news of the first important breeding ground for the hawksbill in Australia.

At the time of writing there are no records of Australian nesting by the leathery turtle. However, there is an important migration route for the species down the east coast of Australia judging by seasonal sightings and reports of capture in shark nets.

We will start our account with the best-known species – the hawksbill turtle. There are many reports of the hawksbill in Australian waters where the species is widespread particularly in the north. However, the reports invariably refer to adults or sub-adults and breeding records are very sparse and then only of stray individuals. Cogger and Lindner (1969) in an account of sea turtles in the Northern Territory of Australia produced no definite evidence of nesting by the hawksbill in Northern Territory waters although they believed that sparse nesting probably occurs there.

Musgrave and Whitley (1926) provided the only published nesting record for Australian waters, they wrote '. . . According to Surgeon-Lieut. W. E. J. Paradice, R.A.N., the Hawksbill lays . . . on Thursday Island, and perhaps breeds southward as far as Low Island, Queensland.' Cogger and Lindner state that two hatchlings (A4905 and A4906) in the Australian Museum collection were collected 90 years ago in Torres Strait by Alex Morton. The actual location is not recorded.

My own investigations show that sporadic nestings occur on the Queensland mainland almost as far south as Brisbane but that these are uncommon. We have no records of nesting on the Capricorn cays where we have worked extensively over many years on the green and loggerhead populations. To date the only important rookery areas I know for the species are in Torres Strait, for instance Long Island and Campbell Island.

Farther south the hawksbill is reported nesting on Little Adolphus Island off the tip of eastern Cape York (10° 35's. 142° 35'e) (John Scott, personal communication). Further efforts to locate hawksbill rookeries in Australia should be directed at the tropical north in view of the more tropical distribution of this species. Although adults do range far south, undoubtedly many of the records attributed to the hawksbill are brightly marked immature individuals of the green turtle, the carapaces of which appear brightly marked when seen in the water. When ashore the hawksbill moves extremely rapidly using normal quadrupedal locomotion – alternate limbs move together.

Although there was considerable exploitation of the hawksbill in Australia at one time for tortoiseshell, it has been little interfered with in recent times. Unless Japanese activities in Australia result in a re-awakening of interest in exploiting this species its future in Australia would seem secure.

The hawksbill is seldom eaten in northern Australia because the flesh of some populations is known to be poisonous at least at certain times of year. In the New Guinea region a number of deaths have resulted from eating this turtle's flesh. Most Torres Strait Islanders avoid the turtle for this reason, but those who do eat it claim that they can render it safe to eat by removing the poisonous portions prior to cooking. The hawksbill is eaten in the Caribbean and in Fiji without, to my knowledge, any ill effects being reported.

The locations of the Torres Strait breeding grounds do not

give cause for optimism with regard to the creation of National Parks to protect the Australian populations. Firstly, the outer islands of Torres Strait are closer to the southern coast of New Guinea (Papua) than they are to Australia (Queensland). Secondly, the Torres Strait Islanders relish turtle eggs. Furthermore, it would be difficult to police any restrictions given the present international climate towards Australian indigenous people and the available conservation resources of the Queensland Government.

The Pacific ridley nests in huge numbers on the Pacific coast of Mexico where it is the basis for an enormous industry. The skin is tanned into a durable leather, the meat used for soups or eaten fresh, the oil is used by the cosmetics industry, calipee is taken from the plastron and even the shell and viscera are utilised commercially. The huge conservation scheme run by the Mexican Government is described on pages 167-9.

Knowledge of the olive or Pacific ridley is sparse and unreliable as it has usually been confused with the loggerhead. Since I have not seen the species in the field, the following account draws heavily on Cogger and Lindner (1969). They wrote,

'It would appear, however, that this species occurs commonly in northern Australia and that it nests in many areas. We have recorded nests at various localities between Gove Peninsula and Coburg Peninsula, while reliable reports have been received of nesting on Bathurst and Melville Islands.'

Cogger and Lindner say that as a result of their colour, adult Pacific ridleys are frequently confused with the flatback by Europeans in northern Australia. They report, '9 sightings of adults at Coburg Peninsula, 7 of which were of specimens basking on the surface of depths exceeding 5 fathoms'. The tracks, nesting sites and eggs of the species are diagnostic. Cogger and Lindner reported,

'More than 50 nests were noted, of which 12 were randomly selected to confirm the accuracy of the nest identifications. All of these proved to belong to *Lepidochelys* (as confirmed by identifications of embryos and hatchlings). Clutch sizes in six nests varied from 50 to 147 (mean 108), the slightly elliptical eggs measuring from 38.5 to 41.0 mm in diameter (mean 38.8). Incubation times (from day of laying to day of hatching) for four nests ranged from 48 to 52 days (mean 50 days). All nests were recorded between January 31st and March 17th, 1967, and during March, 1968.' This presumably reflects the time when the authors looked for nests and is not meant to imply that the nesting season is restricted to such times.

Concerning the future of these Australian populations of the Pacific ridley, Cogger and Lindner wrote,

'At present many of the small islands on which *Lepidochelys olivacea* nests are rarely visited by man and are not inhabited by any of the predators (e.g. dingoes, monitor lizards) which frequently destroy mainland turtle nests. Basking adults are extremely unwary of approaching boats but the flesh is not esteemed by aboriginals and adults are rarely hunted. The main threat to the survival of the species would seem to lie in the population growth and development of the northern coast. However, any conservation program designed to protect important nesting beaches of *Chelonia depressa* would probably also ensure the survival of this more widely distributed species in Australian waters.'

Clearly there is a need for surveys to evaluate the status of the Pacific ridley in northern Australia but the information presented by Cogger and Lindner shows that the species is certainly a well established member of the Australian fauna under no immediate threat. Locomotion is by alternate limbs moving together.

Australian information on the leathery turtle is extremely sparse. This turtle is known to seafaring Europeans and aborigines who periodically sight them from boats and readily recognise it due to its large size, dark coloration, and longitudinally ridged carapace. I know of no records, or even reports, of Australian nesting by the species although I would not be surprised if a nesting colony did occur somewhere in the far north and had been overlooked. Presence of even considerable numbers of leathery turtles seasonally in Australian waters is no indication of the proximity of a nesting beach. The species is a great wanderer travelling far into temperate regions, although it nests only in the tropics. Only the collection of recent hatchlings could be taken as evidence of breeding taking place in the vicinity.

Due to its large size the tracks are distinctive and would readily be picked up during aerial survey work. Its pelagic habits have resulted in the front flippers being proportionately larger and more powerful than in other species (see plate 2/3). Its extreme aquatic adaptations mean that on land it is very clumsy. When ashore the leathery turtle moves by synchronous forward pushes of all four limbs like the green turtle.

The paucity of knowledge on these three turtle species indicates fertile areas for future research in the Australasian region. The fact that all three species, but particularly the leathery turtle and the hawksbill, are seriously threatened throughout most of their range, means that the research would have important conservation impact quite apart from being of considerable scientific interest.

PART THREE

Turtle Research

THIS section of the book deals with research on sea turtles.

Chapter 8 is devoted to the fascinating topic of the eggs and young in which much recent work of general interest has been carried out. The accompanying plates show just how tiny newly hatched turtles are and some of the many predators which attack them as soon as they leave the nest.

Chapter 9 provides an account of our Australian turtle research programme in relation to work going on elsewhere. This chapter and the associated references will place the reader in the van of turtle research.

CHAPTER 8

The Eggs and Young

WITH experience one can distinguish the eggs of most sea turtles on the basis of size and appearance. For instance, in the Capricorn Islands, the eggs of the green turtle are somewhat larger than the size of a ping-pong ball, with a diameter of about 46 mm and an average weight of 52 grams. Loggerhead eggs are noticeably smaller, diameter about 40 mm and weight approximately 40 grams. They have a slightly pink appearance whereas green turtle eggs are whitish. The eggs of the flatback are considerably larger than green turtle eggs, diameter about 52 mm, average weight approximately 78 grams. The hawksbill and the Pacific ridley lay smallish eggs – about ping-pong ball size and the leathery turtle lays large eggs.

Clutch size is also characteristic for each species although considerable variation occurs, and overlap prevents this being a diagnostic feature. In the Capricorns the green turtle clutches average about 110 eggs. This figure is remarkably similar in many parts of the world. The flatback, on the other hand, averages about 50 eggs per clutch.

In reptiles the embryo becomes attached to the inside of the egg-shell at an early stage of development, so that if the egg is turned over, instead of being above the yolk, the embryo will have the yolk resting on top of it. (In birds in which the embryo does not attach itself to the shell, the embryo remains on top of the yolk when the egg is rotated by means of differential yolk viscosity and thicker strands of albumen called the chalazas or balancers.) Fixation to the shell is usually cited as the reason for rotation during development killing reptile eggs. However, additional information is required since a few reptiles which brood their eggs roll them around (such as the American skinks of the genus *Eumeces*).

This question is of more than academic interest in sea turtles since hatchery incubation success is usually much lower than occurs naturally. Hatcheries can play an important conservation and economic role, and it is, therefore, essential to maximise incubation success. An obvious explanation for reduced hatchery viability would be that the eggs have been roughly handled.

Commencing in summer 1965–6, I operated a hatchery at Heron Island which was capable of holding 50,000 eggs at one time. I held permits from the Queensland Government to place 30,000 green turtle eggs in this each season and 20,000 loggerhead eggs. I hoped to greatly increase incubation success in my hatchery compared to the literature record of a mean of 47 percent emergence (Hendrickson, 1958). The procedure used was as follows: The hatchery was a cyclone wire enclosure which extended 18 inches into the sand, roofed with chicken wire, and sited adjacent to the beach where heaviest nesting occurred. This meant that most clutches of eggs had only to be transported between 1–200 yards to the hatchery where incubation resulted from the heat of the sun as in nature.

All eggs were collected immediately after laying. This was done by operating behind the turtle, collecting the eggs as they were laid, and putting them straight into polythene bags. The bags were then sealed and carried to the hatchery. No nests were dug up after the turtle had finished laying and returned to the sea. At the hatchery holes similar to those of the natural nest were dug immediately prior to burying the eggs, which either took place concurrently with egg collecting or immediately thereafter. Hence all eggs had been re-buried in the hatchery within hours of laying – the average time that elapsed between collection and re-burying was under two hours. During handling, the eggs were treated with care to avoid undue bumping. Despite all these precautions, hatchery percentage emergence, although considerably better than the figure quoted by Hendrickson, was significantly lower than incubation of undisturbed nests on Heron Island.

The actual green turtle results for the hatchery were as follows: 1965–6, 67 percent emergence for 29,948 eggs; 1966–7, 65 percent for 17,112 eggs and 1967–8, 52 percent for 29,997 eggs. The poor result for the third year is thought to be the result of prolonged wet weather. Drainage in the hatchery was probably inferior to the majority of natural nest sites. In summer 1966–7, 26 natural nests were followed throughout the incubation period. The eggs were counted as the turtle laid them but were not touched or interfered with in any way; the turtle was allowed to cover the nest in the usual manner and after she had departed a sketch map was prepared to precisely locate the nest site. Percentage incubation success was obtained by waiting until the nest had hatched and then carefully excavating it to count the number of unhatched eggs. By carefully counting the shells a tally could be made to check the original figure recorded at the time of laying. Hence the loss of any eggs, as would result from another turtle digging into the nest, was readily discovered. Emergence for these 26 nests averaged 88 percent or 23 percent better than the hatchery in the same year. This experiment was repeated in summer 1967–8, this time for a sample of 40 green turtle nests. These undisturbed nests recorded 85 percent emergence which was 33 percent better than in the hatchery in that year.

It is my belief that the marked discrepancy between natural and hatchery percent emergence in the above experiments, with the exception of the poor hatchery result in 1967–8, can only be explained as a result of moving the eggs in the few hours following laying. At the time of egg laying, presumably the eggs are not vulnerable to movement or bumping as they fall into the egg chamber from the female's cloaca and subsequent eggs fall on top of them. However, it may be that development proceeds extremely rapidly in the few hours following laying and that even in this short time the early blastocyst has become vulnerable to movement. I have said above 'presumably' the eggs are not vulnerable to movement at the actual time of egg-laying because a number of authors have been surprised at the consistently large percentage of the eggs – about one-third in many parts of the world – which fail to develop. They have considered these as in-fertile eggs. However, the possibility exists that at least some of these eggs might have been killed as a result of rough treatment during egg laying.

When the hatchery eggs are moved from the polythene bag to the artificial egg chamber, this is done by placing the bag in the hole and slowly inverting it. Eggs are, therefore, rotated in the process.

I am convinced that temperature and humidity effects are not involved. The eggs are in sealed polythene bags and the operation is carried out at night when the temperature is about 24°C (75°F). An interesting finding is that eggs brought back to Canberra by air as hand baggage have a similar emergence level to hatchery eggs. This occurs despite a considerably greater movement factor en route commencing with a five-hour boat journey and spread over a much longer period of time. On arrival in Canberra the eggs are placed in incubators at once, however, this is about

24–30 hours after laying. It may be significant that these eggs are not rotated while being transferred from the polythene bags to the incubator. Before removal from the bag, the top of each egg is marked with a pen and the egg is placed in the incubator in an, as nearly as possible, identical position.

The lack of precise knowledge about egg tolerances immediately after laying is an example of the paucity of knowledge on sea turtle biology generally. Yet for both conservation and economic purposes it is essential to be able to operate highly efficient hatcheries. A 25 percent drop in emergence compared to natural nests is a very substantial loss and every attempt must be made to eradicate this or at least reduce it to an acceptable level.

In all natural nests examined in the emergence work described above, and in a random sample of 25 hatchery nests each year, a detailed record was kept of the fate of each egg and hatchling. Failure to emerge from the nest can be the result of a number of causes – infertile eggs, death of developing embryos, deformations, or imprisonment in the nest. In the hatchery, the percentage of infertile eggs varied from 16–21 percent whereas, in natural nests, the figure was seven and nine percent respectively in the two years. Since it is not possible to detect signs of a very early embryo when the nest is excavated some two months after its death, the category 'infertile eggs' includes death of very early embryos.

Dead embryos, usually near full-term, were detected in 3.3 to 11.6 percent of the eggs in the three years. The figure was highest in the third (wet) year when, incidentally, the percentage of 'infertile eggs' was lowest. In natural nests, dead embryos accounted for 2.2 and 4.2 percent respectively in the two years. Apart from the third (wet) year's hatchery results these values are similar for the hatchery and natural nests. Only minor differences were found between the hatchery and natural nests for the other categories examined. This leads to the conclusion that hatchery operations resulted in the death of at least ten percent of the eggs at an extremely early stage of development.

Sand temperature at the depth of the egg chamber does not vary with the 24-hour external temperature cycle; that is to say, sunshine during the day does not result in temperature variations at this depth as occurs near the surface. Sand temperature at the depth of the egg chamber averages 26°C (79°F) during the nesting season on Heron Island. Since the temperature of turtles is slightly above this, when first laid the eggs undergo slight cooling.

Hendrickson (1958) and Carr and Hirth (1961) measured the temperature of developing nests by inserting mercury thermometers into the nest. Both recorded substantial increases in temperature as incubation proceeded. This is not unexpected in view of the large number of eggs all in contact with each other. The heat results from the metabolism of the egg-mass and only becomes conspicuous during the second half of the incubation period. As a result of this metabolic activity, the temperature of the egg-mass becomes much higher than it was at the start of incubation and maintains a substantial differential compared to sand at the same depth not containing eggs. An important result of metabolic heating will be to reduce the incubation period, since incubation rates are closely dependent on temperature in reptiles. For instance, in the laboratory we have shown that green turtle eggs at 27°C (80.5°F) hatch after 80 days, at 30°C (86°F) after 55 days and at 32°C (90°F) after 48 days (Bustard and Greenham, 1968). These experiments were carried out at constant temperature and the eggs were kept in small batches so that metabolic heating did not occur. Any factor which speeds up incubation in the natural nest will have survival value since, while the eggs are incubating, they are at risk from predation.

The nest temperature relationships appeared so interesting that I designed an experiment using a recorder and fine thermistor probes to investigate them in detail. Each recorder had six temperature channels and automatically recorded these six temperatures at hourly intervals. By working behind a nesting turtle (as we do during egg collection) it was possible to locate the probes in precise positions. The turtle was then allowed to cover up the nest in the usual way and to return to the sea. Hence, we had our probes located at known points within the egg-mass of a completely natural nest. The recorder was switched on and operated until the hatchlings emerged. Usually we built a small wire screen around the nest area to prevent other turtles digging up experimental nests and so ruining the experiment.

I anticipated that there would be temperature gradients within the egg-mass which would be warmest in the centre with temperature falling off towards the outside. With this in mind, probes were located in the middle of the egg-mass and also near the edge. Probes were also located near the top and bottom of nests. No probes were located outside the egg-mass (other than controls which were sited at a similar depth in sand not containing eggs).

Probes at the edge, top or bottom, were located one egg in from the edge in order to monitor the temperature conditions being experienced by the outer eggs in the nest.

The temperatures recorded in the middle and near the edge of a developing nest from egg laying until after the baby turtles had emerged and the control are shown in fig. 5 plotted as daily means.

The egg-mass temperatures of this nest started to become higher than the sand about the middle of January and shortly thereafter differences between the middle and edge of the egg-mass became apparent. By mid-February, the middle of the egg-mass was $2.5°C$ ($4.5°F$) above sand temperatures at the same depth. A peak nest temperature of $31.8°C$ ($90°F$) occurred on 29th February, when the difference between the middle of the egg-mass and the sand also reached a maximum. In this particular nest the difference between these temperatures at this time was $5.1°C$ ($9.2°F$). A difference which averaged somewhat more than $1°C$ ($1.8°F$) was also recorded between the thermistor probe sited in the middle of the nest and the probe near the edge. This difference remained similar from 9th February until emergence occurred.

These results, while extremely interesting in their own right, provoked a puzzle. We knew that egg incubation was closely related to temperature in the green turtle so that the eggs in the centre of the nest should hatch well before those on the perimeter. However, we knew from field observations that all the hatchlings usually leave a nest together with only the occasional exception of a few stragglers. Indeed, the remarkable aspect of emergence in hatchling sea turtles is the way in which all the young burst from the nest at once. How is this achieved despite temperature differentials within the nest during incubation?

A likely hypothesis was that communication occurred between the eggs late in development as a result of which the retarded eggs 'caught up' with the more advanced eggs in the middle of the mound. Fantastic though this theory may sound it had been demonstrated for game birds where a similar problem occurs as a result of the mother starting brooding before the last eggs are laid. In the case of birds the communication is vocal. Since turtles do not vocalise we had to look for other means of communication. Movement within the eggs seemed the most probable method and would be effective since the eggs possess parchment-like shells. Furthermore, since the eggs are all in contact, waves of movement could proceed through the egg-mass to stimulate those eggs near the perimeter of the mass which would be somewhat retarded. We examined eggs about a week before they were due to hatch and confirmed that movements occurred within the egg. These were often sufficient to move the egg around if it was placed on a level surface.

In order to test this hypothesis, we set up a clutch of freshly-laid eggs in the laboratory. The clutch was divided into three approximately equal portions. One batch was maintained at the temperature of the middle of a natural nest, as recorded in the field, by means of daily alterations in the temperature of the incubator. The other two batches, both maintained in a second incubator, were kept at the temperature of the eggs near the edge of the same nest. Ten days prior to the anticipated date of hatching one of the latter batches of eggs was stimulated by a mechanical prodder which pressed down evenly on the eggs in the batch at hourly intervals. The other batch of eggs at this temperature was not disturbed and acted as a control. When the eggs from the incubator maintained at the higher temperature of the middle of the nest were hatching, the prodded eggs and controls were watched closely. The following day the prodded eggs commenced hatching but the controls did not hatch for a further four to five days. Hence prodding definitely speeded up late embryonic development allowing somewhat less developed eggs to catch up with others on the point of hatching.

It seems certain that this is the mechanism which occurs in the natural nest. It will be aided by the fact that after breaking their egg shells, the young spend several days in the nest before emerging. This period will allow retarded young to catch up with the rest of the nest and the activity within the nest will provide almost continuous stimulation. Before describing the hatching and emergence process there are several points concerning the nest micro-environment which deserve discussion.

As can be seen in fig. 5, a marked temperature fall was recorded by all three probes between 14th and 15th February. This was the result of a heavy tropical storm. The extreme porosity of coral sand combined with very heavy rain (several inches may fall in a single evening) bring about these rapid temperature falls. In one nest the temperature of the middle of the egg-mass fell by 2.7°C (4.9°F) in twelve hours and in another nest by 1.4°C (2.5°F) in only seven hours. As is shown in fig. 5, the rise of temperature may be

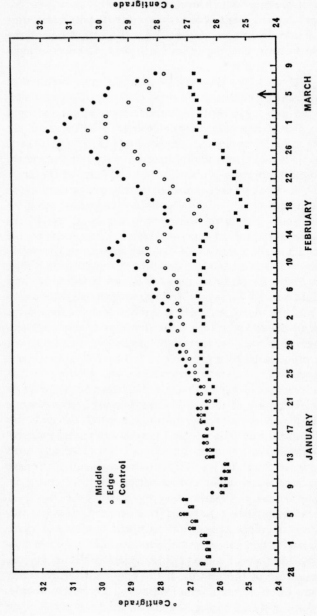

FIG. 5 Temperature recorded throughout the incubation period of an undisturbed natural nest of the green turtle at Heron Island, plotted as daily means. The probes in the nest were located as the turtle laid the eggs. The control was sited two yards from the nest at a similar depth to the middle of the egg mass. Emergence of the hatchlings from the nest is indicated by the arrow.

fairly slow thereafter, the egg-mass taking a number of days to regain its previous temperature level.

The temperature differential exists around the whole circumference of the nest. Temperatures at the top and bottom of the egg-mass are similar to each other and to edge temperature taken at the same level as the probe in the middle of the egg-mass.

Sea turtle eggs must be adapted to incubate over a range of temperatures, due to environmental differences between nest sites (see below), and in order to allow for temperature changes brought about during incubation as a result of metabolic heating. In practice we have found by laboratory experiment that green turtle eggs from the Capricorns tolerate a range of temperatures of about 10°C (18°F). Work was carried out at constant temperature and the lower and upper levels for successful incubation were found to lie between 25 and 27°C (77–80.5°F) and 35 and 37°C (95–99°F).

Long-term environmental differences in the sand at nest depths can be quite considerable even on a single cay as a result of variable exposure to sunshine and shade and wind effects. Clearly, nests in sunny locations with little exposure to wind are much warmer than those in deep shade or windy locations. These factors sufficiently affect nest temperature to approximately double incubation period at Heron Island for nests incubating simultaneously in cool as opposed to warm nest sites. The actual incubation period varies from six to eleven weeks, average eight weeks. In seasons where prolonged rain has lowered temperatures we have recorded nests which took up to thirteen weeks to hatch.

Water relationships of the nest are not usually important. As pointed out in Chapter 4, if the sand is moist enough for the turtle to successfully dig its egg chamber it contains sufficient moisture for successful incubation. The extreme porosity of coral sand prevents waterlogging occurring and when fatalities do occur, as described above for the third year of the hatchery, they may result from the prolonged depressed temperature, resulting from the rain rather than from the water itself.

During very prolonged dry spells the uppermost eggs may undergo desiccation, since the sand dries out from the surface downwards. However, the eggs are able to lose some of their contained water without the embryos dying. When laid the eggs are not quite turgid and in the first 24 hours or so following laying, they absorb several ml of water from the sand, if this is available, and become turgid. Where water content of the sand is adequate for this to occur, incubating eggs continue to absorb small amounts of water throughout the incubation period. I view this absorbed water as a form of insurance policy. If, at a later stage, water is not available and a net loss of water subsequently occurs, they are able to lose this absorbed water plus some of the water contained in the egg at the time of laying and still continue normal incubation. In a laboratory experiment I have reduced the water content of incubating green turtle eggs to eight percent below that at time of laying (measurements are carried out by weighing the eggs) and still obtained successful incubation. Such eggs have lost approximately 7–8 ml of water compared to eggs not under water deprivation. Should water be available subsequently the eggs rapidly regain the lost water.

Very much greater water gains occur in reptiles other than turtles. For instance, in an agamid lizard, I have recorded eggs which increased in weight by 250 percent purely as a result of water absorption, yet these eggs incubate successfully if this additional water is not available (Bustard, 1966). In sea turtle species with which I am familiar weight increases during incubation due to water uptake rarely exceed one-third of the original weight and are generally considerably less than this. It may be that in the relatively constant water micro-environment of the turtle nest there has been little selective pressure for the uptake of water since very large reserves are seldom required, as is the case, for instance, in desert reptiles.

It has been shown that some deformities are produced in testudines as a result of water shortage at certain stages of embryonic development (Lynn and Ullrich, 1950). I know of no work, however, on this topic in sea turtles. Certainly, similar deformities to those described by Lynn and Ullrich are seen in hatchling green turtles and probably have a similar origin. It is particularly interesting to note that some individuals with deformed carapaces survive into adulthood. In one population of green turtles we have several breeding females in which the carapace is constricted somewhat in the middle, an abnormality seen in certain hatchlings.

Albinos are rarely seen. Albinism itself is not extremely rare but it is usually associated with other deformities, particularly of the head, which prove lethal. During the operation of the hatchery we found one full albino which was extremely healthy. The hatchery also produced a partial albino which is shown in plate 22. One further full albino occurred in the hatchery, and one in eggs incubated in the laboratory, but both of these died shortly after hatching. Albino embryos usually develop to full term and then die without breaking the eggshell. We have come across a number during routine examination of hatchery and natural nests after emergence of the healthy hatchlings. We have also recorded them in the flatback (Bustard and Limpus, 1969).

When the young turtles are ready to leave the egg, the shell is slit using a caruncle, the 'egg-tooth' on the tip of the snout. Having slit the shell the baby turtles remain in the shells for about 24 hours. During this time, the yolk sac, two to three times the size of a pea when the shell is slit, is completely absorbed. When they emerge from the eggs they are approximately two feet underground and it is thought that emergence from the sand still takes several days. Group effort (social facilitation) plays a key role in the emergence pattern (Carr and Hirth, 1961). When one turtle moves, contact with others stimulate them and hence a burst of activity moves through the whole group. In this way, a high level of movement can be sustained for long periods of time. The hatchlings on top bring down the ceiling and those below trample down the fallen sand. As a result, all the hatchlings move slowly upwards. On their way to the surface they ascend the neck of the egg chamber dug by the mother turtle. A lift ascending a lift-shaft provides a good analogy.

In our experience, hatchlings very seldom emerge during the heat of the day, and in a sample of 5287 only three percent emerged during daylight. There are good evolutionary reasons for this behaviour as bird predation is high by day but almost non-existent by night. Furthermore, during the heat of the day many hatchlings would die from heat exhaustion before reaching the water. Baby green turtles with their black carapaces absorb radiant heat rapidly and are also very conspicuous against a background of white coral sand. The almost total nocturnal emergence pattern raises the question, how are the hatchlings 'programmed' to emerge at night? Investigations, starting with the work of Hendrickson (1958) and continued by ourselves and others, have indicated that the hatchlings dig upwards at any time of the day or night, but on reaching temperatures above a certain level, above about 30°C (86°F), become torpid and cease digging. When temperatures fall, activity recommences. This behavioural mechanism will result in those that dig up during the day waiting until temperature in the sand near the surface falls before they dig to the surface and emerge. Temperature generally falls to the required levels in the few hours following nightfall hence this is the time of peak emergence.

A problem with this theory puzzled me for a time. The problem resulted from the fact that hatchlings occupy perhaps an eight or nine inch depth of the egg chamber, and our knowledge of temperature gradients in the sand indicated that there would be a well-marked temperature gradient along this. Clearly not all the hatchlings would reach the critical temperature together so when the uppermost hatchlings reached this zone and became torpid, what happened to those farther down in the nest which were still experiencing activity temperatures? I found that social facilitation played an important role in this process. The uppermost hatchlings, on striking high temperatures, became torpid. They acted like a cork in a bottle, preventing upward movement of those below, but equally, if not more important, their complete inactivity dampened down activity in the whole group which became still. This is a reverse of the waves of activity which pass through the whole group in the earlier stages of digging.

Sometimes activity is not stopped until several turtles at the top are almost at the sand surface and their heads and front of the carapace may protrude from the sand. I have shown that these turtles are able to withstand several hours' exposure to the sun. Occasionally a few are completely pushed out of the egg chamber. Unless there is shade near by these are invariably killed by over-heating effects.

This fascinating temperature-dependent emergence mechanism, which I published in *Nature* in 1967, results in the majority of hatchlings becoming quiescent within the nest at a level where no light could penetrate and where temperatures are little different from those experienced in the egg chamber before the upward journey is commenced. It is a most effective mechanism as the very small percentage of daytime emergences quoted above demonstrates.

When the topmost turtles commence activity shortly after dark, this activity is quickly transmitted to the whole brood with the result that they all emerge at once, in practice often in under one minute. This effect can be induced while temperatures near the surface are still too hot for activity to recommence spontaneously, by pulling out several turtles at the top where heads can be seen protruding from the sand. This results in the complete emergence of the whole brood at once, presumably because the hatchlings deeper down in the sand now reach the surface before their body temperatures reach inactivity levels.

Clearly, there will always be some turtles which emerge during daylight hours, especially in the late afternoon. This can result from wind and shade cooling the sand over the nest while only several yards away temperatures in the surface layers of the sand are still well above activity levels. Some of these turtles may reach lethal or near-lethal temperatures before reaching the beach and we have recently discovered remarkable behavioural adaptations which greatly curtail death from overheating in these individuals. However, first I must describe how hatchlings, emerging at the usual time after dark, make their way to the sea. This problem has interested scientists for very many years and it is only now that it is becoming properly understood. So many people have contributed to the work since the early years of the century that it is perhaps unfair to name any one individual.

Many early theories were inadequate as they did not cover all naturally occurring situations. For instance, a tendency to simply move downhill would not suffice since before they reach the bank, hatchling turtles may have to climb upwards. It is now generally accepted, as a result of critical work both in the laboratory and the field, that hatchling turtles move towards the light horizon. In a natural situation this is always seawards since the ocean acts like a huge mirror reflecting available star and moonlight. Even on the blackest night, after one's eyes have become dark adapted, one can detect the direction of the sea from ground level in the tree-bush zone where nests are made. The mechanism is somewhat more complex than this as it takes into account open areas of the horizon as compared with areas where the horizon is obscured by vegetation. (A solid wall of vegetation will usually occur on the landward side of nests.) The mechanism is extremely precise and results in almost all hatchlings taking the shortest route to the sea which must require very accurate levels of discrimination between light intensities.

The hatchlings which emerge during the heat of the day and become overheated (body temperatures above about 36°c (97°f)) reverse this behaviour and seek shade. Once they enter shade their body temperatures quickly return to the levels at which they become torpid and they tend, therefore, to become inactive and come to rest within the patch of shade. When the temperature falls in the evening they become spontaneously active once more and make their way to the sea. I have quite a number of records of turtles which were thus exposed throughout the heat of the afternoon but subsequently reached the sea safely after nightfall. Had they attempted to reach the sea in the heat of the day they would have died of heat exhaustion before reaching the top of the bank.

The main land predator in the Capricorns of those few hatchlings which emerge by day is the silver gull (*Larus novaehollandiae*). This species also patrols the water's edge on nights around full moon when it undoubtedly picks up some turtle hatchlings. The other bird predators are strictly diurnal. We have never seen reef herons (*Egretta sacra*) eating hatchlings which would appear to be far too large for them to swallow. However, occasionally reef herons peck and so kill or maim hatchlings without attempting to swallow them. We have sometimes seen crested terns (*Sterna bergii*) flying with turtle hatchlings held in their beaks but have not actually observed them swallowing them. One of our group on one occasion saw a white-breasted sea eagle (*Haliaetus leucogaster*) take a hatchling green turtle.

Progress to the sea is very rapid once the hatchlings leave the nest, and most enter the water within minutes. However, even during this short space of time they are preyed upon by crabs. The large ghost crab (*Ocypoda ceratophthalma*) is an active hunter and patrols the beach at night on the lookout for food. When one spots a turtle it immediately grabs it in its chelae, usually in the neck region, and drags it towards its burrow. Other ghost crabs in the vicinity usually then become extremely alert, and if this hatchling was the forerunner of a brood of hatchlings scurrying seawards, most other ghost crabs will also secure one. When held in the neck region the baby turtles are unable to do anything effective to escape. They flap their flippers to no avail, while the crab settles down to its meal (plate 21). The crab usually picks out the eyes or attacks the top of the head first, so that although the baby turtle is eaten alive, it dies as soon as the brain is attacked.

Beach rock can be a hazard to baby turtles although they show great agility in climbing over it. Usually, unless there are vertical ledges which they cannot climb, with the result that they have to move along the beach searching for a way through, it does not slow them down much. However, the beach rock harbours a mortal enemy – the red-eyed crab (*Eriphia laevimana*). This species is much more sluggish than the ghost crabs, but a brief delay, such as often happens when a hatchling is trying to climb a ledge in the beach rock, is sufficient, and the red-eyed crab, which lives in crevices between the beach rock, reaches out and clutches the baby turtle in its huge vice-like chelae.

Predation on land in the Capricorn–Bunker Group is nothing compared with the hazards which the baby turtles face on entering the water. Before discussing this, however, a brief description of the hatchlings may be useful as they differ greatly in superficial appearance from the adults on which the colour pattern notes in the key in Appendix 1 are based.

Baby green turtles are blackish above and immaculate white below. The black coloration extends on to the head and flippers as well as the carapace. The hatchlings have a carapace length of about two inches and weigh approximately three-quarters of an ounce as they run down the beach. Flatback hatchlings are very different in appearance from baby greens. Firstly, they are much larger, weighing about half as much again as green turtle hatchlings. However, the most obvious difference is in coloration which is an attractive grey with just a touch of olive on the dorsal surfaces. The joins between the various carapace shields are black. The lower surfaces, as in greens, are immaculate white. The other species lack the white ventral surfaces. Baby loggerheads are brown to red-brown on both dorsal and ventral surfaces, the colour being considerably darker on the flippers. Unlike the green and flatback, which have smooth carapaces, the carapace of the loggerhead is very rough and there are three longitudinal ridges, one passing down the middle of the centrals and one in the middle of the laterals on each side.

Baby hawksbills and Pacific ridleys are superficially somewhat similar to baby loggerheads; however, the features given in the key provide ready separation as in the case of all hatchlings. The ground colour of baby hawksbills is usually a much paler shade of brown with a yellowish hue, than that of loggerheads, and the flippers are also much paler. At hatching there is no sign of the very attractive scales of tortoiseshell in the hawksbill. In the Pacific ridley the dorsal colour of hatchlings is brown, but not the red-brown of baby loggerheads, and the colour is usually much paler, often a dirty pale yellow colour tinged with grey, on the ventral surfaces.

When they enter the sea many species of carnivorous fish attack the baby turtles. Mortality is thought to be extremely high while they are crossing the reef flats towards the open ocean. Once in deep water they are less prone to attack but their size and lack of diving ability make them very vulnerable to any enemy which sees them. The dark dorsal coloration of several species, such as the green, undoubtedly has survival value under such conditions as it blends in with the mass of the sea viewed from above and so camouflages the hatchlings from seabird predators flying overhead. Baby green turtles, like hatchlings of the other species with the exception of the flatback, are sufficiently small to be swallowed whole by gulls. The white undersurface of both baby greens and flatbacks camouflages them from fish swimming below, as from below the surface of the sea appears silvery-white due to the sky above. This type of colour pattern, dark above and pale below, is known as countershading and is of such universal occurrence in surface-swimming fish that it is difficult to explain why it has not been adopted by hatchlings of the other sea turtle species.

In plate 21 a fifty-seven inch black-tipped reef shark (*Carcharinus spallanzani*) caught at Shark's Bay, Heron Island, is shown together with fourteen hatchling green turtles which I removed from its stomach. Twelve of these were in perfect condition and two were partly digested indicating that they had been taken earlier. Since these sharks are common around the Capricorn cays an enormous toll of turtle hatchlings must be taken. Frequently when a brood of hatchlings enters the sea once they get several yards offshore a whole series of popping noises are heard as one after another is taken by large fish.

The high level of predation during the initial period while the hatchlings are crossing the reef platform suggests that it may be important for large numbers of hatchlings to enter the sea from the one cay at the same time and so flood the market so to speak. Once most sharks and other large fish have had a fill then all subsequent hatchlings on that particular night will have a high probability of reaching the reef edge unmolested. If turtles could lay a whole season's eggs at one time and if all nested synchronously (as happens in the ridley (Carr, 1968)) then the hatchlings would all emerge over a short space of time. This would result in a much larger proportion of the hatchlings escaping than occurs when the young hatch over a period of several months. The comparison is effectively between feeding the large predaceous reef fish for a few days or for a few months. This concept may be extremely

13. (a) Loggerhead turtle emerging to lay **on** late afternoon high tide, Wreck Island, Capricorn Group.

(b) Loggerhead commencing excavation of shallow body pit, Wreck Island, Capricorns.

14. (a) Loggerhead raising anterior of plastron well clear of the ground in order to increase downward reach of rear flippers.

(b) Loggerhead leaving nesting site after egg-chamber collapse in extremely dry sand.

important in conservation and may also explain why huge discrete rookeries build up – even to the stage where nesting turtles are so numerous that high levels of egg destruction occur. These large rookeries produce a higher percentage of hatchlings which 'get away' from the island than small rookeries. The lesson for conservation may be that once a turtle rookery is reduced below a certain level by over-exploitation, such as has occurred on Aldabra in the Seychelles, complete protection from human predation may not bring about the desired effect, since a critically high proportion of the small production of hatchlings may be eaten before they reach the deep sea. This is yet another aspect of sea turtle biology which deserves careful investigation. However, I know of no work in this field up to the present time.

As I pointed out in a recent paper (Bustard, 1970a) the dark dorsal coloration of most sea turtle hatchlings probably has important survival value during the early months of life while the young spend most of their time floating at the surface. The dark coloration potentiates radiant heat absorption and so raises body temperature. An increase in body temperature above that of the sea water is beneficial as it stimulates metabolic activity including food digestion. Provided food is readily available, anything which makes the turtle hatchlings more active in searching for food and able to digest it more rapidly (and hence take in another meal), will increase their chance of survival as it will lead to more rapid growth. As pointed out, at hatching baby sea turtles are small enough to fall prey to very many enemies. However, with growth they rapidly out-grow most enemies. Hence rapid growth, especially when very small, will have important survival value. I have presented information based on laboratory work to show that in the green turtle the black dorsal coloration of the hatchlings results in a significantly higher body temperature than light-coloured carapaces.

Remarkably little is known about baby turtles once they enter the sea and they are seldom seen until they are at least one year old. During this initial period of the life history, often referred to as 'the lost year' because of the absence of sightings, we know nothing about the habits or whereabouts of the baby turtles. For this reason recent accounts of the stranding of very young leathery turtles near Capetown by George Hughes, and our own data on the stranding of loggerheads only a few months old on beaches near Perth in Western Australia following severe storms, are of particular interest because they indicate that large numbers of baby turtles are being transported by the prevailing offshore currents.

When green turtles are about three or four years old one commonly sees them on the reefs of the Capricorn–Bunker cays. However, by this time they are well on the way to becoming adults.

CHAPTER 9

Our Research Programme

O ur basic research programme has been centred on Heron Island in the Capricorns over the last eight summers. The work involves tagging and recapturing all the turtles which come ashore to nest during a specified period each summer. Associated with the tagging programme we have collected extensive information on egg production. We have also carried out work on egg physiology and the natural nest together with some work on hatchlings. These latter aspects have been discussed in Chapter 8 and in Bustard (1972) and Bustard, Simkiss and Jenkins (1969).

The tagging work is extremely laborious and its efficient operation requires a high degree of dedication by the staff. Since almost all the results are dependent on its being carried out with a very high degree of accuracy, and with virtually no turtles being missed, the procedure followed is described first.

Turtles are tagged so that we can positively identify them at a subsequent encounter. The tags serve the added function of informing anyone who may subsequently encounter the turtle that we have tagged it so that, hopefully, they will report its tag number to us. The tags we use are cow-ear tags, made of monel metal, to withstand long-term submersion in sea water. Their application to turtles was devised by Tom Harrisson in Sarawak and all turtle workers now use these. Some, however, prefer to have the tags made of plastic.

There are few places to tag a turtle. An examination of the carapace shows that it is a mass of minor abrasions and that anything affixed to it would soon be damaged or lost. Similarly, it would be unwise to fix anything to the plastron lest it be lost when the turtle is resting on the bottom.

When Professor Archie Carr started tagging turtles in the mid 1950s, he bored two holes in the rear of the carapace and fixed a metal label to the shell by monel metal wire passing through these two holes. He did not obtain any recaptures, but in time did recover turtles with holes bored in the carapace.

Having discarded the shell, one is left only with the soft parts, particularly the flippers. Harrisson picked on the front flippers, presumably since these are less frequently damaged, and selected the trailing edge. This proved to be an extremely wise choice. If one looks at a turtle during the nesting procedure, either when it is moving across the sand and/or negotiating rocks, or digging and subsequently filling in the nesting site, one is struck by the fact that only one area of the flippers is free from abrasion – namely, the trailing (rear) edge of the front flippers. The tag is best placed well in from the edge of the flipper. Different turtle workers, however, use different sites, some siting it well up the flipper near the 'shoulder' whereas we site it about mid-way.

Tags are applied using a specially designed pair of pliers. Once again practice here differs. Some workers prefer to make a hole first and then to insert the tag while the turtle is on its back awaiting the taking of various measurements. My own philosophy is rather different. As a population ecologist I like to think that I keep any possible effect on the animals I am studying to an absolute minimum. For this reason I never turn turtles over, and as described below, contact with them is reduced to a minimum. We apply the tag, which has a sharp piercing point, in one sudden motion. We do this just after the turtle has finished laying at which time it seems to be particularly insensitive to disturbance. Typically it either gives no noticeable reaction or shows a slight flipper withdrawal movement. Incidentally, it is extremely rare for any bleeding to occur when a turtle is tagged.

Let us now go back to explain the operation. Heron Island is some 1300 miles from my base (the Australian National University in Canberra). During the summer a number of assistants, usually promising zoology undergraduates or graduates, and myself, move up to live at the Research Station on Heron Island. Our first task is to become nocturnal since as mentioned in Chapter 4 green turtles do not leave the water during daylight hours. The task is somewhat more difficult than a straight shift of hours, since the work periods change virtually from night to night. On a coral cay with extensive associated reef, like Heron Island, turtles cannot come in on low or near low tides. The turtles show a well-marked response to the tide cycles, and about ninety percent come ashore between one hour before high tide to two hours after high tide. The time of nightfall and dawn are further complicating factors as the turtles show behavioural modification of the basic cycle firstly to avoid coming out of the water until it is dark and secondly to reduce the amount of time they must remain ashore after egg laying in order to complete the filling-in process.

When high tide is about 11 p.m. we start work at 9.30 p.m. and patrol continuously round our area of beach. Patrols continue until we have tagged or noted the recapture of our last nesting turtle. However, the last patrol will not begin until at least 1.30 a.m. Clearly turtles which come in late or experience trouble in completing an egg chamber may keep us up most of the night.

When the time of high tide is between 3 and 4 a.m., a change in the beaching behaviour becomes noticeable in that turtles tend to come in rather earlier than one would anticipate. As high tides become later this trait becomes more pronounced so that when the time of high tide approximates dawn most of the turtles are up a couple of hours prior to high tide. On these tides we start work correspondingly earlier, and subject to turtle nesting activity, start the last patrol once it is broad daylight.

A similar phenomenon occurs in reverse when high tide is in the late afternoon before nightfall – turtles wait until it is dark to leave the water. Incidentally, there are three or four days in each fortnightly tide cycle when we have to work extremely long hours since turtles come in on both tides (there are two high tides every twenty-four hours). This is because one high tide occurs in the few hours preceding nightfall, and the tide is still high when darkness falls to activate turtles which are ready to lay. The other high tide, approximately twelve hours later, occurs in the early morning around the time of dawn bringing in turtles before first light. During these three days the turtles all switch over from the one tide to the next. The typical pattern is that on the first of the customary three days of 'double night tides' virtually all the turtles appear on the early morning high tide (which has been the only night high tide for about ten days). On the second day they are split fairly equally between this tide and the new evening tide, and on the third the majority come in on the evening high tide there being few on the morning tide. Since we are forced to follow the tides in order to see all our turtles, we work rather irregular hours, some days being up until after daylight and having worked through from sunset, perhaps with a rather annoying few hours' lull during the night. At other times we work in either the first or second half of the night depending on the stage in the fortnightly tide cycle.

The small size of Heron Island (beach perimeter just over one mile) means that two trained observers can operate the tag-re-capture scheme. When turtles are seen for the first time they are tagged on the left front flipper after egg laying. The left flipper is selected since this is much easier for a righthanded person to tag. The tag bears a serial number on the upper side and a return address together with the word 'REWARD' on the lower side. Currently we pay a reward of four dollars (Australian) – about £2 Sterling – for the return of the tag together with date and the locality at which the turtle was caught, provided the turtle has been legally butchered. Under Queensland law only aborigines and Torres Strait Islanders can take turtles, and then only for their own use. The reward scheme does not operate in the Capricorn Group of islands and people are requested never to remove tags from living turtles. Since human population density is low in northern Queensland, there are few recaptures other than those we record ourselves back at the breeding beaches. This topic is discussed further below.

When a turtle is tagged, a record sheet is completed on the individual as follows; tag number, date of tagging, species, length and breadth (measured over the curve of the shell), presence or absence of barnacles and their location if present, injuries if any, notes on coloration, carapace shape and number of postoculars (in the green turtle), and number of marginals and inframarginals in loggerheads. Subsequently this information is transferred to a card in Canberra which is maintained for each individual tagged turtle. Each time the turtle is recaptured the date is noted together with other relevant information such as whether the turtle succeeded in nesting, and, if the individual is under detailed study, the number and weight of the eggs laid may be recorded.

During patrols, as far as possible, the operators move without lights, although they are issued with dim torches for writing and reading tag numbers when necessary. On most nights moonlight is quite adequate for normal activities. Great care is taken not to disturb beaching turtles, which sit at the water's edge and scan the landward horizon before emerging. Similarly, turtles moving up the beach are avoided by entering the vegetation zone and thereby bypassing them. Patrols are carried out by moving along the top of the beach adjacent to the vegetation zone. The best way to scare away turtles which are moving shorewards to nest is to walk along the water's edge where one is clearly silhouetted against the white coral sand. This process can be made virtually one hundred percent effective by periodically shining a bright torch on the water.

The above statement brings me to a question I am frequently asked – the effect of tourists on turtles. It is impossible to generalise as there are many variables. However, we have extensive experience of the effect of tourists on Heron Island as this is a tourist resort. On the whole, tourists have not had a deleterious effect on the Heron turtles. Firstly, they only go out to see turtles on nights when the high tide is in the early evening – only the keenest turtle watchers are prepared to rise in the middle of the night! Secondly, and most important, the owners of the resort have been most conscious that the marine life is their greatest potential asset and have been keen to preserve it. They have worked in with us to advise tourists how to watch turtles without frightening them. We give talks to tourists, as does the resort management, and most tourists meet some of my assistants on the beach within minutes of going out turtle watching. However, it must be remembered that Heron Island is a small cay situated about forty miles offshore. All tourists (other than scientists visiting the Research Station) must live at the guest house as the rest of the island is a National Park and camping is prohibited. The effect would be quite different on the mainland where people could drive cars down on to the beach. Without a full-time warden, a mainland turtle National Park would serve little purpose if the public were granted unlimited entry.

Over the years we have guided very large numbers of tourists round the Heron beaches. We have certainly met many charming people and we send our publications to a number of these. Apart from everything else, we feel that this meeting ground is an excellent way of making people aware of the problems of conservation. Many people, who had never seen a turtle before, go away thinking it a very great shame that these huge, harmless beasts should be killed for soup in most parts of the world. Since these people all have votes, the conservation impact must be positive. Overall we feel privileged to be able to work in an environment where we meet such interesting people and are able to tell them about our work. Quite apart from discussions on the beach, when time permits, we hold weekly or twice-weekly informal talks with tourists and any questions they may have relating to turtles are answered to the best of our ability.

Many people think of a Barrier Reef island as being hot at

night. In fact after nightfall there is frequently quite a cool breeze and I wear a jersey most nights. Popular imagination also tends to omit thoughts of rain, often torrential downpours which soak you to the skin in seconds, and which may continue for a large part of the night. This is particularly the case in the latter half of the nesting season (January, February). It is remarkable just how put out man is by rain. Work becomes much more tedious. Wet sand seems to get literally everywhere. Note taking is much more time consuming. It is interesting to note that this also reduces the turtles' 'efficiency'. If they are already about to lay or at a subsequent stage in the nesting process they do not appear to be disturbed. However, turtles coming up during or following torrential rain usually wander about aimlessly and often return to the sea without attempting to nest. They appear to require dry sand in order to start to dig. Since this is an impossibility on such nights digging attempts are scant.

Earlier I mentioned that turtles can be frightened away before beaching by shining bright lights on the water. Consequently, they are greatly disturbed by lightning. Prior to severe storms, dry storms with thunder and lightning often occur. If these take place before the turtles have emerged from the sea beaching is greatly impaired.

Our initial contact with the turtles gives us a mass of information on physical features. Furthermore, by plotting the numbers of newly tagged turtles each night throughout the time we are there, we can show that we 'tag out', that is tag all the individuals. This is accomplished after about one month, commencing with a completely untagged population. The time taken to tag the population is a reflection of the interval between laying (discussed below), since, until they have beached on the island in order to lay eggs, we have no opportunity to tag them. For this reason the work is restricted to female turtles. During the first cycle, if the nesting female population is a large one, we may be unable to cope with every turtle. Those missed are then all caught up with the next time round.

We have no data on weights because we have always felt that weighing constitutes a major disturbance to the turtle. Nevertheless, we now plan to weigh a small series for completeness of information on the population.

The 'green turtle' may constitute more than one species. Periodic attempts have been made to separate populations of this circum-

15. (a) Torres Strait Island turtle programme trainee, Nancy Pilot recording data on nesting loggerhead, Great Barrier Reef.

(b) Portrait of an old loggerhead. Note the pronounced 'beak'. Great Barrier Reef.

16.(a) Flatback (*Chelonia depressa*) emerging from the surf.

(b) Flatback (*Chelonia depressa*). Note the greatly flattened carapace, numerous small scales on front flippers and three large postocular scales immediately behind the eye.

global inhabitant of tropical and subtropical seas as a new species or subspecies. In view of this it is essential to have detailed information on the variation in features, which are used from time to time in attempts to separate populations, within individual populations. The shape of the carapace is one such feature which we have noted subjectively. For five years we recorded each turtle as having either a flattish, steeply rounded, or intermediately-shaped carapace. The information collected indicated that two-thirds of our green turtle population possessed intermediately-shaped carapaces with the rest split evenly between flat and steep. Of extreme interest was the fact that the percentages with each carapace shape varied greatly in different years. To demonstrate the significance of these variations a definite length/height ratio would need to be measured. Nevertheless, the crude observation made did not appear to be subject to bias especially since the same observers made the reports in several subsequent years and any new observers' data could be checked against this for bias. For instance, in years 1 and 2 the percentages with flat, intermediately-shaped and steep carapaces were 16, 35 and 49, and 25, 62 and 13 percent respectively – markedly different.

A feature often said to be diagnostic of the flatback is the presence of three scales behind the eye known as postoculars. Green turtles are said to have either four or five postoculars. This feature was checked in 1375 green turtles and 88 percent were found to possess four postoculars and seven percent possessed five. However, five percent possessed three as in the flatback. In a few individuals the postocular count differed between the two sides of the head.

In the loggerhead turtle populations a study was made of the number of marginal shields which edge the carapace and also the number of inframarginals which form the bridge joining the carapace to the plastron. A five-year count based on only 144 turtles indicated that 60 percent possessed 12 marginals, 22 percent 11 and 17 percent 13. Only one turtle was found with 10 marginals. The percentages varied between the populations visiting the island in different years. Twelve marginals was always the most common count but this varied from 51 percent in year 3 to 74 percent in year 5. The percentage of turtles with 11 marginals ranged from 12 to 32 percent and with 13 from nought to 37 percent. Eighty-three percent of the loggerheads examined in the five years possessed 3 inframarginals and 16 percent had 4. Only one turtle had an inframarginal count of 5. However, as in the

case of the marginals, there were differences in the relative pro-
portions of 3 and 4 between populations of different years. In
years 1, 2 and 3 respectively the percentage with 4 inframarginals
was nought, 10 and 4 percent respectively whereas in years 4
and 5 it was 40 and 47 percent! Differences of this nature would
seem to be the result of distinctive populations nesting in separate
years. This topic is taken up again towards the end of this
chapter.

During routine observations on each turtle, presence or absence
of barnacles, and the location if present, was recorded. In both
green and loggerhead turtles there was not a marked increase in
the percentage with barnacles with increasing size (age) of the
turtle as one would expect if the incidence of barnacle infestation
was cumulative. In the green turtle the figure was similar in all
size-classes of breeding females. In the loggerhead the figure
appeared to fall somewhat as the turtles became larger. In both
cases this would tend to suggest that either barnacles are acquired
at a specific immature stage of the life cycle only, or that incidence
of acquisition is balanced by rate of loss, either through barnacle
death, or loss when scutes are shed. As was the case with certain
other features described above the percentage occurrence of
barnacles varied considerably between populations in different
years.

There are several factors which affect the number of turtles
coming ashore to nest each night in addition to the aspects of
weather referred to previously. In my experience green and loggerhead turtles dislike high winds, probably due to wind action on
the sand. Winds of velocity above 25 knots cause the surface sand
to become airborne. Since the experience is quite painful to bare
skin if one sits on the ground, the effect on turtles' eyes is probably
severe. Turtles that emerge under such conditions invariably
change direction so as to put their backs into the wind and shield
their heads. This behaviour often results in them moving parallel
to the beach. They may return to the water without reaching the
vegetation zone. On windy nights the majority of the turtles
which would be expected to arrive on the windy side of the island
move round to the lee side and nest there.

Numbers of nesting turtles also vary greatly but predictably
during each tide cycle. On Heron Island with a large nesting
population the peaks are around one hundred turtles per night and
the troughs less than ten. This has important bearings on survey

work – one must be able to specify the state of the tide at the time of the work. It is extremely important if only a few nights' observation are carried out, otherwise one could come away with a completely unrepresentative picture of the abundance of turtles. In our experience, the greatest number of turtles usually beach on the second night following the end of the double tides. The following night numbers are often considerably less, but still high, and numbers then generally remain similar for several nights before starting to drop off. Numbers may reach a low point about midway through the fortnightly cycle or this may not occur until the double tides. The phenomenon is well illustrated in fig. 6 based on the Heron Island green turtle data for summer 1965–6.

We understand the fluctuations in number of nesting individuals of the much smaller loggerhead population at Heron Island less well. We have noted what we call 'loggerhead nights' on which a number of loggerheads come ashore to nest, whereas on adjacent nights there may be none. At the present time we are unable to explain these variations.

There is also a fluctuation in the number of turtles nesting throughout the season. Since all turtles do not arrive simultaneously, and depart together, there is a build up in numbers at the start of the nesting season and a gradual fall towards the end. The first green turtles to arrive are seen at Heron Island generally during the last week of October. For the first few days no nesting takes place, although some turtles may emerge from the water and crawl up the beach, only to return to the sea without making any attempt at nesting. By late November the population has built up to its maximum size and remains at this level until mid to late January when it starts decreasing. Some nesting, however, occurs until at least well into March and sometimes a few turtles are nesting until the end of April.

While on the subject of beachings it may be of interest to discuss exploratory beachings. This is the term we use for turtles which emerge, apparently to nest, but make no attempt to do so. Dampier (1697) noted the phenomenon. He wrote, 'sometimes they come up the night before they intend to lay, and take a view of the place, and so having made a Tow, or Semi-circular March, they return to the sea again, and they never fail to come ashore the next night, to lay near that place'.

These turtles frequently wander long distances in the course of which they often accidentally bump into other nesting turtles and

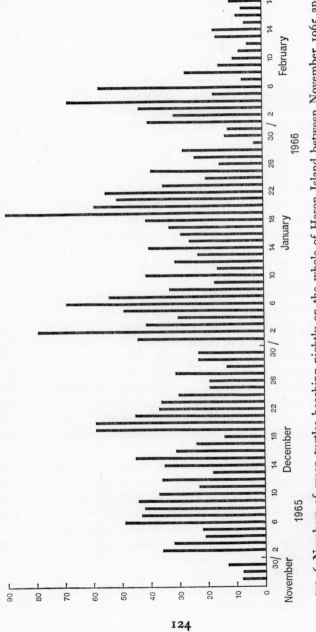

FIG. 6 Numbers of green turtles beaching nightly on the whole of Heron Island between November 1965 and February 1966 (see text).

disturb them. During this wandering they either make no attempt to dig or make only cursory front flipper movements at a few sites before moving on again. Detailed observations have shown that these particular turtles almost always emerge again the following evening, haul-up just above the spring high-tide mark, and dig their nests at once with no exploratory activity. The marked contrast between the two nights' activity is most conspicuous. Provided weather conditions have resulted in the sand being suitable for nesting activity, we can only assume that on the first night they were not quite ready to lay their eggs whereas on the second night a strong laying urge was present.

During nesting, turtles have to avoid hazards such as fallen trees, roots, large impenetrable bushes and even other turtles. This results in considerable movements within the nesting area which is best shown by an actual record of one night's activity by all the turtles on the beach (fig. 7). This beach was accurately surveyed and the turtles' movements plotted, without causing disturbance, as they occurred during the night. As can be seen from the figure some turtles carried out lengthy and complicated movements. Different symbols are used to separate tracks which might otherwise be confused. Since the time of beaching is noted and also the time of egg laying, if this occurred, the time that elapsed can be calculated. The figure gives a graphic impression of green turtle nesting movements and should be examined in conjunction with Chapter 4.

Most species of sea turtle lay a number of clutches of eggs in a breeding summer. The time interval between successive clutches is usually about two weeks. At Heron Island the majority of green turtles lay again after 14 or 15 days, although exceptionally this may be after as few as 9 days or as many as 21. Very few turtles fall outside an interval of between 12 to 18 days. For loggerheads the mean interval is 15 days with most re-nesting after an interval of 12 to 17 days.

Probably the question we are asked most frequently about nesting behaviour is whether the turtles return to the same spot or general area on the island to lay successive clutches of eggs. For convenience we have divided the beach perimeter of Heron Island into sixteen beach areas and the area in which each nesting occurs is noted. Observations of 2120 subsequent nests of green turtles over three years has shown that there is no well-marked return pattern to the same area, although more return to nest in the same

FIG. 7 Turtle movements on an area of high beach platform at Heron Island on one night to show their complexity. Times at foot indicate emergence from sea, bracketed numbers are turtle tag number. 'X' indicates site of laying, time is given and the arrow shows direction of turtle's head. Square with diagonal line indicates unsuccessful nesting attempt. Records were made by watching turtles carefully at night.

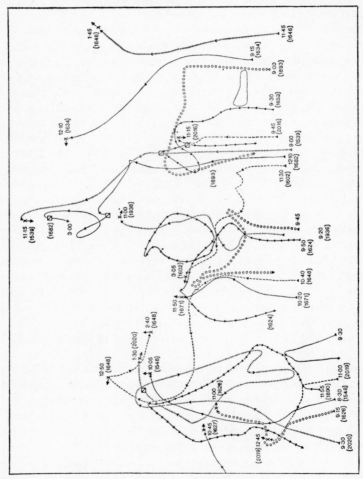

area or area immediately adjacent thereto than would occur randomly. The figures recorded were as follows: returns to the same area 21 percent; to adjacent area 22 percent; to completely different area 57 percent.

Any mathematical calculations on the above data would be heavily biased by a number of factors. Firstly turtles do not beach randomly on Heron Island for nesting. Numbers are most dense in the Shark's Bay area where there is good access to deep water without intervening coral. On areas of the island where there is extensive beach rock (plate 1) the numbers nesting depends on the height of the night tide and, therefore, on the state of the tide cycle. When the tide covers the beach rock, nesting takes place at quite substantial density. However, when the high tide leaves large areas of beach rock exposed then much sparser nesting takes place in these sections of the beach. Green turtles will crawl across large areas of beach rock, but not unnaturally there is a tendency to avoid this where possible. Once they are on beach rock they will continue across it, but if the tide is below the start of the rock – which often makes climbing on to it difficult – they generally swim parallel to the beach rock looking for a way through. In our experience loggerhead turtles seldom cross beach rock, and since this occurs on a large proportion of the Heron beaches, their main nesting area is restricted to a small part of the island.

We have carried out considerable work on egg production by the green turtles at Heron Island. Production per female is the number of clutches produced in a season multiplied by the number of eggs per clutch. Information on the first is obtained as a result of the tag-recapture programme, but the latter requires counting eggs in successive clutches. Initially this work was greatly aided by the hatchery programme, described in Chapter 8, in which large numbers of eggs were collected from known females for hatchery incubation. All these eggs were counted during collection and a random sample from each clutch was weighed in order to establish the mean egg weight.

In the green turtle we have found that the mean number of clutches of eggs deposited differs between years. In three successive years it varied from between three and four to between five and six clutches. The third year was intermediate. In two of three years the greatest number of loggerheads were recorded only laying one clutch although some individuals laid as many as four or five times. In the remaining year most laid two or three clutches of eggs. At the present time we are not able to explain these inter-year population differences. The observation period was the same in each year and there is no reason to doubt the efficiency of the tag-recapture operation in any year. It may reflect population differences, or perhaps is a result of variation in the quantity and/or quality of food supply.

We found that a number of factors affect clutch size in the green turtle. One of these is the size of the turtle, larger turtles producing larger clutches of eggs. Carapace length is plotted against clutch size for the green turtle population at Heron Island in summer 1965–66 in fig. 8. As shown in the figure large turtles lay up to twice as many eggs in a clutch as small females. Since turtles, like other reptiles, commence breeding long before they have reached maximum size (most reptiles subsequently continue to grow slowly throughout adult life) 'small' is probably equatable with 'young' and 'large' with 'old'.

The average size of the eggs remains similar despite changes in size of the mother. That is to say, larger turtles produce a much greater mass (weight) of eggs. Clutch size, in the sense of biomass of the clutch, is probably a result of the physical space available to house the developing eggs as well as a result of the amount of reserves which the turtle can make available for egg production. Both these factors would promote larger clutches by bigger females. It is not surprising that average egg size remains similar, as this will be determined by natural selection at a size which produces the greatest number of surviving progeny, bearing in mind that the amount of egg material is fixed and, therefore, that if the eggs were smaller there could be more of them and vice versa.

In the loggerhead the relationship between clutch size and carapace length is much less pronounced than in the green turtle.

In addition to studying the turtles' way of life at the nesting beach, we are interested in where they go and what they do while at sea for several years between nesting cycles. Tagging helps to provide some data on this as recaptures give an indication of the distance moved. Carr (1968) has shown that the Costa Rican green turtle population moves as far afield as Mexico, adjacent to Yucatan, southern Florida and Isla de Margarita, Venezuela. Furthermore, work by Carr and associates discussed in Carr (1968) has indicated that Brazilian green turtles travel to Ascension Island in the mid-Atlantic to nest. This information was gained by tagging green turtles on Ascension Island, where there are no nearby feeding grounds. Turtles tagged on Ascension Island have been recaptured on the coast of South America and have also been recaptured nesting again at Ascension after an interval of several years. The shortest distance between Ascension and the coast of South America is about 1400 miles. Navigational problems in the journey to a small island like Ascension must be immense but turtles appear to be adept at this.

Recaptures of Australian tagged turtles are shown in fig. 9. In examining the figure one must bear in mind that the human population in Queensland is heavily concentrated in the south-east of the State. There is accordingly marked bias in reporting recaptures in the south as compared to the north. The fact that

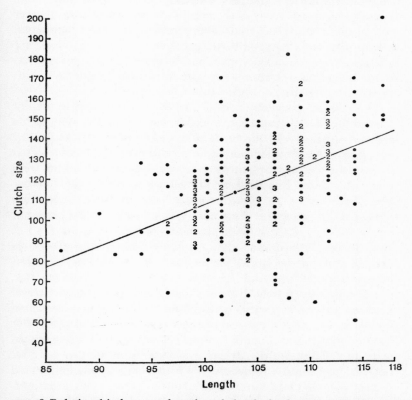

FIG. 8 Relationship between length and clutch size in a green turtle population at Heron Island showing that larger turtles lay appreciably more eggs. Numbers where several points are superimposed.

despite this bias most recaptures come from considerable distances from Heron Island is good evidence of lengthy migration by the vast majority of turtles. Apart from those individuals which move out into the Pacific (such as the three New Caledonia recaptures) the trend is unmistakably to move northwards. Some knowledge of local geography is necessary to appreciate this. The Capricorn–Bunker cays are situated astride the Tropic of Capricorn and as such are relatively far south for major green turtle rookeries. Certainly the major feeding grounds are well to the north. One might wonder why turtles feeding say, north of Townsville, would come as far south as Heron Island to nest. The reason for this is that cays which provide ideal nesting conditions for turtles are not common throughout the length of the Great Barrier Reef. The main aggregations occur in the extreme south (Capricorn–Bunker group) and in the far north. In between there are many continental islands often lacking good turtle beaches, but no cays. There are of course numerous sandy mainland beaches but the green turtle shows a marked preference for nesting on small isolated islands compared to mainland nesting (see Chapter 10).

The recaptures recorded in fig. 9 are not of nesting turtles. Except for an occasional turtle which may be caught in a net, its capture recorded and the turtle liberated (unless drowned), they are taken on the reefs for food by aboriginal people. The two dotted lines in the figure represent recaptures of loggerheads which were tagged by Colin Limpus near Bundaberg in south-east Queensland. Both turtles had travelled great distances from the location of tagging, the recapture from near Weipa being the first record of a turtle rounding Cape York peninsula and entering the Gulf of Carpentaria. The limited data on recaptures of loggerheads in various parts of the world, summarised by Bustard and Limpus (1970) and Bustard and Limpus (1971), would indicate that this species travels long distances. Furthermore, the time interval between last sighting at the nesting beach and recapture elsewhere indicates that deliberate long distance migrations take place. For instance Hughes et al. (1967) reported recapture of a loggerhead tagged in Natal, South Africa, at a distance of 1650 miles after only 91 days and the recapture of a Bundaberg tagged loggerhead in the Trobriand Islands off eastern Papua–New Guinea, a straight-line distance of 1100 miles, took place after a lapse of only 63 days. If, as appears likely, the turtle followed the coast for much of the way the distance covered would have been much greater – up to

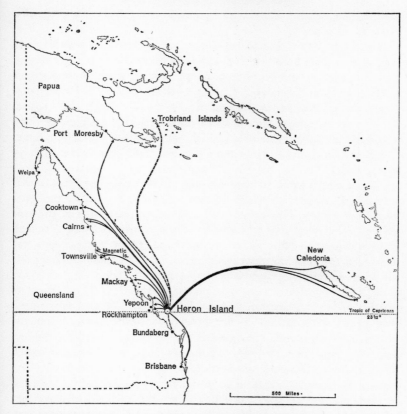

FIG. 9 Recovery sites of green turtles tagged at Heron Island and adjacent cays (continuous lines) and loggerheads tagged at Bundaberg on the mainland (dotted lines). The lines do not necessarily indicate the route followed.

2000 miles. Furthermore, at the time of year that the movement took place, the prevailing current is travelling southwards down the east coast of Australia, so, far from travelling on the current, the turtle would have to swim against it.

It has been known for many years that turtles may return to the same beach to nest in subsequent nesting seasons. This information has been substantiated by tagging programmes. However, most reports gloss over the very low proportion of returns recorded. The low returns are puzzling in view of the probable longevity of the adults and would tend to indicate that the return pattern to the same island may be much weaker than has generally been supposed.

The best data are those of Carr (1968). For the Costa Rican population Carr has recorded 447 individuals back at the nesting beach in subsequent years from a tagged population of 5758 green turtles. It should be noted that 55 of these returns did not occur until a lapse of between five and nine years (Carr and Carr, 1970). Of 635 green turtles tagged on Ascension Island only eight were recaptured at Ascension after periods of two to four years. Similarly, Harrisson in Sarawak recorded a low level of recaptures in subsequent years.

There could be a number of reasons for this poor level of recapture. For instance, the tags could fall off as a result of destruction by sea water. However, I know of no evidence for this. Indeed, individuals recaptured by us, either back at Heron Island – where I have examined most of the tags personally – or taken elsewhere, in which case the tag is returned to us, have all shown the tags to be in excellent condition with no signs of deterioration or wear.

At the end of the 1969–70 nesting season we had 3825 green turtles and 665 loggerheads tagged in the Capricorn cays. However, since they do not re-nest for several years these are not all immediately available for recapture at the nesting beaches. Allowing for a lapse of four years – the commonest for the green turtle in our limited Queensland experience – we have a marked population of 859 greens 'available' for recapture at Heron Island. During summers 1968–69 and 1969–70 only nine recaptures were recorded. It will be recalled that due to the small size of the cay it is easy to see all nesting turtles at Heron Island. Furthermore, the fact that it is an island means that turtles cannot be missed by beaching just outside the study area as could occur on the mainland.

In 1965–66 we tagged 139 green turtles on North-West Island, the largest of the Capricorn cays. In summer 1969–70, four years later, only two tagged turtles were present in the nesting population.

Loggerheads appear rather more prone to return to nest subsequently than greens but even with them the percent recapture rate is low. In our experience they nest again after intervals of two or three years. On this basis we had 153 tagged individuals available for recapture by summer 1969–70 yet recaptures totalled only ten. One loggerhead returned after one year and laid, and this same individual was recorded at Heron Island for a third season two years later.

The geography of the Capricorns – there are seven islands in the group used by nesting turtles – provides some additional information of great interest. One reason which could be put forward to explain the small number of returns to specific beaches in subsequent nesting seasons would be that turtles have a tendency to return, not to the exact location of previous nesting – perhaps they have difficulty in locating it – but to the same general area. Hence there would exist not populations of Heron Island turtles but Capricorn cay turtles. Since the various cays are situated only 8 to 17 miles from Heron – quite trivial distances in view of migrations of many hundreds of miles from the north – they provide an excellent situation to test this theory. One would expect many 'misses' in which turtles tagged on one island return four years later to another cay in the general area. During summer 1969–70 we were able to test this possibility since we carried out tag-recapture operations on four of the seven nesting cays. During the summer all recaptures bar one were made on the island where the turtles were originally tagged. The sole exception, a loggerhead tagged on Heron, was recaptured eight miles distant on Wreck Island. Hence, there is no question of most turtles returning to the general area but using another island. If they returned to the general area they nested on the same cay used several years previously. Despite this we have several records of turtles tagged on one cay subsequently nesting in the same season on an adjacent cay.

As stated in Chapter 2 the past fifteen years have seen a tremendous advance in knowledge concerning sea turtle natural history, particularly as a result of the work of Carr. The following accounts are of particular interest: Carr (1962), Carr and Giovannoli (1957), Carr and Ogren (1960), and Carr et al. (1966). Other important accounts include Harrisson (1951, 1954 and 1956) and Hendrickson (1958).

Our major interest in Queensland has been to utilise the large unhunted turtle populations to carry out a detailed population ecology study. This would advance knowledge very considerably without merely repeating in Australia work carried out or in progress elsewhere. Queensland offers very great advantages for this work not enjoyed elsewhere which is why we started the programme there. Firstly the State is huge with a seaboard of 3250 miles. We have assumed that most of our tagged turtles remain within or adjacent to Australian territorial waters throughout their life. There is no European fishery for turtles permitted in Queensland (see Chapter 10) and the aborigines no longer take many. This means that marked animals are not subject to a substantial but imprecisely known predation rate as a result of human hunting effort as occurs in most other countries. Furthermore, the small size of our study area, together with the information given above that turtles returning to the Capricorn Group of islands in subsequent nesting seasons return to the same cay once again, allows us to effectively monitor a discrete population.

As detailed above the reproductive pattern is now fairly well known. It is interesting to note that the length of the nesting season differs considerably in various geographic locations probably as a result of latitude. As one moves towards the equator the nesting season is prolonged and in such areas as Sarawak some nesting occurs in every month of the year but with pronounced peaks in certain months. As well as the spread in nesting season, the number of clutches laid by each female also shows geographic variation.

In view of a presumed optimum size (weight) for the egg as a result of natural selection (see discussion above) it is extremely interesting to note that egg weight and, therefore, size of the hatchling, varies in different localities. For instance, Hendrickson (1958) gave a mean of 36 grams (range 28.6–44.7) for Sarawak which compares with 51.6 grams (range 44.0–60.4) for the Heron Island population. This very substantial difference could perhaps be related to differences in the mean number of clutches laid by a female in a nesting year, however, this is not borne out by Hendrickson's data.

An extremely interesting facet of the population ecology is the enormous numbers of individuals nesting at undisturbed rookeries. The discrete nature of these rookeries, combined with the limited area available for nesting – a narrow strip between the spring high-tide mark and the vegetation zone – results in many subsequent nesting females digging where a female has previously deposited eggs. Thus appreciable destruction of incubating eggs occurs, as was first pointed out by Moorhouse (1933). We have studied this situation on Heron Island and using computer studies have confirmed that nest destruction is dependent on population density (Bustard and Tognetti, 1969). It may be that this phenomenon is important in limiting production of any one rookery and hence playing a role in population regulation. However, the situation is extremely complex as the density of hatchlings entering the sea has also to be taken into account. For some time I have seen the progressive build up of a rookery, with the resultant flood of hatchlings entering the water, as an important way of reducing neonatal predation by flooding the area with hatchlings. The hatchlings are most vulnerable when still in fairly shallow water on and around the reef platform – that is, during the first few hours of life. When a rookery produces more hatchlings per night than the carnivorous fish on the surrounding reef can eat, then clearly many will certainly survive and reach deep water. As long as the numbers of hatchlings are inadequate to feed the local fish then any hatchling entering the sea has a finite chance of being eaten while crossing the reef. Clearly there must be a population level at which the reef platform is regularly flooded with hatchling turtles. The relative importance of egg destruction by subsequent nesting turtles will depend at what adult turtle population size 'flooding' by hatchlings occurs.

Where two species of turtles share the same nesting beach, competition between them for nesting space may be important, especially if their behaviour differs sufficiently for one to be markedly adversely affected by the other. Bustard and Matters studied the interaction of green and loggerhead turtles nesting at Heron Island where the loggerhead population is always much smaller than the population of nesting green turtles. The field data were simulated on the computer to provide extensive quantitative information. Loggerhead turtles usually nest much nearer the sea than green turtles. At Heron Island they usually lay just above the low bank which encircles the island. Some green turtles nest in this zone but most move farther inland. Hence the nesting loggerheads potentially affect only a fraction of the green turtles. Furthermore, due to the small numbers of loggerheads their effect is minimal. However, although many green turtles move considerably farther inland before nesting, they frequently dig a first egg chamber in the main loggerhead nesting area. Naturally this results in a tendency to dig up and so destroy incubating loggerhead eggs. Since green turtles are proportionally much more numerous than loggerheads, and since the total loggerhead lay is aggregated in this narrow area above the bank, the effect of the green turtles on the loggerheads is proportionately large.

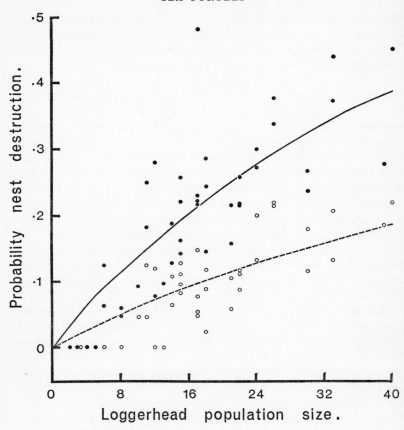

FIG. 10 The probability of nest destruction resulting from intra- and inter-specific competition for nesting sites on a cay (Heron Island). Graphed are the destruction of loggerhead nests by subsequent nesting loggerheads (lower broken curve) and total nest destruction suffered by the loggerhead population (upper continuous curve). The difference between the curves is the result of very substantial interaction (nest destruction) by a nesting population of green turtles.

The effect of this interaction is illustrated graphically in fig. 10 in which the probability of nest destruction (a figure of 1 would represent one hundred percent) is plotted against the size of the loggerhead turtle population. The lower dotted curve shows the loss of incubating loggerhead eggs as a result of destruction by other nesting loggerheads, whereas the upper continuous curve shows the total level of egg destruction suffered by the loggerhead population. The difference is due to interaction with green turtles. As is shown in the figure the green turtle effect is substantial. For instance, with a loggerhead population of only 18 animals on the nesting beach studied, the probability of nest destruction by subsequent nesting female loggerheads is of the order of 1 in 10. However, the effect of the green turtles is to more than double the destruction to between 1 in 4 and 1 in 5. This is the same as saying that there is considerable competition between green and loggerhead turtles for nesting space and that the competition adversely affects the loggerhead population.

Growth is another fascinating topic about which little is known. A small number of turtles have been reared in captivity in various parts of the world. The resultant information is open to criticism on the grounds that there is no indication of the relationship of captive growth rates to growth in nature. Indeed it is known that captive growth rates vary enormously depending on the conditions under which the turtles are kept and the food supply.

On the basis of growth rates obtained by Les and Dorothy Tanis who provide ideal conditions for their turtles (see Chapter 10) I would give a tentative age at first breeding for Australian green turtles as not less than eight years. This is much slower growth than figures arrived at by Carr and Hendrickson and may merely reflect slower growth in captivity. Carr (1968) thinks that Caribbean populations of the green turtle reach maturity at about five years of age and Hendrickson (1958) has suggested between four and six years for Asian populations of the same species.

Turtles reared in captivity from hatching and then subsequently released into the ocean may maintain similar growth rates to captives kept under ideal conditions. Of a number liberated at the age of one year or more we have so far had only one recapture. The turtle was hatched on 24th March, 1965 and released at Heron Island on 9th January 1967. At the time of release it weighed $4\frac{1}{2}$ lb and had a carapace length of $9\frac{5}{8}$ inches. Another hatchling from the same clutch of eggs also reared in captivity weighed $9\frac{1}{4}$ lb and had a carapace length of $11\frac{3}{4}$ inches on 9th January. The foregoing turtle was recaptured on the reef at Masthead Island, Capricorn Group, on 6th May 1969 and sighted there again on 8th and 9th May. On 6th May it was measured, the length over the carapace being $19\frac{1}{2}$ inches. At this time the captive sibling had a carapace length of $21\frac{1}{2}$ inches. Hence, the overall difference in carapace length had remained similar indicating that the individual at liberty was showing a similar, or marginally better, growth rate to the captive individual.

There are no data as yet on growth to breeding size by wild individuals. In an attempt to get this information I operated a hatchery at Heron Island for three years from 1965–6. All hatchlings were marked immediately following hatching and then liberated into the sea at the water's edge. Recaptures will provide information on growth to maturity and hopefully also on survival. The hatchlings were marked by removing part of a marginal shield of the carapace. Evidence suggests that this does not regenerate well and that the clip can be picked out readily many years later. Use of a different marginal each year will allow us to age the individuals if these are subsequently recaptured.

On the Great Barrier Reef nesting female green turtles vary from 35 to 50 inches in carapace length (measured over the curve). The commonest size is about 42 inches, and above this size the addition of only one or two inches makes the turtle appear very much larger and greatly increases its weight. Tag recapture data can provide information on growth of these turtles between nesting seasons. Since reptiles, like other ectotherms, continue growth throughout life and typically reach sexual maturity long before attaining a 'maximum size' one would expect considerable growth to be recorded, at least among the smaller females. Once reptiles reach a certain size, often referred to as the 'adult size range', growth becomes extremely slow and indeed it may be difficult to measure. Young nesting female green turtles might be expected to show fairly rapid growth until they attain a size of 40 to 42 inches. Our very limited recapture data is extremely interesting but difficult to interpret. We have recaptured eleven green turtles after intervals of up to four years at sea. Nine of these definitely showed no measurable growth. In only one was there a strong indication of an increase of one inch, from 45 to 46 inches. The remaining individual apparently increased by 0.5 inches but since this is at the level of accuracy the apparent growth might have been due to experimental error.

The loggerhead recaptures provide similar information. In only two of eleven recaptures is there definite indication of growth. One increased by 1 inch from an initial carapace length of 41.5 inches and the other by 1.5 inches from 38 inches.

The above information can be interpreted as meaning that growth is generally extremely slow in both species once sexual maturity (minimum breeding size) is reached. On this interpretation large individuals are extremely old. On the other hand, the data can be taken to mean that there is markedly different growth during immaturity, perhaps as a result of food supply, with the result that size at sexual maturity varies widely. On the latter interpretation little growth would be expected after attainment of sexual maturity – only the extremely slow growth characteristic of reptiles throughout adult life. An age determination technique is required to settle this problem and we are currently investigating skeletal ageing techniques in sea turtles.

The frequent high density of nesting turtles on rookeries not subject to intensive human predation – which quickly wipes out the turtles if applied to the nesting females – leads to two important situations. Firstly one is usually struck by the shortage of nesting area. Only a narrow strip between the spring high-tide mark and the vegetation zone, the latter usually forms an impenetrable barrier, is available to the turtles. Furthermore, green turtles have a tendency to nest beside vegetation hence increasing egg destruction even further. It is possible to design an ideal beach which has a greater nesting area, with vegetation so arranged that the same area can support a much larger volume of developing eggs without a concurrent high rate of egg destruction by nesting turtles. Clearly this could have important practical applications. There is no question but that the productivity of most island (or mainland) nesting beaches could be increased at little cost. At the simplest this would involve removing debris in the form of tree trunks and the like from nesting beaches and laying areas. We have carried out an investigation of ideal nesting area configurations using computer techniques (Bustard and Matters, in prepn.). The other situation is beach erosion which was discussed in some detail in Chapter 3.

The relative occurrence of turtles of various sizes in the population provides additional information on the growth-age problem. In both green and loggerhead turtles at Heron Island there are extremely few individuals of about first breeding size, which may be young females breeding for the first time. This could suggest that few juveniles survive to join the breeding population which would, therefore, need to have a long life span. However, as mentioned above, it could merely mean that many females attain a considerably larger size before commencing breeding. The size–frequency distribution data, shown in fig. 11, also show a very small number of large individuals. This means that most individuals are lost from the population before they attain a very large size. On the other hand this could reflect a fairly rapid loss, so that even with a recordable growth rate adults tend to be lost before a large size is reached, or it could result from a slow growth rate with the result that the turtles seldom live long enough to attain these large sizes. Once again only an ageing technique applicable to adults will solve this problem.

Some information can be obtained, however, by an examination of the information on injuries grouped according to turtle size. A cursory examination of these data show that incidence of injury is definitely not cumulative throughout life as could be expected. Injuries are highest in the smaller breeding female green turtles. As the turtles become larger the percent with injuries drops steeply and then remains similar throughout life. The fall in percentage with injuries above this size grouping is clear evidence that there is considerable loss of young breeding female green turtles from the population and that a lower rate of loss occurs throughout later life (to offset those contracting new injuries) or that sharks seldom attack larger green turtles. Both factors may be important. In loggerheads, injuries reach a peak somewhat more than half-way through the breeding size range. This would tend to indicate that little loss from the population occurs prior to the size (age) class represented by the peak but that after this size (age) is attained substantial losses occur. The above statements will only hold good if the hypothesis that the larger turtles are older is shown to be correct.

The problems raised above show that a great deal remains to be elucidated about the lives of sea turtles. Their relative inaccessibility during their life at sea is largely responsible for this paucity of information. However, greatly increased tagging effort at many more locations should provide considerable information to fill present gaps in our knowledge. For instance I have remarked above on the poor recapture rates recorded back at the nesting beaches. Do these reflect dispersal to other nesting beaches or death? This is yet another problem which we are not able to answer at present. The definite characteristics of a nesting population in any one year, outlined earlier in this chapter, together with the fact that these characters tend to repeat themselves when that population would

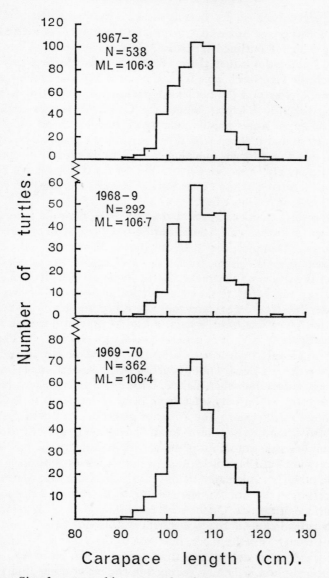

FIG. 11 Size-frequency histograms for three years' populations of the green turtle at Heron Island. The virtual absence of small breeding females (new recruits?) and the fall-off in size above about 105 cm (41.5 inches) should be noted.

be expected back at the nesting beach – four years later in the case of the green turtle in Queensland – suggests an interesting theory which I outlined tentatively in a review paper (Bustard, 1972). I pointed out that there are pronounced currents moving towards the Capricorn cays from the north and the north-east at the time of year that the turtles are presumably migrating to their nesting beaches. I wrote, 'Hence the Capricorn turtles could be parts of much larger populations which happen to get caught in this current and proceed with it to the nesting cays . . . The hypothesis raises a further question which cannot be answered at present, namely, what happens to the turtles which do not reach the southern area of the Great Barrier Reef in a nesting year? Do they breed, and if so, where?'

For several hundred years there have been periodic records of adult green turtles lying ashore during the daytime in areas of the Pacific (viz. Dampier, 1697). In one part of their range – the outer Hawaiian Islands – green turtles are well known to come ashore during the day time when they lie in the sun (Kenyon and Rice, 1959; Parsons, 1962). Since green turtles, as described above, take considerable trouble to carry out their nesting activities during darkness, observers have been at a loss to explain this behaviour and particularly why it is observed solely in areas of the Pacific. One would only expect to observe the phenomenon in isolated regions where turtles are not disturbed since they are shy creatures and very vulnerable when ashore. This could be sufficient reason for the trait, which may once have been widespread, to be little seen now. Furthermore, the evidence given below shows that the trait also occurs in northern Australian waters, and Mr Robert Poulson has seen numerous green turtles basking on the reef – out of the water – at Bloomfield Reef in the Capricorn Group.

The obvious explanation of the phenomenon is that the turtles are basking in the sun. Turtles are frequently recorded sleeping at the surface of the sea. Under such conditions their body temperature is considerably above water temperature due to absorption of radiant energy. Furthermore, heat loss to the water is reduced, as the surface waters are warmer than deeper down. However, basking opportunities are much reduced in the water compared to on land as heat loss to the surrounding water is always substantial. On land in the presence of a radiation source, heat loss is much reduced. Basking is well known in many reptiles as a means of elevating their body temperature. This can result in much faster digestion. It would seem feasible, therefore, that after eating a large meal green turtles in remote areas haul out to lie in the sun in order to speed up digestion.

In 1969 the Lardil aborigines on Mornington Island told me that, during the winter, green turtles hauled ashore far from the settlement and lay on the beach during the day. In the course of a discussion I asked them why the turtles did it. Without hesitation they said the trait was only shown by females which came ashore to escape the attentions of the promiscuous males. I was most intrigued by this explanation which I had never heard advanced before and determined to investigate at the first opportunity.

In winter 1970 during turtle survey work I was flying over Mornington and neighbouring islands in the Gulf of Carpentaria and sure enough on the outer islands there were turtles lying ashore on the beaches. The following day we landed our light aircraft – a Cessna 182 – on the beach at Bountiful to investigate. I wandered up to two large turtles lying on the beach and to my disappointment both appeared dead. I gave one a push with my bare foot and to my surprise it quickly came to life, grunted and lumbered down the beach towards the sea. The other turtle responded similarly. Both were females. During our stay on Bountiful we walked right round the island's beaches and observed many turtles lying ashore in the sun often fifty to one hundred yards from the water. We were able to observe exactly what happened.

Firstly, we corroborated the Lardil story – all were females. In the morning we observed the situation just after the tide turned. High tide was about 8 a.m. Shortly thereafter turtles came up to the wave wash and generally turned round to face seawards where they remained stationary in extremely shallow water in which swimming was impossible. At this stage they were alert and the sight of humans sent them lumbering into deeper water where they swam out to sea. However, as the tide receded these turtles were left high and dry and by early afternoon many were considerable distances from the sea as we had observed the previous day. Since male turtles never leave the water there is no doubt about the efficacy of this behaviour against sexually active males. Indeed the females do not need to actually leave the sea to escape the attention of the males. Males cannot mount females unless they are in about two feet of water, and by resting in extremely shallow water in which males cannot swim, females can completely avoid their attentions. We observed many males swimming along parallel to the beaches, in water just deep enough for efficient swimming, undoubtedly looking for females. They passed a number of females at the water's edge without noticing them. The fact that the females become stranded at some distance from the sea is quite incidental – the result of the tide cycle. Unless the females keep crawling seawards to compensate for tide fall this is bound to occur. As a result of these observations I am now convinced that my aboriginal friends are correct.

We have seen many female turtles deliberately enter shallow pools which become cut off from the sea by the receding tide. There is no basking advantage in these pools as their carapaces remain covered or largely covered all the time, although the shallow water becomes somewhat warmer than the sea. This behaviour, like stranding, is clearly carried out to avoid male attentions. Sometimes several males enter these pools before the tide cuts them off. Females cannot subsequently escape and there is pandemonium until the tide comes in or darkness falls. One can tell at a glance if males are also present. If not, the females are all asleep often with part of the carapace completely dry and projecting from the shallow water. If males are present the females' carapaces are usually wet due to continuous assault, and activity in the pool is generally pronounced.

Remarkably little has been written about sea turtle courtship. Indeed I know of no detailed account for any species of sea turtle. Photographs of copulating turtles are fairly common, as are accounts of several males swimming around a single female in the water. On remote Bountiful Island I was lucky enough to observe courtship and copulation many times, often from a distance of less than six feet. Incidentally, I had never observed this at Heron Island. This is because the main mating areas are often at some distance from the nesting beaches. In the Capricorns, Broomfield reef is renowned as a mating area.

When a male green turtle first approaches a female it swims round to face the female and nuzzles her head, rather like rubbing noses. Usually the female shows no response whatsoever. After a short period of nuzzling, the male then makes 'bites' in the region between the female's shoulder and neck. Little attempt appears to be made to actually grasp the female in the jaws. Rather the process is an extension of the nuzzling first observed but now no longer directed at the head. Undoubtedly the procedure is intended to arouse the female. After a variable time the male then swims to the rear of the female and makes some biting actions at one of the rear flippers. Sometimes the flipper is taken loosely in the jaws. At this stage the female frequently swims away at speed, chased by the male. In the sea males are never able to mount an unwilling female, but due to their persistence and the fact that many males are always looking for females they must have very considerable 'nuisance value'. Presumably this explains the female haul-out behaviour. However, in land-locked pools the female is less readily able to escape from the male although she can certainly frustrate actual copulation attempts.

If the female does not swim away when the male nuzzles and bites a rear flipper, the male then attempts to climb on top of the female. This manoeuvre is only possible if the water is somewhat deeper than the depth of the female's carapace. Due to the highly domed carapace of the female and the bony plastron of the male, the manoeuvre is difficult at the best of times. The male attempts to gain momentum and literally swim up, and on to, the female's back. Once there he hooks on with the large thumb claws of the front flippers. These are hooked over the front of the female's carapace between the shoulder and neck region. As a result of this, nesting females are seen with anterior marginal areas of the carapace chipped and the soft parts raw from the male's claws during copulation. The male also maintains his position on the female by hooking the horny end of his tail under the posterior marginals of the female's carapace. The greatly elongated tail of the male has a pronounced horn-like distal portion. Sometimes a male may go right over a female and, following a chase, not infrequently fails to approach from behind but makes a sideways approach. This results in the male not being able to maintain his position and he slides off to try again. Once a male has firmly positioned himself on a female, copulation can begin. As pointed out above, males never succeed in reaching a stage where copulation is possible unless the female is a willing partner to the act. The courtship behaviour is illustrated in plate 6/7.

In view of the general paucity of information on sea turtle biology in many parts of the world, the small number of scientific turtle workers have an obligation to set some time aside for investigations outside their main study region. The large gaps in our knowledge reflect lack of personnel just as much as lack of funds. Indeed it would seem that personnel are more at a premium than availability of funds. However, the two are often related.

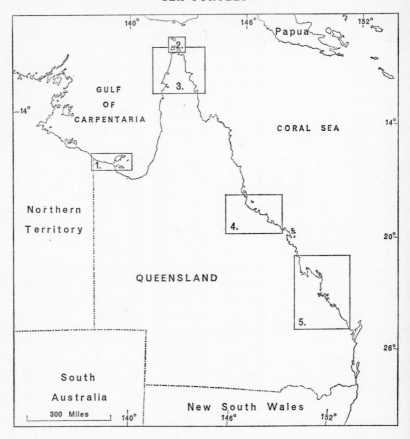

FIG. 12 Map of Queensland, Australia, showing areas (boxed) with turtle nesting aggregations in December 1969.

Perhaps it may be of interest to readers to know what we are doing in this regard. In June 1970, with financial support from the United States National Appeal of the World Wild Life Fund, we started an investigation of the sea turtle resources of the whole of Queensland. This work involved aerial surveys of all mainland beaches and off-shore islands together with extensive ground follow-up work and is expected to take about eighteen months to complete. When complete it will be written up as a report to the Government of Queensland and also published separately to act

146

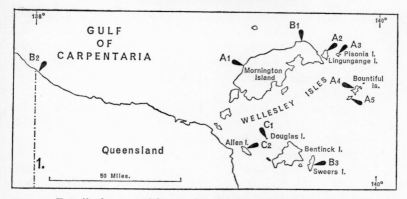

FIG. 13 Detail of area 1 of fig. 12 showing locations of specific rookeries, which are categorised A, B or C in descending order of importance. The Bountiful and Pisonia rookeries are large by world standards.

as a guide to others of how we feel this sort of work should be undertaken and the results evaluated.

It is readily possible from a height of about 500 feet to count individual turtle tracks from the air and usually to state the species involved. Before writing our report we will have seen all of the State's beaches and islands between three and six times from the air. Survey work has been arranged so that the various areas of the State are investigated at different periods of the breeding season since seasonal differences in time of breeding between species are known to occur.

A major result of the work so far has been to show that nesting only occurs to any extent in certain areas of the State and that, as anticipated the main rookery areas are closely circumscribed. This information has two important bearings on conservation or any rational exploitation schemes which may be investigated. It would be easy to virtually wipe out the present large turtle populations in Queensland. Alienation of only two rookeries – geographically very small – Bountiful and Crab Islands, would probably reduce the Queensland populations of green turtle – the economic species – by one half! On the other hand, since the important areas are small and remote, it would be a simple procedure for the Government to protect the turtle populations by declaring these remote areas, which form such key nesting rookeries, National Parks. In fig. 12 the main areas used by nesting turtles during the first surveys are indicated by boxes 1 to 5. Outside of these areas no

147

nesting was recorded during this survey. The Capricorn–Bunker cays were not included in this survey. Maps of each of these areas are then prepared to cover each survey. For instance, area 1 for the June 1970 survey is shown in fig. 13. Major rookeries are indicated by the letter A, smaller nesting aggregations by B and some nesting by C.

It is extremely important that applied research of this nature be carried out. Since the scientific workers are the best qualified, and usually the only people available, they must be encouraged to participate wherever possible. After completion of our statewide investigations in Queensland, I have plans to carry out similar work in Western Australia and then in the Northern Territory. I have also been providing some help to other turtle bearing countries overseas. For instance, during 1970 I spent several weeks in Fiji investigating the status of sea turtles there (Bustard, 1970b) and also visited the Trengganu rookery of the leathery turtle on the east coast of West Malaysia to see what could be done to further safeguard the future of that population (Bustard, 1971a).

PART FOUR

Turtles and Man

CHAPTER 10 brings together the many facets of sea-turtle conservation, past, present and future. Our own experiences in Queensland are used to illustrate the sort of problems which one encounters in this kind of work since these are of universal occurrence. We differ in that we have been exceptionally fortunate in the enlightened attitude we have encountered towards turtle conservation by the Government of Queensland and its officers.

The chapter starts by reviewing past legislation. Current conservation achievements are then considered together with relevant background information. The chapter concludes with a species by species survey of the future of the world's sea turtle resources. Since turtle farming – by satisfying the demand for commercial turtle products – can greatly reduce the hunting pressure on wild turtles, and perhaps ultimately replace wild turtles as a source of commercial product, it is strongly linked to conservation in my view. Of course, the way in which the farms are run is vitally important and as always political considerations must also be borne in mind. Because of the future importance of turtle farming to turtle conservation, a section of Chapter 10 is devoted to this topic.

CHAPTER 10

Conservation

Sea Turtle conservation prior to 1964

THE aim of this section is to outline the sea turtle conservation
situation up till the time that I started an Australian research
programme on sea turtles. This information provides a background
to our own work and shows why I became interested in the
conservation aspects of the study from the outset.

As Professor Archie Carr has pointed out, the legislation passed
by the Bermuda Assembly in 1620 against the killing of young
turtles below a specified carapace size was the first recorded conservation legislation for sea turtles anywhere in the world. However, the slaughter continued, in the Caribbean and elsewhere, as
a source of fresh meat for European navies and garrisons. An early
account of turtle taking is given by Fryke and Schweitzer (1700) in
'Voyages to the East Indies'. On arrival at the island of Onrust from
Batavia they noted, 'the only pastime we could have was catching
tortoises, of which there are vast numbers there. When it is fair,
and the sun shines bright, they come out of the water, and lie in the
hot sand. So when they were all very quiet and settled, we came
upon them of a sudden with Sticks and Iron Bars.' It should be
noted that early navigators frequently called sea turtles tortoises.
Incidentally, this account also provides an early reference to
diurnal haul-out, presumably by the green turtle. Power (1835) and
Brandreth (1835) provided information for Ascension Island where
during the height of the nesting season two men turned forty to
fifty green turtles each night making a total of about 2500 a year.
Brandreth noted, 'The numbers caught year after year have frequently staggered belief. The supply in general is so abundant
as to be issued to the ships and troops as fresh meat.'

A masterly account of the virtual extirpation of the green turtle
from the Caribbean was provided by Carr (1954). Writing of the
Cayman Islands, Carr said, '. . . for three hundred years the vast
"flotas" there – the fleets of breeding green turtles – were a prime
factor in the growth of the Caribbean. As the settlements grew and
got hungry, ships of half a dozen flags converged on the untended

islands in June. They took away as many as their holds and decks would carry. The turtle flotas were as infinite as herring schools. Or so it seemed.

'The vitamin hunger of sailors, which came from nowhere and made men's gums grow over their teeth, and could send a corpse a day sliding over the rail, practically disappeared in the Caribbean after the discovery of *Chelonia*, the green turtle. No other edible creature could be carried away and kept so long alive. Only the turtle could take the place of spoiled kegs of beef and send a ship on for a second year of wandering or marauding. All early activity in the new world tropics – exploration, colonisation, buccaneering and the manoeuvrings of naval squadrons – was in some way dependent on the turtle. Salted or dried it everywhere fed the seaboard poor. It was at once a staple and a luxury – a slave ration, and in soup and curries the pride of the menus of the big plantation houses. More than any other dietary factor the green turtle supported the opening up of the Caribbean.'

On the progressive loss of the green turtle from its Caribbean strongholds, Carr wrote, 'The documentation of the decline of *Chelonia* is voluminous and clear. One by one the famous old rookeries were destroyed. The first to go was Bermuda and next were the shores of the Greater Antilles. The Bahamas were blanked out not long after, and boats from there began to cross the Gulf stream to abet the decimation in Florida, where vast herds foraged in the East Coast estuaries and on the Gulf flats of the Upper Peninsula and a great breeding school came each year to Dry Tortugas.'

What was probably the earliest regular collection of statistical information began in Sarawak in 1927 under British guidance. These data have been assembled continuously since then. After the second world war until recently the Turtle Board was extremely fortunate in having the services of Tom Harrisson, Curator of the Sarawak Museum and Government Ethnologist. Mr Harrisson, who possesses tremendous energy and drive, has played the key role in the conservation activities on the Sarawak turtle islands as well as drawing attention to the plight of the green turtle worldwide. His pioneer role included the tag which most of us now use to permanently identify adult turtles and the operation of hatcheries whereby a percentage of the annual egg production was set aside for incubation in the absence of predators. The hatchling turtles were then liberated in deep water off the islands to reduce shallow water predation by carnivorous fish. The aim of this programme was to try to offset, at least to some extent, the inroads made into the population by virtually total egg collection for human consumption.

In Sarawak turtle eggs are prized as food, and egg collection takes place to supply this market. Adult turtles, however, are never killed. It should be possible to sustain populations in which adults are safeguarded, and only eggs utilised, since the chance of any one egg producing a mature turtle is so small. However, the populations, judged by annual egg 'take', have declined sharply over the last forty years (Harrisson, 1962). On the assumption of a three-year breeding cycle, there are three populations using the Sarawak islands for nesting. The population which nested in 1927, then in 1930, 1933 etc., I shall call population A. Egg collection in 1927 was about 2.1 million, there are no data for 1930 and in 1933 the figure was 1.5 million. In 1936 it was 3 million. No data exist for the war years but it fell each time from 1948 to 1954 when it was 1.1 million. In 1957 the figure climbed marginally to 1.4 million and in 1960 and 1963 it was 0.5 million. Population B which nested in 1928, 1931 etc., has similarly shown an overall decline from 2.3 million in 1928 and 3.1 million in 1934 to 0.3 million in 1964. Population C (1932, 1935 etc.) has been erratic. However, once again an overall decline appears to have occurred. The figures were 2.25 million in 1932, 0.9 million in 1935, an estimate (judged to be low) of 0.7 million in 1947 with a climb to 2.35 million in 1950 and 2.05 in 1953. In 1956 the take was down to 0.7, in 1959 it rose to 1.3 but in 1962 was only 0.55 million. With the possible exception of population C, which might reflect merely a fluctuating population (except that the 1968 figure was down to 0.2 million!), the trend appears to be unmistakably downwards.

Harrisson's work attracted Hendrickson's attention to sea turtle ecology. Hendrickson's 1958 paper is a model for subsequent turtle researchers and Professor John Hendrickson has played an important role in green turtle conservation. He was also responsible for the initiation of the vital leathery turtle hatchery scheme in Trengganu, and has continued to play an active role in sea turtle conservation.

The motivation for conservation usually arose directly from economics, and in this Harrisson's work was no exception. Its special feature was that it was carried through over a period of many years and Harrisson himself was interested in fundamental problems of turtle research. Many fisheries people have from time to time made recommendations for putting turtle fisheries on a rational exploitation basis, outstanding among which is Hornell's 1927 publication dealing with the Seychelles. However, as has happened elsewhere, Hornell's views were not acted upon. Similarly the extensive review assembled by Ingle and Smith (1949) for the Caribbean did not have the anticipated conservation impact.

The first major long-term investigation of sea turtle ecology divorced completely from economics came from Professor Archie Carr at the University of Florida. Carr started tagging turtles in Costa Rica, which is still his headquarters, in the mid 1950s. The greatest tribute one can pay to Archie Carr is to say that looking back to the mid 1950s it seems incredible just how little was known then about almost every aspect of turtle biology. Carr would say that we still know all too little to-day, but to my mind the significant thing is that solid foundations have been laid since then. The general natural history of at least some species is now well documented. Tagging programmes have provided a wealth of new information and above all there is a general awareness of the plight of the world's sea turtles. Professor Carr is the leading authority on sea turtles and is Chairman of the I.U.C.N. Marine Turtle Group. He is totally committed to turtle conservation.

The sea turtle conservation situation in Queensland is rather different for historical reasons. Australia was the last Continent to undergo European settlement. Although Dutch and Portuguese sailors had visited other parts of the Continent much earlier when trading with the Spice Islands (Indonesia) it was not until 1770 that the east coast of Australia was charted by Captain Cook. As a result Australia did not experience the gross over-exploitation of sea turtles by the navies of European powers in the sixteenth and seventeenth centuries which occurred in the West Indies. As mentioned in Chapter 2, Bermuda first gazetted protective legislation for the green turtle in 1620 by which time it was presumably becoming scarce.

Following settlement in New South Wales there was a period in which the Royal Navy was active in charting the Australian coastline. This was done by a very small number of extremely talented people such as Flinders who extended Cook's earlier work and is credited with first calling the Continent 'Australia'. The fact that Cook claimed the entire eastern seaboard on behalf of the British Crown also resulted in little foreign shipping being active in the area.

After this period of early exploration little was heard about the Barrier Reef and northern Queensland. For instance the London Missionary Society – the first to reach the islands of Torres Strait – did not arrive at Darnley and Murray Islands until 1871 (a hundred years after Cook's voyage of discovery). Queensland, at first part of New South Wales, did not become a separate state until 1859.

In addition to late settlement of the Continent, two additional factors were important in greatly slowing down European inter- ference with tropical fauna. Firstly, Australians settled in the south. This is still the pattern to-day. The capital city of Queens- land, Brisbane, is in the extreme south-east of the State. Secondly, due to the small number of people, there was little incentive to push north in order to secure land. This is not to suggest that northern Australia to-day is all virgin bush – much of it is taken up by cattle stations, the larger the size of European kingdoms – but the population density in the north has remained extremely low. For Australia as a whole the figure was only 3.9 people per square mile in 1966. This compares with 575 and 54 people per square mile for the United Kingdom and the United States respectively in 1964.

Australia has not avoided what may be called the exploitative stage of development. It is fast coming, and mining ventures are rapidly springing up in many parts of the far north of Australia. The threats to the fauna are only now becoming obvious in the north and soon the pressure will be on, at least on the mainland.

Having put the subject matter in historical perspective, the object of this section is to explain what has and is being done to conserve sea turtles in Queensland and what action will be needed in the future.

Heron Island and North-West Island, off Gladstone in central Queensland, were the sites of turtle soup canneries in the 1920s and early 'thirties. An excellent account of what occurred at North-West Island was given by Musgrave and Whitley in 'From sea to soup' (1926), from which the following extract is taken,

'Turtle-hunters patrol the beaches of the islet nightly, turning over all the turtles they find *en route*, and leaving them out of reach of the tide. There they are helpless, and lie on their backs, their flippers scooping up the sand with great force, until exhausted. They are often left in this position for a whole day or more, in the heat of the tropical sun, and their plight as they lie with drooping heads, often gasping for breath, is one which cannot fail to excite one's pity. Later, several members of the party left the islet in a boat carrying a load of turtles to Rockhampton. The unfortunate animals lay on their backs arranged around the decks between the deckhouse and the railings, ever and anon emitting long-drawn sighs or slapping their flippers against the decks or their plastrons. The hold, too, was full, and on the trip over several died. With their eyes exuding long trails of mucus, and so distended with blood that they protruded beyond the orbits, these helpless creatures aroused our sympathy. During a night spent on the boat, the turtles kept up an incessant tattoo against the sides of the deckhouse, making sleep an impossibility.

'The turtles are killed by decapitation, and later butchered. First the lower shell or plastron is cut around and lifted off like a lid. Then the limbs and flesh are removed; the head and entrails, including the ovaries with their numbers of unlaid eggs, are buried in the sand. The shells and flesh are loaded into a punt, and towed to the wharf near the canning shed, where fifteen men are employed. Here the meat is cut off the bones and boiled slowly in large wooden vats overnight, forming the soup which passes into a galvanised iron tank where it is flavoured with pepper, onions, arrowroot and other herbs. It is poured into sixteen ounce tins and sterilised for forty minutes before being sealed up. The tins are then labelled and ready for sale. Twenty-two to twenty-five turtles, a good day's catch, produce about nine hundred tins of soup. Last season (1924–1925), thirty-six thousand tins were prepared.'

These statistics indicate that about 1000 turtles were taken from North-West Island during summer 1924–5 which approximates the size of the entire breeding population at the present time. Clearly the removal of virtually the whole breeding population each year was the surest way to wipe out the resource! Musgrave and Whitley continued,

'Besides soup the turtle furnishes many by-products. The flesh of the breast, called calipash, is dried and used to make mock-turtle soup. That of the flippers is called calipee, and is sold dried and makes excellent eating when cooked, having the appearance of fried fish and tasting almost exactly like veal. The green fat of the

17. (a) Legalised egg collecting by licensee at leathery turtle rookery near Dungun, Trengganu, West Malaysia. The eggs are taken as the turtle lays them.

(b) Leathery turtle laying eggs. The turtle's tail is to the right of the back projection at the rear of the carapace.

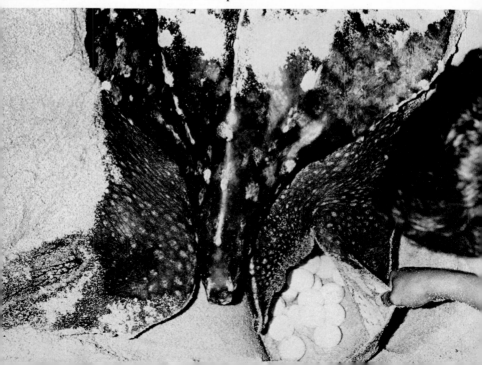

18. (a) Nesting olive ridley (*Lepidochelys olivacea*) in Surinam. Note the large area of the carapace missing above the hind leg. This is almost certainly the result of shark attack. P. C. H. PRITCHARD.

(b) A group of olive ridleys (*Lepidochelys olivacea*) nesting at Eilanti beach, Surinam, South America. This species, like Kemp's ridley, nests in groups or 'arribadas'. P. C. H. PRITCHARD.

turtle is rich in flavour, and lubricating oil is extracted from it, while fertiliser is made from the shell and bones.

'Each of the twenty-five odd turtles which are killed daily during the breeding season, is the potential mother of about one hundred and fifty young (they did not realise that multiple nesting occurred) so that unless drastic measures are taken, the species in the long run will become extinct.'

This article, and others like it, were important in creating an atmosphere receptive to conservation. When authoritative statements are made, even though they seek no specified solution, they can do a lot to achieve public and Government awareness. Indeed when no particular solution is proposed the authors may have even more influence since clearly they have no personal axe to grind. Important pioneer work on sea turtle biology was carried out on Heron Island during a three-and-a-half month period in summer 1929-30 by Mr F. W. Moorhouse, a Queensland Government biologist. The fact that the Queensland Government initiated an investigation on sea turtles showed that they were conscious that the resource might be being over-exploited.

Moorhouse was alone in carrying out detailed field work. Other fishery people had superficially investigated the problem of over-exploitation in other parts of the world. In some instances, such as Hornell (1927), excellent and detailed reports had been published but without the results of detailed field work to back them up. Moorhouse had field information to back up his recommendations that some degree of protection be given to the green turtle and, furthermore, he did not make the mistake of asking for too much all at once.

In my opinion it was no accident that Moorhouse's pioneer field work resulted in the first conservation legislation for sea turtles in Queensland being introduced by the State Parliament, while Hornell's recommendations were ignored for forty years until I drew the British Government's attention to the report. Moorhouse's success illustrates the effectiveness of using information from the field to document (support) a case for conservation. He wrote,

'Canning of turtle soup had been carried on at Heron Island for some years, work commencing early in November and finishing in February. During the 1928-29 season, so scarce did the turtles become towards the end of the season that periodic visits had to be made to the neighbouring islands in order to obtain sufficient animals to keep the factory in active operation. In view of the facts that the last season's animals were wiped out and that there was a considerable number present this season, one deduction is that turtles seen in any one season on any given island do not necessarily return the following year to lay, but that there is a period of rest between laying – that laying seasons are separated by some years. This is offered tentatively and can be proved or disproved only after some years of investigations.'

We now know that Moorhouse was correct in deducing that there is an interval of some years between nesting seasons for any given turtle (see Chapter 9).

By marking animals Moorhouse was able to record that many animals laid up to seven times in a single season, which at Heron Island commenced in late October and lasted until mid-February. He pointed out that the breeding population of any one island is very much smaller than would appear to be the case, as so many of the females lay six or more times in a season. Moorhouse's work had important conservation impact both in Queensland and overseas. This concept of a limited number of breeding females and not an inexhaustible supply was to prove a vital starting point for conservation in Australia, and I am accordingly quoting his conclusions in some detail:

'The following definite results are here presented for the first time:
(a) A very limited number of animals visit any one island during the breeding season.
(b) The same animals return again and again, seven being the maximum returnings recorded.

With this information now available these deductions can be drawn:

1. The idea now prevalent that there are thousands of turtles visiting any one island during the breeding season is quite erroneous and must be replaced by *a limited number of turtles make many visits to any one island during the breeding season.*

2. Had the factory on Heron Island operated right through the 1929–30 season, there would have been seen towards the middle of the season that dearth of animals that has marked previous years when continued canning operations were carried out, mention of which was made in the Introduction of this paper (quoted above).

3. Since the 1928-29 season's limited number of animals that visited Heron Island was completely wiped out, and yet some hundreds of animals were seen there the following season, then we are confronted with the following probabilities:

(a) Turtles do not lay every season.
(b) Turtles that laid on an island in one season go to some other island the following season.
(c) Sufficient young mature each season to take the place of those adults killed during the immediate past season.
(d) There is a combination of (b) and (c) – i.e., some turtles that laid elsewhere during the previous season, together with some lately-matured young, go to any one island for the next season;
or
(e) Turtles that laid some seasons ago, together with some lately-matured animals, visit an island during the season.

Of the five points in No. 3, all that can be said at present is that (c) is the only point that can be definitely ruled out, for the turtles that came up to lay during the season varied, as shown in an earlier portion of this paper, from 35 to 48 inches in length of carapace, so that all those laying were not newly matured; in fact, only a small percentage of the laying females found on Heron Island was of such a size as 35 inches. It is a tentative hypothesis that 35 inches is the size of newly-matured animals – i.e., in so far as Heron Island observations allow, green turtles first mature when they have reached a length of 35-inch carapace measurement.'

Moorhouse made recommendations for conservation of the green turtle in Queensland. Writing in the same paper, he said:

'At present in Queensland there is no restriction on the taking of turtles, and there is further no regulation forbidding fishermen from taking animals before they have laid the eggs that they have come to the island to deposit. Though the short-sightedness of killing the turtles before they have laid is admitted, even by the hunters themselves, this unwise practice is still followed. If it is continued, especially early in the breeding season, it must in the very near future deplete our stock of turtles to such an extent as to wipe out this branch of our fishing industry; therefore, a regulation should be framed in order to prevent the extermination of the turtle.

'Any regulation regarding the taking of turtles should be such that a breach of it will become patent without the added expense of policing the waters to enforce it. In so far as turtles are concerned the matter appears simple. At Heron Island turtles are taken on the beach as they come to lay, and since the laying season commences at or about the close of October in these waters, no turtles are seen upon the beach before that date. It is not till the middle of November that all the animals have been to the island to lay the first batch of eggs, so that by preventing the taking of turtles till the close of November all will have had the opportunity to have laid once, while many will have laid their second set. (N.B. – At the commencement of the season turtles were scarce, five or six being the normal number seen each night. The numbers gradually increased till early in January, when as many as fifty-one were seen on the beach in one night, after which the numbers began to decrease again rapidly till towards the close of the season only six or seven were seen each night.)

'But the coast of Queensland is some thousands of miles in length, so that what applies in southern Queensland does not necessarily apply in the north. The writer saw turtle eggs that had been laid in May in the Torres Strait islands, so, either the season is much more protracted in north Queensland or it occurs in different months. If, then, regulations are to be framed they must state clearly that they apply to that part of the coast of Queensland south from Cairns at least (or latitude 17 degrees South) until such time as the length of the season in North Queensland is definitely known.

'The regulation recommended should, therefore, be similar in form to that suggested hereunder:

"No person, south of latitude 17 degrees South, shall take, or offer for sale, and no person shall purchase, kill or attempt to export, between the dates of 30th September and 30th November of each year, any turtle of the kind known as the Green Turtle (*Chelonia mydas*). Penalty £10 for each animal found in possession."

'This close season is absolutely essential, for it is the only definite means of ensuring the laying of some of the eggs normally produced by the turtle. But if the fishermen and factory authorities could be compelled to plant the eggs from the killed animals, since it has been demonstrated that such action is advisable and profitable, then the yearly production of young turtles can be appreciably increased. It does not appear wise at the present juncture, owing to insufficient knowledge, to frame regulations to limit the *number* of turtles that shall be taken each season, or the *size* of animals permitted to be taken.'

Then, Moorhouse greatly strengthened his case by citing many instances of protective legislation then in force in other parts of the world, notably the West Indies where turtle stocks had been greatly depleted by centuries of over-exploitation.

Moorhouse's recommendation of a close season during the early part of the nesting season was accepted by the Queensland Government and legislation was gazetted to provide for this south of latitude 17°s. To the best of my knowledge no investigation was ever carried out in north Queensland – it was certainly not published – and until 1968 all legislation was restricted to south of 17°s.

The close season during October and November which resulted from Moorhouse's work permitted some eggs to be laid before the breeding female turtles were butchered. In normal years the first turtles reach the Capricorn cays about the end of the third week in October, but it is some weeks before large-scale nesting gets underway. Thus the turtle canneries could obtain virtually no turtles during October anyway. Closure during November was important, and would allow each female to deposit an average of two clutches of eggs before being killed. However, in order to be strictly objective one is forced to state that populations subjected to such a regime would still be exterminated, although more slowly than if butchered before any eggs were laid. This is because turtle populations are not geared to withstand a virtual total loss of their reproductive females in each nesting year. Furthermore, hunting effort was still concentrated exclusively on the females. Moorhouse's work did not, therefore, solve the green turtle conservation problem, but it did provide a secure foundation on which to build. It provides a valuable lesson for conservationists, namely that some legislation is better than none, and that once legislation is on the statute books it can be improved upon. This is usually much easier than getting over the initial hurdle of successfully introducing legislation where none exists.

Professor Tom Harrisson told me that his own work on sea turtles was greatly influenced by Moorhouse's pioneer study. Professor Harrisson has had a great impact on the sea turtle conservation problem. Furthermore, it was Tom Harrisson's work which first attracted me to sea turtle research. Hence Moorhouse's influence, through his pioneer field work on Heron Island, has played a key role in sea turtle conservation. Needless to say the fact that Moorhouse's early work had been carried out on Heron Island, now largely a National Park, influenced me in favour of making this cay the headquarters of my own research.

The next phase in sea turtle conservation in Queensland did not come for about twenty years. It has been carefully recorded by Frank McNeill (1955) in an article entitled 'Saving the green turtle of the Great Barrier Reef'. Frank McNeill, lately Curator of Invertebrates at the Australian Museum, began his interest in the Great Barrier Reef over 40 years ago and was a member of the 1928 expedition to the Low Isles. This British expedition organised by the Great Barrier Reef Committee was the most exhaustive expedition yet to visit the reef.

In McNeill's words,

'In a corner of Gladstone Harbour, Port Curtis, "the creek" is a backwater flanked by a big sprawling mud bank. From seawards it gives ready access to town for dozens of fishing and pleasure craft which moor at the small wharves and jetties or tie up along the opposite bank to numbers of tall piles provided for their accommodation. Most activity centres around the so-called town jetty, and on a steaming hot mid-day in January 1950 this place presented a sorry sight. Lying helplessly on their backs upon the decking under the sub-tropical sun were eleven live Green Turtles. All were in an exhausted and pathetic state, with mucus streaming from eyes and nostrils. The spectacle was only too familiar to most local residents and caused them little or no concern. But by a strange quirk of fate, this particular occasion was not to pass un-noticed. It was to prove fortuitous for future generations of green turtles along Australia's Great Barrier Reef – a day which was to mark the turning point in the heartless suffering and trading of harmless creatures long prized as one of our major tourist attractions.

'By chance some strangers were destined to come upon that deplorable scene. They were among a number of passengers who disembarked from the motor cruiser *Capre* – holidaymakers homeward bound to a southern State from coral-girt Heron Island in the Capricorn Group. Away from the tempering sea breeze, the general discomfort of the still heat caused an immediate and sympathetic reaction to the plight of the suffering turtles. The newcomers watched resentfully while a miserably small stream of water from a hose was played on the captives by a woman in attendance. Instead of alleviating the creatures' distress, it seemed only to aggravate their disablement. They impotently responded by thrashing about with their flippers and struggling in a hopeless way to escape from their tormentors. Here was proof of an ill-considered and cruel exploitation – a practice calculated to endanger the very existence of a quaint edible marine reptile in one of its last world-strongholds.

'Cruelty of this kind has a way of continuing unabated until noticed by somebody determined enough to take decisive action. There were two people among those eye witnesses from the *Capre* who made an immediate resolve to bring to official notice the alarming details of a trade that was long overdue for correction. One was a university Professor of Zoology; the other a museum curator having accredited affiliation with the government-sponsored Great Barrier Reef Committee of Brisbane. No time was lost in gathering convincing data for the strongest of protests. It was learnt that a dozen to eighteen green turtles came through Gladstone every week during the summer egg-laying season and passed on south by rail to Brisbane. The agony endured by the luckless overturned reptiles during lengthy and changing forms of transport must have been intense. Some crude rope bridles looped behind the front flippers and still attached to the captives seen at Gladstone were proof of the painful manner in which they were dragged and hauled about on their backs. The tragedy of the trade was the senseless capturing of only breeding females as they came ashore to deposit their eggs in the sands of the coral island cays; the smaller bodied males avoid the land and are quite inaccessible. While ashore the females face the risk of being rudely overturned and rendered helpless, often immediately upon leaving the water and before their eggs are laid.

'Inquiries made in Brisbane disclosed that the turtles arriving there were slaughtered and shipped to England, and probably elsewhere in Europe, as a luxury export. A news item, detected in the local press of a few weeks before the Gladstone incident, carried an illustration of overturned turtles lying forlornly on a factory floor. Finally, in Sydney more details were gathered from reliable sources, and a protest sent in the strongest possible terms for consideration by the Great Barrier Reef Committee. This had been preceded by a report to the Royal Society for the Prevention of Cruelty to Animals. It was represented to the Committee that over the previous forty years the green turtle population of the Capricorn Group area had been systematically exploited with either indifferent or no planned official supervision. The result had been a marked reduction in numbers, slow but inexorable. No sooner had the population partially recovered from one period of concentrated butchering than another began. At least three island processing factories had been operating prior to 1930, and had failed – two on North-West Island and one on Heron Island. In addition, certain large meat works on the mainland had, over the years, been buying turtles from fishermen. These turtles were sent as carcases overseas direct in the refrigeration holds of ships which transported export beef. A special point made to the Committee was that reasoning local residents had expressed their distaste of the cruel trade. Some had voiced their relief that only a few fishermen had been tempted to cooperate. They predicted dire results if higher payments were to attract a greater number of turtle hunters. . . .

The deliberations of the Great Barrier Reef Committee on the question of turtle slaughter took place in May, 1950. By that time newspaper publicity had attracted the attention of the Queensland Government Department of Harbours and Marine, a body concerned with the control of fisheries and relevant matters. The combined interest in the humanitarian campaign produced spirited and lengthy discussion. The cruel nature of the trade was given particular emphasis. A parallel was drawn between it and whaling, sometimes stated to be one of the cruellest forms of hunting. It was disclosed that green turtles were protected in Queensland waters by government regulation for two months of the year – October and November – *and that some sort of investigation on their numbers and habits had taken place, but had not been completed.* (My italics.) A healthy reflection voiced at the meeting was that the tourist trade was likely to outweigh the turtle trade by ten to one. On a sounder basis it was argued that in the past every form of exploitation of other than domestic animals had been unconsidered, and that this lack of concern had led in all instances to population disturbances which had had a very deleterious effect upon the trade concerned. It was felt that, as the revived turtle trade was in an early stage of development, it should be placed on a reliable and scientific basis before it increased.

The final and welcome outcome of the Committee's discussion spelt success for the campaign. Recommendations (carried unanimously) were that *an investigation into the ecological and economic status of the green turtle along the Great Barrier Reef should be undertaken, and that, pending the investigation, the green turtle should be placed on the list of protected animals under the relevant Government Act.* (My italics.) Crowning success came on September 7, 1950, when a Queensland Government Order in Council was gazetted. This rescinded the earlier Order relating to the taking of green turtles and stated that the law 'doth absolutely forbid the taking of any of the species of Turtle known as 'Green Turtle' (*Chelonia mydas*) or the eggs thereof in Queensland waters or on or from the foreshores of or lands abutting on such waters'. This legislation only referred to south Queensland.

McNeill's account is particularly interesting and shows the part that tourist interest played, and has continued to play, in conservation of the Barrier Reef. Experts are, of course, needed to make authoritative statements and to provide advice, but public interest once aroused is an excellent way in which to ensure Government action. It is interesting to note in McNeill's article (first italicised section) that Moorhouse's work had never been completed; in fact, no investigation had taken place in the north of the State in the intervening 20 years. Furthermore, the ecological and economic status survey of the green turtle along the Great Barrier Reef was not initiated prior to the commencement of my own work in 1964.

This section may tend to give the appearance that little was achieved prior to 1964 and that when I became interested in turtles the situation was rapidly deteriorating. While the latter is true, the former is far from being the case. It is only fair to point out that Harrisson had to operate a Turtle Board whose main responsibility was to provide eggs for human consumption. Similarly Carr, an American citizen, was operating in Costa Rica, where obviously he had to move with great diplomacy. The pioneer work, particularly by Harrisson and Carr, had wide repercussions on the international scene. Perhaps this can best be illustrated by pointing out that at the 1969 I.U.C.N. Turtle Specialists Working Meeting eight representatives were present from six countries where active sea turtle conservation programmes were being practised, namely, Australia (Queensland), Costa Rica, Malaysia (Sabah, Sarawak and Trengganu), Mexico, South Africa (Natal) and Surinam. Additional research workers presented reports on other areas of the world. Furthermore, the work of Moorhouse had provided a firm basis for sea turtle conservation in Queensland.

Recent Conservation Achievements

There has been a marked increase in sea turtle conservation in recent years largely as a result of Professor Archie Carr's eloquent pleas on the turtles' behalf. Very recently (since 1969) the work of I.U.C.N. and its sea turtle group has made an important contribution to conservation. This contribution will continue to expand.

In December 1964 I commenced a long-term study of green and loggerhead turtles in Queensland with field headquarters at Heron Island. At the outset the Government was informed that it was envisaged the work would extend over a period of ten to twenty years. When in summer 1967–68 Mr G. T. T. Harrison, Chief Inspector of Fisheries in Queensland, was on Heron Island seeing our programme, he asked whether we had yet come to any conclusions on the conservation requirements of the species. Mr Harrison is deeply interested in conservation. It was clear that any depositions which would be made were to receive the most careful consideration. It was answered that our work had confirmed earlier feelings that it was not practical to operate a fishery based on taking breeding female green turtles from the nesting beaches. Turtle populations could not sustain any substantial loss resulting from such activities. Therefore, a total protection for the green turtle was favoured in order to conserve the substantial Queensland populations of this species until such time as turtle farming had been scientifically worked out. Approved farms, which would have their own breeding stock and which thus would not cause any depletion of natural populations, could then be licensed by the Government. As most Queenslanders do not know the differences between the six species of sea turtles occurring in Queensland waters, protection if it were to be effective should be extended to all species and in the whole of the State. These proposals were duly accepted by the Government, and legislation to this effect was gazetted on 18th July 1968.

This conservation action by Queensland is by far the most significant legislation in the field of marine turtle conservation that has yet been enacted anywhere in the world. Six species of marine turtles are now totally protected (except from aborigines, see below) along a coastline of 3,250 miles, as well as along 1,250 miles of the Great Barrier Reef. This immense area embraced by the Order in Council guarantees the future of very substantial turtle populations.

Part of the significance of the legislation results from the fact that large populations of several species of sea turtles presently occur in Queensland waters. So often legislation does not come until the species in question are greatly decimated or even on the verge of extinction. This is not the case with the sea turtle legislation in Queensland. I doubt that our Queensland populations are bettered anywhere in the world. The wise action by the Queensland Government has incidentally safeguarded an important tourist attraction. The tourist potential of the Great Barrier Reef, which is just starting to be tapped, is truly enormous, and every tourist wants to see turtles. Tourists want to be able to go out at night and watch nesting turtles and to be able to see these huge creatures swimming lazily on the reef platform during the day. They can certainly do this in Queensland, where seeing turtles is an integral part of a Barrier Reef holiday.

The importance of the 1968 Queensland sea turtle conservation legislation will become more apparent later in this chapter when it is seen in the context of the overall plans for sea turtle conservation in the State. Firstly, however, I would like to mention some other conservation achievements elsewhere.

Professor Archie Carr has stimulated the Costa Rican Government, through his intensive studies at Tortuguero, to declare a reserve over part of the beach where he works and to prevent the harpooning of turtles immediately offshore. This is a most valuable achievement. Professor Carr has also played a key role in trying to bring about an international agreement to control sea turtle harvests between the Governments of Costa Rica, Nicaragua and British Honduras under United Nations (F.A.O.) auspices.

Dr Pritchard has been responsible for protection of sea turtles in French Guyana where there is an extremely important leathery turtle rookery. Indeed it is fair to say that every member of the I.U.C.N. sea turtle group is trying to bring about conservation legislation, have important rookeries created reserves, and, by pure or applied research, improve the survival outlook for the world's turtles.

Since 1966 the Fisheries Department of the Government of Mexico has been carrying out large-scale research on its turtles, particularly the Pacific ridley (*Lepidochelys olivacea*). The sheer scale of operations is most impressive. Although the work was initiated to conserve a resource which had suddenly become in great commercial demand, many basic data are being collected. Since the work is being carried out on the Caribbean coast of Mexico as well as on the Pacific the very localised Kemp's ridley (*Lepidochelys kempi*) is also being investigated.

In 1962 Mexican sea turtle products became an important commercial product. In the 1950s the annual capture was about or below 600 tons. In 1962 it was 1,400 tons, in 1965 2,200 tons and in 1968 15,000 tons! Their takes consist almost entirely of Pacific ridleys.

In 1965 much of the beach area of the country was explored in order to locate the main nesting areas. The next year turtle camps were set up at some of the major areas in order to protect the eggs from human collection and the nesting females from slaughter. The turtle camps include a detachment of Marines and Infantry soldiers who patrol the nesting beaches and guard the camp. In 1966 three such camps were established one of which had the purpose of protecting nesting Atlantic ridleys (*Lepidochelys kempi*). The camp observed and protected 1,265 Atlantic ridleys and transplanted 29,937 eggs for hatchery incubation. The two other camps hatched 25,000 Pacific ridley eggs. Nineteen sixty-seven saw a huge increase in activities with six camps established, 375,000 eggs of various species transplanted for safe incubation, and about 25,000 natural nests protected from human and animal predation resulting in a total hatch of 1,600,000 young turtles. In 1968 the scheme resulted in more than 9 million hatchlings reaching the sea and in 1969 (the last year for which data are available) more than 4 million hatchlings resulted from hatchery schemes together with protection of natural nests.

From 1966 to 1969 inclusive 3,688 nesting turtles were tagged, 61 of which have been recaptured.

The Mexican fisheries biologists hope to see positive results from this programme starting in a modest way in 1972, by which time they calculate the hatchlings released in 1966 should have reached sexual maturity.

The Mexican Government is to be congratulated on the way in which it has accepted the challenge of utilising its sea turtle resources in the most effective manner. This is not to suggest that all the problems have been overcome – they are well aware that management of this kind is only in its infancy – but an important start has been made and large sums of money are being expended annually on sea turtle biology and conservation.

When I started my research programme, Queensland had a history of protective legislation for the green turtle extending back to the 1930s as a result of Moorhouse's work. Thus I was building on what had gone before as did those who secured the 1950 legislation. Secondly, the legislation would not have come about without the active conservation interest of the Chief Inspector of Fisheries, Mr G. T. T. Harrison. It was further aided by Dr Robert Endean, then Secretary, and now Chairman of the Great Barrier Reef Committee which has long been active in safeguarding the Great Barrier Reef and in carrying out, or providing facilities through its Heron Island Research Station for others to carry out, research on the Great Barrier Reef.

This was a particularly happy occasion in that no outside support was necessary. So often in Australia overseas advice or appeals seem to be essential to obtain Government action. In this case everything took place within Queensland.

An important result of the 1968 legislation is that it legally prevents people from 'interfering with' sea turtles at any time. Prior to this legislation it was not possible to prevent vandalism from taking place even when one was aware that it was of common occurrence. I shall quote one example. At the Mon Repos loggerhead rookery near Bundaberg, it was common practice extending over many years for boys to dig up turtle nests, collect eggs, and throw them at each other on the beach. Such fights, I am reliably informed, resulted in the destruction of very substantial numbers of eggs. The local Inspector of Fisheries can now prevent any such activities since they are a breach of the law.

Most tourist resort islands take a responsible attitude to conservation. This is clearly in their own interests since tourists come to the Great Barrier Reef to see the remarkable fauna and flora. It is essential, if the management are to remain in business, that this is safeguarded for future visitors. However, it is often difficult for them to assume the role of policemen with their own clients. Hence protective legislation, which can be prominently displayed and quoted in their brochures, plays a most useful role.

Interference with sea turtles is clearly going to grow with increasing tourism and population expansion on the eastern seaboard. Further safeguards are needed for the turtles in the form of

National Parks. Several exist at present and others are now being actively sought.

In the Capricorn–Bunker Group of Islands at the south of the reef (where development threat is high due to proximity to centres of population in the south) most of Heron Island is a National Park. The exception is five acres leased to a tourist company and several acres leased to the Heron Island Research Station of the Great Barrier Reef Committee. Lady Musgrave Island has been declared a National Park recently. Two other islands in the Group are wanted as National Parks because of their sea turtle rookeries but, of course, their gazetting would serve a much wider purpose. There are extremely few examples of the Capricorn–Bunker cay-type on the reef, and there is an urgent need to see that several of these are rigidly protected.

The experiment of having a tourist resort permanently sited on a National Park Island (Heron) has been shown to be only a partial success. In the case of Heron Island the National Park area is littered with rubbish from the resort including many piles of old building material, old trucks, tyres and other waste which should have been otherwise disposed of. The National Park has doubtful value except that it does prevent the spread of actual buildings. There is, of course, a need for such inland National Parks to be subjected to thorough inspection from time to time. Certainly such a state of affairs would not have been allowed to happen on one of Queensland's well known mainland National Parks. However, surely the real lesson is that these tiny cays (Heron is forty-four acres) are just too small to allow any development without con-taminating the whole cay. Once this view is generally accepted by the Government we can perhaps proceed to develop some islands for tourism but ensure that other similar islands nearby are rigidly protected. At present, far from this being the case, the 'contamina-tion' of a tourist resort is not restricted to the island on which it is sited.

Taking the case of Heron Island once again, the resort uses another island regularly for picnics (Wilson) and sometimes goes to different islands such as Wreck. Wilson Island shows the signs of these activities, bottles, beer cans, and other debris spoiling the glade formed by the *Pandanus* vegetation which is dominant on the island. Recreational use of such islands by established com-panies should be strictly on a 'no rubbish' basis. Periodic inspec-tions must be made. Furthermore, Heron Island tourist resort

wanted to site an air strip on an adjacent island (Wreck). Wreck
is a narrow sand bar rising to about thirty feet. Once an air strip
was built (which would require the island to be 'levelled') there
would be nothing left. Permission to go ahead with this project
was granted and then speedily withdrawn. Had it gone through as
planned then one resort would have seriously contaminated two
islands and a third to a lesser extent. The Queensland Government are to be congratulated for saving Wreck Island from that
hazard.

Wreck Island was also the site of oil drilling in recent years.
Fortunately nothing was found, but the activities resulted in the
introduction of rats to the island where they are now extremely
numerous. Rats pose a real threat to ground nesting birds such as
mutton birds (*Puffinus pacificus*) as well as attacking hatchling
turtles making their way across the high beach platform to the sea.
The rats are excellent climbers and probably enter the nests of the
white-capped noddy tern to eat the egg or the chick.

Wreck Island is an important rookery for both green and loggerhead turtles – in summer 1969–70 we tagged 413 greens and 289
loggerheads during a 3 week period – as well as being an interesting
island structurally. Its very small size (6 acres) precludes any
economic development, and I am pressing for it to be gazetted a
National Park. An attempt will be made to exterminate the rats
using an anti-coagulant bait.

North-West Island, the largest of the Capricorn–Bunker cays
(227 acres), is the most important green turtle rookery known to us
in the whole of eastern Queensland, south of Coen, a north-south
distance of 1000 miles in a straight line. Its declaration as a
National Park would be of great value to the future of the green
turtle throughout eastern Australia and simple to plan but for
the fact that the Heron Island tourist resort has a ten-year lease
over part of the island. Were they willing to relinquish this, then
presumably it would be possible to have North-West made a
National Park.

Hence the total number of cays which are 'affected' by the
Heron Island resort is four. This is out of a total of eleven cays in
the whole of the Capricorn–Bunker Group excluding North Reef
which is little more than a lighthouse. One-tree cay totally lacks
sand, it is difficult to land at tiny Erskine (5 acres), and Fairfax is
used as a bombing base by the Royal Australian Navy. Against this
utilisation only Lady Musgrave, extensively damaged by goats,

Fairfax (the effect of the nearby bombing range is unknown) and Hoskyn, all in the Bunker Group, are uninhabited National Parks. Clearly there is urgent need for the National Park situation to be strengthened by the designation of further cays in the Capricorn Group.

It is, of course, much easier to get land set aside as National Parks before there is any demand for land development in the area. Australia has the great advantage that there are still substantial tracts of Crown Land available, particularly in the north. These areas can be gazetted as National Parks at a stroke of the pen without the huge costs involved in land purchase which characterise the creation of National Parks in so many parts of the world today. (Crown Land is already vested in the Government and no purchase costs are involved.)

Already, in the south of Queensland, development greatly complicates the issue. For instance, following the discovery of flatbacks nesting at Mon Repos beach, near Bundaberg in southeast Queensland in 1968 (see Chapter 6), we tried to get the area set aside as a National Park. Mon Repos is also the site of an important loggerhead rookery, and under proper management the rookery could have been an important tourist attraction like the fairy penguins on Phillip Island in the Bass Strait. We needed only about 100 acres of coastal sand dune, consisting of a strip about one mile long, going far enough back from the beach so that lights could not prevent the orientation of hatchlings towards the sea or frighten adults coming out of the water to nest. However, some of the land was already owned by the Woongarra Shire Council and most of it was owned by a sugar cane grower who was not using it and was prepared to sell to the Government at a fair price. However, there was a fly in the ointment. An individual had purchased between five and ten acres in the middle of the proposed National Park for real estate development (beach-side houses). He was not prepared to sell at a reasonable price. Furthermore, it turned out that the local council had plans to build a scenic road right along the top of the unconsolidated sand dunes, and greatly favoured obtaining revenue through collecting rates from beach-houses instead of the establishment of a National Park.

Mr Allan Limpus of Bundaberg organised a very active 'Mon Repos National Park Committee', and their representations, backed by various other organisations and myself, resulted in the Minister for Conservation announcing that Cabinet had agreed to the

19. (a) The forerunners of a nest of green turtle hatchlings breaking through the sand surface.

(b) The same hatchlings photographed only seconds later; already the first ones are completely out of the nest and beginning to disperse.

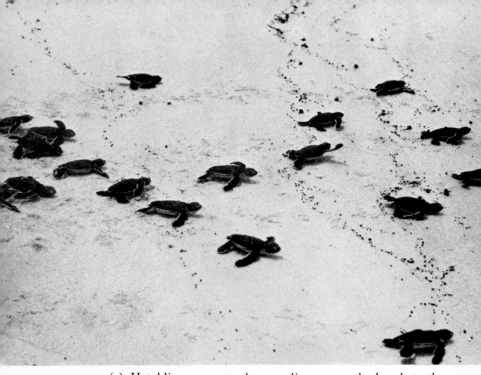

20. (a) Hatchling green turtles scuttling across the beach to the sea.

(b) Baby flatbacks moving to the sea at Mon Repos beach, near Bundaberg, S.E. Queensland. C. LIMPUS.

proposal for a Mon Repos National Park. This statement was bitterly opposed by the Woongarra Shire Council together with the local Member of Parliament. Although I met the full Council I was uncertain what their objections to the scheme really were. I did learn that an important objection was that since the National Park was sited on their land they would lose revenue from rates, whereas any tourist activity which the National Park might generate would flow into Bundaberg (a different Council)! Financial considerations, therefore, appeared to be at the root of their objection together with the desire to build a scenic road along the top of the dunes.

At the time of writing (October 1970) Mon Repos has still not been officially designated a National Park, although the statement of the Cabinet decision was issued by Mr Richter, then Minister for Local Government and Conservation, in November/December 1968. Clearly the lesson of Mon Repos is that it is much easier to obtain land for National Parks before the land speculators and energetic councils move in! This brings us to our present programme.

Two years ago I decided it was now urgent to carry out a sea turtle resources study throughout the whole of Queensland. This investigation would be spread over at least 18 months due to the enormity of the project. The major purpose of the work would be to map all the important rookeries for sea turtles throughout the State. This information would then allow applications to be submitted to the Government to gazette key areas as National Parks now before development threatens the rookeries. This work was made possible by the World Wildlife Fund which is interested in conservation of animals and habitats worldwide. Its associate, the International Union for the Conservation of Nature and Natural Resources (I.U.C.N.), operates a Survival Services Commission which has Specialist Groups for threatened animals or groups of animals. The S.S.C. has a Sea Turtle Group of which I am a member. The World Wildlife Fund operates National Appeals in many countries (unfortunately Australia is not yet among these), and support for the Queensland sea turtle study came from the United States National Appeal to which I am greatly indebted.

The programme includes aerial surveys of the whole of the mainland beaches (Queensland has a coastline of 3,250 miles) together with many offshore and Great Barrier Reef islands. By flying at about five hundred feet at a speed of about 140 miles per hour one can readily detect and count fresh turtle tracks on the beaches. Flights are carefully planned to take place in the early morning when the tide is low following a night high. Work can only be done at a certain time in the fortnightly tide cycle when the tide has receded considerably before the turtles are returning to the water so that they traverse an area of sand on the beach, leaving distinctive tracks, before re-entering the sea. Since the survey work is carried out before the tide rises again these tracks are all exposed.

To date aerial survey work has been carried out at two times of the year (November/December and June). All mainland beaches and most offshore islands in the State have been examined at least twice and many as often as four times. In general, little mainland nesting was found to occur despite the presence of many miles of ideal beach with no habitation within miles. Most rookeries, and all important ones, were located on islands. Apart from the Capricorn–Bunker cays, there are few suitable islands on the southern half of the reef. There are many islands, but they are of mainland origin with steep sides and generally little or no beach area. By far the most important rookeries outside the Capricorn-Bunker Group occurred in the Gulf of Carpentaria. These were on Pisonia Island, 15° 30's, 139° 48'E, and Bountiful, 15° 40's, 139° 51'E (see Chapter 9), where 250–300 and about 600 tracks respectively had been made over the two preceding nights when the islands were flown over on 31st November, 1969. (The figure for Bountiful includes adjacent Rocky Island). Both Bountiful and Pisonia are Aboriginal Reserves which cannot be developed. However, they are no longer used by aborigines and it seems that Bountiful never was (Chapter 9). It is important to ensure that if, and when, they cease to be Aboriginal Reserves they automatically become National Parks. A legislative arrangement to try to ensure this will be worked out if at all possible.

A third island, equally important as a major sea turtle rookery, is Crab Island situated off the coast of the north-west of Cape York (north-east of the Gulf of Carpentaria). Crab Island, 11°s, 142° 6'E, was covered in a mass of tracks when examined from the air on 14th December, 1969. Indeed it was impossible to obtain a reliable count, but tracks from the preceding few nights appeared to number many hundreds. Crab Island is also an Aboriginal Reserve.

Once a suitable series of sea turtle National Parks have been gazetted by the Queensland Government sea turtles will be completely safe in this large region of the world. The present legislation providing total protection is insufficient by itself, although, of course, it prevents any commercial exploitation. The habitats must also be protected. 'Protect the habitats' is now a familiar cry among conservationists. However, sea turtles are perhaps fortunate that their rookeries are relatively few in number and occur in discrete, usually small areas. The total land area required to protect most of the important rookeries in Queensland is smaller than the acreage required for *one* viable mainland National Park for a large macropod (kangaroo).

Undoubtedly the greatest threat to the future of Queensland's large sea turtle populations is land alienation – development of the rookery sites. Since, as pointed out above, three key rookeries are situated on islands in the far north of the State, all of which are Aboriginal Reserves, this threat is not as serious as it could be. However, the discovery of a commercial oil well in the vicinity of any of these islands would spell the end of the rookery. On the Great Barrier Reef itself, both the Commonwealth Government, following personal interest shown by the Prime Minister, Mr Gorton, and the Queensland State Government, appear to be taking a hard line towards oil drilling. It appears likely that no further drilling may be permitted. For some time now no further oil lease applications have been granted on the Great Barrier Reef and the problem has hinged round what to do about leases granted previous to this decision. Public opinion in Australia has crystallised and hardened against drilling on the Reef, partly as a result of the wide publicity which followed the Torrey Canyon Disaster in Cornwall and the oil leak near Santa Barbara in California.

On the mainland, coastal development, particularly in the form of beach-side housing developments and mineral sands mining, will accelerate. Any areas needed for National Parks must be gazetted soon. We are fortunate that most rookeries are situated on islands. This also prevents interference from introduced and native predators (dingoes, fox, pigs, monitor lizards (goannas)).

Although it would appear unlikely that a fishery for the green turtle on the previous basis will ever be permitted again in Queensland, certain other types of fishery activity result in turtle deaths. Offshore trawling over sandy bottoms results in many loggerheads being taken in the trawls and drowned.

In the future it is to be hoped that applications to take turtles can perhaps be channelled into farming ventures. However, I am not in favour of this being undertaken in Queensland until the methodology has been worked out fully and the financial return is known. This preliminary stage should be carried out by non-commercial bodies. Needless to say, I would not back any farming venture which intended to parasitise the natural populations for eggs and was merely a 'rearing station', thereby imposing yet another drain on natural populations. However, it would be permissible to take a quota of wild laid eggs if a specified percentage of the resultant young were liberated, at say the age of one year, *provided it could be clearly shown that these survived and offset the eggs taken by the commercial enterprise.* The key point is that farming must not impose any further drain on the already depleted wild populations. Ideally a farm should have its own breeding stock (taken initially under permit) and, after an initial period, produce all the eggs it requires in the farm. In this way the enterprise can be carried out without jeopardising natural populations (see next section).

Effective conservation of the major green turtle rookeries becomes all the more important in view of the sustainable value of the resource when it is exploited by farming techniques. The potential for a turtle farming industry in Queensland is very substantial.

The status of the Australian aborigines and Torres Strait Islanders and their effect on conservation programmes deserves explanation, particularly for the benefit of non-Australian readers. Aborigines and Islanders are exempt from the fauna laws in all States. This means that they can take totally protected fauna at any time *for their own use.* It is illegal for them to take it and sell it. However, as can be imagined, the law is open to flagrant abuse. Europeans wanting to take protected game (in small quantities, of course) may employ an aborigine as a 'front'. Furthermore, aborigines sometimes offer meat from protected game for sale to Europeans. It is difficult to bring about alterations in the conservation laws in the present social climate since governments are loath to introduce any legislation which might appear to penalise aborigines.

While it is clearly correct for aborigines living a tribal way of life to be able to continue to take their normal food even when this is totally protected from use by Europeans, it is not correct for assimilated aborigines to be able to do this. The law makes no distinction between a completely tribal aborigine and an aborigine living in a residential area in a large city. The latter, living in

Brisbane for example and drawing the same wage as a European on a similar job, is still allowed to go out and harpoon turtles at the week-end although any European found doing this would be prosecuted at once. Together with many conservationists, I feel that this situation is quite wrong and poses a serious threat to the safety of certain native fauna. Aborigines who adopt a European way of life must forfeit their rights under the Act. The ambivalent position of detribalised aborigines presents numerous fauna problems which require urgent action. Basically, I am advocating that once aborigines and Islanders voluntarily leave their reserves they should automatically forfeit their rights to take protected game.

This situation becomes absolutely crazy in Fauna Reserves or National Parks since, under the Acts, aborigines are not disallowed from taking *totally protected game while it is in the sanctuary of a Fauna Reserve or National Park.* As I wrote in a previous book (Bustard, 1970), 'Under the Acts, aborigines can come into a National Park in a vehicle, blast away at the relatively tame game, and go away again having undone the painstaking efforts of many years' conservation effort in a week-end'. I even know of cases where their European Mission superintendents, who should know better, have driven them to such localities 'in order to get their own food'. This behaviour shows a total lack of responsibility.

Looking at this from a turtle conservation viewpoint it means that if and when Mon Repos is declared a National Park there will be nothing to prevent families of aboriginal descent from entering the National Park to collect eggs.

The obvious solution to the problem would be for the Commonwealth (Federal) Government to take the initiative in calling a conference of State Fauna Authorities to clear up this anomalous situation.

Overseas colleagues often see the aboriginal situation as a serious loop-hole in the Queensland turtle legislation and frequently ask me about it. In practice it is of little importance for sea turtles at the present time. I would see its major disadvantage as coming when most aborigines are assimilated and become a rapidly growing segment of the Australian population. They will still retain privileges enacted originally to help tribal aborigines. It is at this stage that a serious conservation threat could arise.

Turning to tribal aborigines, which occur only in the interior and in extreme northern Australia, where most are now settled around Missions, I consider that in general they now pose little threat to the native fauna including sea turtles. Most of these as yet unassimilated aborigines are rapidly losing their ancestral ways, and instead of going out to hunt for food they prefer to accept meals from the Missions or buy tins in the Mission or Government store. This has resulted almost everywhere in reduced hunting pressure even though they are now equipped to go further afield due to the possession of outboard motors. The Mornington islanders provide a good example of this situation. When first contacted by Europeans they possessed only rafts – dug-out canoes were not known to these people – and most of the turtles were taken when ashore laying their eggs, although they were also speared from rafts whenever possible. The aborigines are now losing their skill at, and incentive for, hunting. This is somewhat offset by the possession of dinghies and outboard motors which allow them to reach the turtle feeding grounds much more rapidly. However, the availability of beef (the Mission raises cattle) and tinned foods means that failure to catch wild game does not mean that the family group will go hungry. Hunting has become rather more a spare time occupation, almost a form of relaxation. They enjoy hunting but are no longer prepared to put into it the time and effort which formerly was necessary to obtain sufficient food.

Turtles usually do not nest close to permanent settlements, hence on Mornington and many other islands a walk of some miles may be necessary before one reaches the main nesting areas. It is amazing to me how seldom many aboriginal groups now make this sort of effort even though they may have little else to occupy their time. They are happy to take visitors, such as myself, to these places but seldom now go there themselves. The overall picture is, therefore, one of increasing settlement and reduced hunting. Most Torres Strait Islanders also now hunt turtles much less than formerly.

I would summarise the future outlook for sea turtle conservation in Queensland as follows: Provided the most important rookery areas can be gazetted as National Parks, and provided these Parks remain inviolate from mining and oil seeking interests, the outlook looks extremely secure, comparing very favourably with anywhere else in the world.

There is a marked reaction in Queensland, as elsewhere in Australia, to what might be termed 'mining unlimited'. The tremendous mineral discoveries to date, together with the overall strength of the Australian economy, means that it is not imperative to exploit and hence destroy all the virgin land. Australians are becoming aware that not only do they want to set aside areas of Australia which remain more or less as they were before colonisation, but that Australia is a rich nation with plenty of land and can well afford to do this. Hence the 'ifs' at the start of this paragraph may not be insuperable and we can conclude the section on a cautiously optimistic note.

Turtle Farming

By turtle farming I mean an establishment in which all turtles used to produce commercial products are hatched from eggs laid in the farm by a captive breeding stud. A 'farm', therefore, operates quite independently of natural resources. Establishments which merely parasitise wild populations for eggs were designated as 'ranches' by the I.U.C.N. sea turtle specialists meeting in 1971. The meeting deplored ranch-type activities, except on a pilot research level, as they place a further strain on rapidly depleting natural turtle populations.

It is important to explain at the outset that for about fifty years scientists have thought that turtle farming was feasible, and that it was probably the best way in which to exploit sea turtles commercially, nor had people been slow to push the idea. For instance, Dresden and Goudriaan (1948) writing about turtles in the Netherlands Antilles said (in translation), 'Systematical breeding of turtles deserves serious consideration with regard to both meat and shell. In a period of 3 years the turtle already has grown sufficiently (approximately 55 lbs.). For breeding purposes certain parts of a bay should be fenced in and closed off with wire-netting. Personnel would be required to guard against thieves . . . For further protection it would be advisable to prohibit buying and selling of turtle eggs and turtles, as well as having them in one's possession with a view to sell them. An exception could be made by the issuance of permits.'

It would seem that Dresden and Goudriaan, who were not zoologists, supposed that it was sufficient to fence off a bay and add some turtles to have a turtle farm. Following a report by Bocke (1907) an attempt at turtle farming was made in Curacao but this failed. It is, of course, essential that any farm have the best scientific advice and if possible be under scientific direction until the teething problems have been overcome.

After spending a year on the Great Barrier Reef, C. M. (now Professor Sir Maurice) Yonge wrote (1930) of the green turtle, 'Turtles are very numerous in the northern regions of the Barrier and in the Torres Strait, and again in the far south' (the latter refers to the Capricorn cays). He also wrote, 'If some measures were taken to protect the young turtles in this early stage of their existence their numbers, and so the potentialities of the fishery, would be greatly increased. *Fortunately there is every hope that this will soon be done*'. (My italics.)

Yonge's remarks did not lead to any action to protect young turtles in Queensland waters or elsewhere. Indeed the world's first properly planned turtle farm was only recently established (in 1968).

When I advocate farming some animal, I am often asked why farming was not started a long time ago. There is no adequate answer to this question except to reply that man has been exceptionally conservative in this respect, and throughout recorded history the number of animals which have been domesticated has remained extremely small. An outstanding example of this is the way in which cattle adapted to the British climate, were taken to many parts of Africa where tsetse and other ailments afflicted them, and to tropical Australia. It is only very recently that people are realising for example, that the native antelopes of Africa may offer much better opportunities for beef production than cattle, while in Australia Brahmin and other tropical-adapted crosses are being introduced in increasing numbers. The list of animals that could be farmed is extensive. With a little experimentation many of these would amply repay the investment. For instance in Australia attention should be directed at various sea foods, such as crayfish, as well as sea turtles, and certainly at crocodiles and kangaroos.

Returning to sea turtles it is important to appreciate that growth rates of captive turtles are generally poor. The majority of turtles have been kept in zoos where the conditions are very far from ideal. Turtles may live for many years under such conditions, but growth is poor, and those obtained as juveniles frequently become stunted. The best growth rates will occur in the tropics, not in aquaria in temperate climates. Growth in reptiles is extremely dependent on the conditions being right. This is demonstrated by crocodiles, which when kept in small aquaria, may show extremely little growth over long periods of time. Even in the better zoological gardens crocodile growth is generally slow. The heated reptile houses are cramped and often badly designed. This has led people to question if a farming venture could expect a growth rate of even a foot a year while the crocodiles are in their maximum growth phase. I have frequently been told this is too optimistic. Yet the world's only commercial crocodile farm raises saltwater crocodiles (*Crocodylus porosus*) to a belly skin width of 12–20" at two years old and 20–30" at three years old, achieving much faster growth rates than occur in the wild. Furthermore, farm-reared crocodiles are of a stockier build than wild ones. This means that they reach a specified belly size at a considerably smaller overall length than wild individuals. However, these belly sizes are equivalent to wild saltwater crocodiles of between about five feet to seven feet six inches and seven feet six inches to ten feet respectively!

In view of my remarks above I reserve judgement on the growth potential that turtle farms could obtain. However, it is my belief that it would be adequate to make them an attractive commercial proposition.

I would like to digress at this stage to provide some information on captive-reared Australian turtles. These turtles were not over-fed to try to obtain maximised growth, and although heating was provided during the winter, the turtles were not nearly so warm as they would be in Torres Strait for instance. However, every care was taken to see to their welfare and detailed data were kept on their growth and weight increases.

It was in summer 1964–5 that I met Les and Dorothy Tanis who had holidayed at Heron Island each year since 1946. They had been keen observers of marine life including the turtles for many years, and Les Tanis knew more about the Heron turtles than anyone else alive, with the possible exception of F. W. Moorhouse then in retirement in north Queensland. The Tanis's had collected a hatchling green turtle when it emerged from its nest and reared it in Brisbane. The baby turtle, christened 'Tommy', had hatched at Heron Island on 11th January 1963, so was almost two years old when I first saw it. Clearly it was in superb condition – so different from the stunted unhealthy young turtles which are the result of most captive rearing attempts under quite unsuitable conditions. I was so enthusiastic about this that I talked the Tanis's into rearing additional turtles in conjunction with us. I say 'in conjunction with us' but since the Tanis's kept the turtles and had all the day to day problems, I certainly had the easiest end of the stick!

We were keen to know more about growth rates and their variability under different conditions. I wanted to have some loggerheads reared and, furthermore, to be able to observe the appearance of clips made in the marginals of day-old turtles some years later. This work could be so much better attempted in Brisbane than in southern Canberra, where, being an inland University, we lack marine facilities.

In this brief account I will only refer to green turtles, although I find it hard to disguise a marked partiality for loggerheads.

Tommy increased from about $\frac{3}{4}$ oz. at birth to $13\frac{1}{4}$ oz. at one year old, 6 lb at two years old, 20 lb at three years old, $42\frac{1}{2}$ lb at four, 103 lb at six and 131 lb at seven. Now at an age of $7\frac{3}{4}$ he weighs 140 lb. I say 'he', as before the age of five his tail started to elongate and well before six was quite unmistakably the tail of a male turtle. It is only fair to point out that subsequent turtles (with my encouragement the collection increased from 1 to 21 turtles!) probably as a result of ever increasing 'turtle know-how' on the part of the Tanis's, showed more rapid growth rates. Furthermore, it is difficult in a private home in Brisbane to provide facilities to sustain rapid growth rates once turtles reach a comparatively large size. Let it suffice to say that the Tanis's subsequently succeeded in at least doubling the growth rate of young turtles compared to Tommy. At present the record stands at just over 2 lb at the age of one year. Furthermore, I am convinced that under tropical conditions, caged in the sea, we can do substantially better than the best growth rates obtained in aquaria in Brisbane. This has now been verified, as described below.

The major contribution of the Tanis's has been a mass of detailed information on changes which occur with growth – in appearance, habits, and relative growth of parts. By their skilful rearing of day-old hatchlings they were able to demonstrate the effectiveness of our marginal clipping procedures. Quite apart from greens they have reared a fine pair of loggerheads, now $5\frac{1}{2}$ years old and a flatback now $2\frac{1}{2}$ years old.

In 1968 the world's first turtle farm got underway at Grand Cayman Island in the British West Indies. The concern – Mariculture Ltd. – contends that 'the once great turtle fleets of the Caribbean may be brought back in a short time by rearing large numbers of hatchlings in protective custody, then releasing them on the *Thalassina* beds at a year of age'.

Dr Robert E. Schroeder, then Managing Director of Mariculture Ltd. wrote to me (May 1969),

'At present our eggs come from natural rookeries, although we intend to establish our own breeding colonies as rapidly as possible. In return for 15,000 Costa Rican eggs, for example, we are returning 500 yearling turtles that will be tagged and released on the rookery beach. The turtles to be returned were hatched naturally and allowed to enter the water before being caught and pen-reared. We have a similar arrangement with Ascension Island.

'The balance of the turtles we rear are to be released around Grand Cayman Island. The site was chosen because it is surrounded by deep sea. At a year of age, the turtles will, presumably, be ready to stay in the grassbeds. The Cayman government has passed the necessary protective legislation, and extended to us the requisite franchise, to make such "Open-range ranching" of the grassbeds feasible.'

I cannot do better than let Dr Schroeder explain how it all came about in his own words.

'My wife and I got hooked on green turtles quite by accident while working on the ecology of the trematodes of lutjanid fishes in the Florida Keys. One of Archie Carr's some-time students (Wayne King) gave us a few hatchlings.

'They grew so well in a spare fish pen that we got 600 more from Archie the following year. Then, rather as a lark, we went to Tortuguero to photograph his work for the National Geographic Society. There we found ourselves in the thick of discussions with Archie and his associates that covered the Caribbean turtle problem from ecology to sociology.

'It became clear to us that no conventional conservation methods will do much good in Central America. There is a population explosion unmatched elsewhere in the world. Grinding poverty is the rule. Law enforcement along the wild, primitive coasts is all but non-existent. The number of nesting turtles falls markedly each year.

'I have data on survivorship in captivity, and tag returns from all over the Florida Keys, the Florida Gulf Coast, Cuba, Honduras, and Nicaragua. I cannot give figures on the survivorship of released pen-reared turtles, but my data do make me dead certain that they do a whole lot better than hatchlings just out of the nest. A little simple arithmetic shows that hatchling survivorship cannot exceed four or five per thousand, and probably is more like two per thousand. Otherwise there would be plenty of turtles. My data suggest that at least 40 or 50% of released pen-reared yearlings survive a year of freedom. Unless there are some very radical kinks in the survivorship curve, pen-rearing must increase overall survivorship something like 50 to 100 times.

'A pen-reared turtle does not behave exactly like a wild one, but its behaviour when released is wild enough. Later, it may calm down and even hang around a wharf as does no wild turtle. About 80 yearlings released nearby in Florida Bay returned to our dock, and hung around waiting for a hand-out. Twelve of these were from a group of 67 released 35 miles away across the bay. We re-caught and weighed many of these turtles repeatedly. Obviously they were not behaving like wild turtles, but they were not suffering any noticeable predation either. All were in excellent health.

'Tag returns from the Keys and from the Gulf Coast all came from turtles that were caught on a hook and line from docks. Wild turtles never are caught in this fashion, but all were in good condition except for a hook hole in the side of the mouth. All had grown at rates comparable to captive turtles of similar size. The random scattering of recoveries suggests that the turtles that found their way home probably did so by accident, following the chain of keys until they blundered back to our dock.

'Many turtles released in the vicinity of the dock did not hang around but established themselves in the local shallows. Although I was not able to study their progress statistically, survivorship appeared good. As they grew larger, they gradually moved out into deeper grassbeds. That they did not return would indicate that perhaps the majority of turtles released took up a normal chelonian existence, rather than coming home to beg.

'Last September we released 125 two-year-old turtles and 250 yearlings in Grand Cayman waters. We have recovered 47 yearlings and 16 two-year-olds during the past 10 months. All were in good health and growing rapidly. We occasionally see turtles bearing our tags in the Great Sound of the island, a shallow grassbed area of about 20 square miles. They are found in areas of a depth and bottom type characteristic of turtles of their sizes.

'Tag returns from Cuba and Central America indicate that even small green turtles will cross sizable bodies of deep open water, which I did not expect from juvenile turtles ready to live in the grassbeds. Perhaps the establishment and maintenance of migratory patterns is more complex than I suspected. The sustained level of tag returns suggests that the released population probably remains essentially intact.

'Turtle farming deserves a fair chance to prove itself. Mariculture Ltd., will give it that chance. I have very little patience with theoretical objections, especially from people whose answer to the problem is to dump cans of turtle soup on the floor in supermarkets. If the species does not become extinct, I do not believe the motives of the people who save it will make very much difference an eon or two hence. If it does become extinct, it will be extinct forever more, the grand gesture of the indignant notwithstanding.

'As Archie Carr pointedly wrote to our Directors, "If Mariculture does not breed turtles in captivity, it has no future." We certainly cannot rely on wild populations indefinitely to supply us with eggs and hatchlings, even though the number of eggs we take right now are inconsequential. In a very few years, despite our best efforts, the natural rookeries no longer will support us. We are spending fifty thousand pounds on experimental breeding facilities during the next three years. We hope to fly wild breeders here from Costa Rica in August or September. Our first pen-reared breeders should be old enough to breed in three years.

'Each year we return 250 tagged yearlings to Costa Rica for release on the rookery beach. These turtles are reared from a special stock, hatched on Tortuguero Beach, and given their first swim in Tortuguero water. These yearlings serve two purposes: they recompense the Costa Ricans for the eggs they give us, and they eventually should give us some data on this means of restocking.

'Mariculture Ltd. is intended to be a profit-making concern, and will rear turtles for slaughter. Its investors are business men who look forward to a return on their investment. But they are not small businessmen: they are thinking of the day when the Caribbean will be a vast turtle ranch producing millions of turtles per year. They realise this will be possible only if the survivorship of hatchlings is raised many times by a year's headstart in captivity, and if adequate legal protection can be obtained for the stock.

'They are not interested in exploiting wild populations. The new Cayman Islands turtle law, which we wrote for the Cayman government, gives the wild turtles absolute protection. We will be entitled to turtles bearing our tags only. As this industry grows, the old-style turtler will be run out of business in any case.

'I do not believe that natural populations, even very large ones, can support a satisfactory sustained yield. The animal's reproductive ecology is predicated upon the adult's having a long reproductive life. Natural predation on adults is small, and recruitment correspondingly low. Unsupported populations, therefore, will not stand up to harvesting of adults. But the marine grassbeds will rear and support huge numbers of turtles, provided that recruitment can be raised.

'If Mariculture is successful, nothing will prevent others – governments, granting agencies, private investors – from taking advantage of the knowledge that it can be done. They all will know that the great turtle fleets of the past can be brought back and maintained by headstarting. Everybody, including the I.U.C.N., will get that much for free. If we are not successful, *all* our data will be available for other approaches.'

I have been extremely enthusiastic about Dr Schroeder's work since it first came to my notice. This is because I believe that in the long term farming the green turtle will prove to be the most effective method to conserve this animal. Farming must, however, be under proper Government control so that after a 'breathing space' of several years the eggs come from a captive breeding herd. If the commercial demand can be totally or largely met from farms then wild populations will not be hunted to extinction.

Mariculture has now moved all its turtles into tanks on the land and does not plan in future to liberate turtles to feed and grow on the natural grassbeds. Excellent growth rates are currently being achieved – between 60 and 80 lb net weight at two years old and about 120 lb at age three.

However, there is another reason for my interest in turtle farming. Farming ventures offer employment and a cash crop to maritime people, and in the tropics these people are usually very poor. Yet they are living on the edge of riches. If farming is to be carried out solely by large international corporations, then I think a great opportunity to help these people help themselves will have been lost. This is not to suggest for one instant that I am in any way opposed to Mariculture Ltd. However, I want to see large and small farms operate side by side much as happens on the land. The rights of the original inhabitants may need to be safeguarded by legislation.

The results of my own work will be made available to help Torres Straits Islanders set up turtle farms. My role will be simply that of advisor. To get the programme under way it has been agreed that for an initial period of about three years the farms will be under my direct supervision and the people running them will work for a salary. However, after the farms are demonstrably viable operations it is hoped that these Island farmers, and many others who have been interested observers as the scheme got under way, will elect to become turtle farmers in their own right. The first farms are scheduled to commence in December 1970. Initially there will be six pilot schemes three each on Darnley and Murray Islands in eastern Torres Strait. It is intended to investigate both battery-type pen-rearing to a commercial size, and free range farming, from the outset. In the latter, the hatchling turtles will be pen-reared for about one year during which they will be fed fish then tagged and liberated. As pointed out by Schroeder, pen-rearing for a year should increase survivorship by an astronomical fifty to one hundred times! In the free range farming venture each farmer would own those turtles bearing his tag number. Only tagged turtles could be used for commercial purposes but untagged, that is wild turtles, could still be used for food by the local population. The costs of the programme are being met by grants from the Commonwealth Office of Aboriginal Affairs.

Quite apart from carrying out pilot farming investigations, we intend to monitor the wild populations in the area most carefully from the outset. We want to know exactly what effect our operations have on them. For instance can the productivity of the turtle grassbeds withstand this phenomenal increase in turtle numbers? Furthermore, we must show that our activities are not deleterious to the natural population. Initially we will use wild-laid eggs. Subsequently eggs may come from a domesticated breeding stock. It would be invaluable to know the effect on the natural population of taking a certain percentage of the eggs and subsequently releasing a known percentage of the hatchlings at an age of one year old. Present arguments about the effect of actions of this nature on the wild populations are futile since the information is simply not available. Until the effects are known conservationists have no alternative but to adopt an extremely cautious attitude.

What is proposed, therefore, for Torres Strait, is turtle farming ventures, initially of a pilot nature, to enable the people to become used to the idea and develop the necessary expertise. However, this work will not be carried out in a vacuum. We will carry out extensive research in the area as an integral part of the proposed development so that we will hopefully be able to predict the turtle carrying capacity of the area, and to meet potential problems before they arise.

Since all species of turtles are totally protected in Queensland (see below) the pilot research farms can only be operated by means of annual permits issued by the Queensland Government. These permits will be subject to receipt of satisfactory annual reports. Hence the Queensland Government is in a position to ensure that the proposed farming ventures and commercial farms which may result from them, do not in any way conflict with the Government's role in conserving sea turtles throughout the State.

I am extremely confident that the turtle-farming scheme will be a great success. Its ultimate success or failure will probably depend on the people initially selected as farmers, and for this reason we are choosing these people with great care. The Torres Strait Islanders are a delightful people – happy, intelligent and without a grudge against the world despite their socio-economic problems. Lack of jobs has caused a drift away from the islands and a separation of families as men move south to find work. It is my hope that turtle farms will provide sustained employment enabling at least some communities to continue to live on their islands yet achieve a satisfactory level of income. Incidentally turtles are something for which the Islanders have a strong affinity, and I anticipate that they will show considerable aptitude for work with them. It is only just that they should be helped to exploit their own resources on a sustained yield basis for their own good.

Further encouraging success has been achieved recently of major importance to long-term farming of the green turtle. The species has now laid eggs in captivity. That this has never occurred in any zoological garden is further evidence of the totally inadequate conditions provided. Professor Hendrickson in Hawaii was the first person to succeed in getting green turtles to lay in a pool with an artificial beach. This success has since been duplicated by Mariculture Ltd. in the Cayman Islands. It seems that it may not be long before the green turtle is added to the short but growing list of animals domesticated by man.

21. (a) A 59″ black-tipped reef shark (*Carcharinus spallanzani*) with 14 green turtles hatchlings removed from its stomach.

(b) A ghost crab (*Ocypoda ceratophthalma*) with a hatchling green turtle making ineffectual attempts to escape.

22. Katie Pau, a turtle farming trainee from Darnley Island, Torres Strait, with a four-year-old partial albino green turtle reared by Mr and Mrs O. L. Tanis.

The Future of the World's Sea Turtle Resources

The Survival Services Commission of the International Union for the Conservation of Nature and Natural Resources (I.U.C.N.) held a working meeting of marine turtle specialists at Morges, Switzerland in March, 1969. The following are among the proposals which were deemed necessary to safeguard the future of sea turtles:

1. increased incubation and hatchling programmes, using proved techniques;
2. study and analysis of world exploitation patterns;
3. beach surveys where data are lacking, followed up by expert advice as required;
4. establishment of special sanctuaries under scientific management.

The situation varies so much in different parts of the world that it is extremely difficult to generalise. There are also species differences which tend to complicate the situation further. To simplify this I am considering each species separately below, and in a preamble I am giving examples of the types of situation facing sea turtle conservation in different parts of the world. I will start with Queensland, Australia, where my own knowledge is greatest.

In Queensland, the 1968 legislation protecting all species of sea turtles and their eggs throughout the State prevents any commercial exploitation. Clearly it is impossible to detect every infringement – if someone wants to take a turtle for meat there are many areas of the State where the chance of detection is low. However, infringements of this nature are considered to be insignificant at present. Aborigines and Torres Strait Islanders may still take turtles for their own use but their effect does not appear to impose any problems for the turtles at the present time.

The greatest threat to sea turtles in Queensland has yet to come but will not be long delayed. This is from development, particularly in the form of mineral exploitation. Huge areas of the State, at present virgin bush, will be exploited in the next decade. When these areas involve beach-sand mining operations, then they pose a real threat to any turtle rookeries in the area. A less immediate, but none the less extremely serious threat on the longer term, is pollution, particularly in the case of small islands.

Real estate development is also important although its effects will take longer to reach the north of the State than mining activities. Seaside homes are always popular and significant areas of nesting beach can be quickly alienated as a result of their development. Tourist activity, unless most carefully planned, can also quickly spoil the natural resources of an area of beach or an island. This is particularly the case with small islands which form key breeding places for sea turtles.

In view of these threats, and to determine where the best nesting places were in the State, and what action was needed to conserve them, I commenced a detailed sea turtle resources study of the whole of Queensland with financial support from the World Wildlife Fund (United States National Appeal). It is hoped to submit a detailed report to the Premier of Queensland early in 1971. However, I have already been able to state that a number of rookeries are of such importance that they should be gazetted as National Parks without delay. These proposals are currently under consideration by the Government. The reason that I am discussing this work here is to give an example of what would be the ideal. Protective legislation, which is uniform throughout such a huge area as Queensland (coastline 3250 miles, plus 1200 miles of the Great Barrier Reef), is extremely meaningful biologically. If one can complement this by gazetting the key turtle rookery areas as National Parks then one has the maximum possible safeguards to ensure the turtles' future. Of course, there will always be other problems to face, such as pollution, but these are part of a much wider canvas.

I am not against rational exploitation and will return to this topic later. Firstly I would like to give an example of a situation which on a world basis is certainly much more typical of the problems facing sea turtles than the Queensland picture. The following quote is from Professor Archie Carr's book *The Turtle* which gives an eye-witness account of poaching near his sea turtle research headquarters in Costa Rica. Professor Carr was walking some visitors along the beach to see nesting green turtles when they saw the torch of a poacher up ahead. Professor Carr takes up the story,

'I thought of the mess he would have left, and again was about to say maybe there was no use going any farther, when I saw the backwash curling white fringe around a dark body on the sand ahead, and then it was too late.

'It was a calipeed turtle. I ran up and pulled at one of her limp flippers, and there was no life in it and the head was washing loosely with the surf. So at least the turtle was dead. They were not always dead when you come on them that way. You can find them lying there back-down with the belly shell gone, the flippers waving, the many-coloured viscera glistening, and the heart beating staunchly on in the ruin.

'Everybody crowded around the corpse ... I turned the other way and trotted on up to the point alone. I found two more turtles both dead. It was a humane poacher, this time; but the point is, for the sake of half-a-peck of hard gelatin to be sent off to make soup for a few people thousands of miles away, three full-grown, nesting female turtles that weighed, say three hundred pounds, had been killed and left for the next morning's buzzards to fight about. And this had taken place on the only remaining breeding beach of the green turtle in the western Caribbean, on a shore that is better protected from poaching than almost any other sea turtle beach anywhere. Dried on a rack in a secret place and taken out to Limón or Barra del Colorado, where nobody can tell illegal calipee from that of turtles lawfully harpooned or netted, those scraps of cartilage would bring more money than the poacher could make in any week of other work he would be likely to find.'

Professor Carr in the above statement has summarised the crux of the problem facing sea turtle conservation in many parts of the world – the turtles' economic value. Particular attention should be directed at the last two lines of his statement. This situation provides a classic case of the incentive to poach. What can be done about it?

Legislation is relatively worthless (except as evidence of an enlightened Government) if the animal it supposedly protects is subject to large-scale poaching and the legislation is unable to deal effectively with this. Unfortunately this is all too frequently the case. This is such a fundamental point that it deserves some elaboration. Clearly it will never be possible to catch all poachers all the time. Success can be claimed if one catches a substantial proportion of poachers some of the time. Poachers weigh up the possibility of being caught (and convicted) against the potential gain from poaching. Hence effective legislation involves much more than an honest, hard-working cadre of fauna wardens who manage to catch a substantial proportion of the poachers. In the most 'advanced' countries magistrates only too often impose only nominal fines against poachers whose income from poaching may be many times that of the magistrate. Clearly fines which can be recouped by part of one night's poaching are no deterrent to the poacher. Worse, they ruin morale among the fauna wardens. What is the point of tracking down and apprehending poachers, tedious and usually difficult work at the best of times, if you know that they will receive only a nominal fine? The warden has a good knowledge of the profitability of poaching, he also knows the effect that it is having on the animals he is supposedly there to protect. Can you wonder at his bewilderment and dismay when only nominal fines are imposed? In time he comes to realise that all the dice are stacked against him and in favour of the poacher and becomes apathetic about his work.

Any government passing protective legislation must be prepared to follow through and see that realistic fines are imposed. In saying this I am fully aware that this can be a complicated task as many magistrates have no interest in conservation and are quite likely to consider someone who poaches, for instance, a rare species of crocodile, as doing a service to mankind! However, it is quite wrong to ignore these issues. They must be brought out, discussed, and means found to remedy them. Wherever possible, statutory minimum fines should exist, and these should be substantial enough to actually deter poaching. However, they must be accompanied by information to the magistrates to advise them of the potential gains to be made from poaching. The main problem in a number of areas where I have acted as adviser is that the poachers are streets ahead of the conservation service, and more particularly the law, in terms of professionalism. Almost all of this can be attributed to the failure of the Government to secure adequate fines when poachers are convicted.

In deciding on the level of fine to be levied, which will, of course, differ from case to case, one should carefully weigh up not only the number of animals with which the poacher is actually apprehended but his probable activities. Minimum fines for first offence convictions should be sufficient to more than offset several months' poaching revenue. Unfortunately many, if not most, magistrates still seem to think that if they confiscate the proceeds of a single night's poaching and impose some trivial fine, the person will be deterred from further poaching. Of course, this idea is quite erroneous as any fauna warden can confirm!

A crocodile shooter, who agreed with me in strongly advocating a Fauna Reserve for the saltwater crocodile (*Crocodylus porosus*), and who knew the way poachers' minds work, appealed to me to tell the Government to impose fines ten times greater than normal for any poaching within the Reserve. Needless to say few governments would be prepared to take such action.

To summarise: poaching is a fact of life. However, it can be greatly reduced – hopefully to a level that the protected animal population can withstand – by efficient apprehension of poachers combined with stiff penalties from the Courts for those convicted of poaching.

Rational exploitation

No sensible conservationist is against rational exploitation. By this I mean exploitation adjusted so that the species or population in question can maintain its numbers and withstand continued exploitation in the future. An analogy can be made with mining – a once-only operation, equivalent to shooting all the animals in the population – as compared to carefully husbanding the breeding stock and culling off only the surplus each year. Of course management can greatly increase the annual 'surplus'. Although man has practised this with domestic stock for a very long time the idea of applying it to natural populations of animals has been extremely slow to catch on. The mining approach is usually still dominant even to-day.

Ecological studies have now progressed to a stage where it is often possible to manipulate the population to maximise the production of the particular end-product sought, that is to produce much more of it than would be produced in a natural population of the species. Unfortunately, the necessary legislation and controls to make this sort of operation possible usually require Government action and governments have been extremely slow to take the necessary steps to make this sort of approach possible.

It is essential to face up to the fact that the operation of any 'rational exploitation' schemes require careful policing and hence Government interest if they are to succeed. The problem is particularly difficult politically when the resource to be cropped has already been heavily over-exploited (this usually happens before expert advice is sought). Clearly it may be politically and socially unpalatable to take the obvious remedy and completely close the resource for a number of years until it has recovered.

Faced with these problems several alternatives are open to the sea turtle conservationist. He will say that the critical situation facing sea turtles to-day is a result of the fast growing demand for turtle products – calipee for soup, oil for the cosmetics industry, leather for modern accoutrements, meat for tourists plus rapidly growing coastal human populations. Thus he may decide to try to depopularise turtle products – which to me is a negative approach. Alternatively he can try to devise and implement a scheme whereby certain areas are set aside as total sanctuaries whereas other areas are exploited. Such a scheme has the inherent weakness that unless the sanctuary areas are uninhabited and outside the hunting province of the neighbouring people it will appear that they are being made to leave the turtles in order to benefit someone else (which may indeed be the case). The conservationist may decide that he should try to combine the above with quotas on the catch permissible from the non-sanctuary areas.

There is yet another possibility – to realise that the demand exists for turtle products and that properly utilised, these products can provide a valuable cash crop for people living adjacent to tropical and subtropical seas, who are themselves often intimately connected with turtles through tribal customs. In this approach one will go all out to meet the demand. This positive approach has a number of decided advantages. First and foremost rational exploitation of the resource, conservation, and a cash crop and/or sustenance for the local people, can all go hand in hand. This approach is based on farming.

As described in Chapter 8 sea turtles produce very large numbers of eggs. In nature a large proportion of the natural egg lay is destroyed by predators and the loss from predation is very high in the hatchlings. If one could prevent or greatly reduce egg predation and completely prevent predation on the very young turtles, then the high reproductive rate of the species would quickly result in the world's oceans becoming clogged up with turtles! In my belief farming offers this sort of solution.

In this chapter I have briefly described work that is getting under way in Australia under my guidance. Quite apart from substantially helping Torres Strait Islanders and Australian aborigines, it is my belief that this is a very important development for conservation generally.

Clearly farming must be controlled. As delegates to the Morges sea turtle specialists' meeting were quick to point out, farms which merely rely on the collection of vast numbers of naturally laid eggs will wipe out the species just as surely as a high level of human predation on the adult turtles. The meeting took the view that all such farms should have their own breeding stock so that they operated completely independently from natural populations. This is the wise international aim. However, purely scientifically, there are other ways that farms could be managed. The above-mentioned method is to be preferred because it obviates the need for many controls and political decisions.

Scientifically, farms could operate under permits which allowed them to collect a specified number of naturally laid eggs provided they liberated a proportion of their juveniles at an advanced age to offset the eggs taken. The figures could be set under the terms of the permit to take eggs. This is the way in which the world's first sea turtle farm (Mariculture) got under way at Grand Cayman Island in the West Indies. However, this farm is already starting to experiment in producing eggs from captive breeding stock.

Starting with the eggs, there would appear to be two ways in which farming can proceed, subject to large, readily caught supplies of fish throughout the year. It is essential in initiating any farming scheme to collect freshly laid eggs and to protect these from predators during the incubation period. It is equally important that the hatchling turtles be pen-reared at least to get them through early infancy, when, as a result of their small size, they are extremely vulnerable to a large number of predators. However, when they are about one year old, two alternatives become possible. They can be pen-reared until they reach an economic size for utilisation, or they can be tagged and liberated to be fished at a later date.

Much of the knowledge needed to conserve sea turtle populations is already known. As is clear from the previous statements, the big hurdle facing conservation is political – the implementation and enforcement of suitable legislation by governments.

However, knowledge is still inadequate to permit scientific management of any sea turtle resource. For instance no one has data to allow one to state confidently that x turtles liberated at an age of 1 year are equivalent to y hatchlings. Information on the subsequent survival under natural conditions of pen-reared hatchlings is still inadequate. This is one field where further data are urgently required.

The seven species of sea turtles are discussed separately below:

THE GREEN TURTLE

In planning for the conservation of the green turtle it is important to realise that a number of well-differentiated populations exist and what is currently called the 'green turtle' could prove to be a composite of two or more quite distinct species. It is not enough, therefore, to say, for instance, that there are plenty of green turtles in Queensland so the future of the species elsewhere does not matter. Every effort should be made to see that each well differentiated race survives.

The green turtle is the main commercial species (see also the hawksbill) being in great demand for traditional purposes such as meat and calipee for turtle soup as well as for more recent uses including oil for the cosmetic industry and leather which affect the other species to a varying degree. This is obviously the species to use for any research farming efforts (see above).

The maintenance of substantial populations in a number of world locations will require well co-ordinated international action as well as dedicated work by individuals. It is my belief that farming offers the best middle-term solution for this species. If it proves practicable to farm the animal on a sufficiently large scale then demand can be supplied entirely from the farms and the incentive to hunt wild populations for commercial purposes will decline. This process can be hastened politically once the farming outlet is available. Whereas it is politically very difficult to cut off access to a resource, particularly if traditional usage is involved, if people are given a clear-cut alternative such as farming, it would then be possible to cut off or greatly restrict access to natural populations after a period of years. People who had not followed the farming alternative would have only themselves to blame.

There is a further consideration. I am firmly in favour of rational exploitation of animal populations where this is clearly practicable on a sustained yield basis because politically it is most useful to have an actual price tag placed on a species or population. Most governments act to a large degree on expediency, motivated by a cash consciousness, so that it is much easier to obtain legislation for a 'useful', that is, exploited, rather than an unexploited species. Furthermore, once it is demonstrated that a species can be cropped or farmed successfully, governments are prepared to put teeth into legislation in order to make it effective, with the motive of protecting the 'industry'.

While farming ventures are still at the research stage every effort must be made to bring down protective legislation and to see that this is accompanied by some well-policed National Parks so that at least parts of the populations can be protected. In my view an important task of the Survival Services Commission Sea Turtle Group, and particularly of the Executive Officer, is to keep a constant check on legislation in force throughout the world and to encourage, through people on the spot wherever possible, improvements in the legislation and its enforcement. Properly carried out, this work would have tremendous conservation impact for all species of sea turtles.

In some areas of the world such as the Caribbean and the western Indian Ocean (the Aldabra rookery) the green turtle has been almost exterminated. Conservation can hope to encourage the regeneration of the remnants of once huge populations by explaining the eventual benefit to the local inhabitants. Once again the possibility of farming ventures when the populations have made substantial recovery is a sound argument for conservation now.

The Red Data Book of I.U.C.N. lists the green turtle as status category 3. This reads as follows: 'Depleted. Although occurring in numbers adequate for survival, the species has been heavily depleted and continues to decline at a rate substantially greater than can be sustained.'

THE FLATBACK

Species like the flatback and Kemp's ridley, both of which have a very restricted distribution, are potentially extremely vulnerable and in my view should not be exploited at all. I.U.C.N., through its Survival Services Commission, should ensure that the respective governments, where these species occur, accept full responsibility for them and guarantee to ensure that exploitation is totally prohibited.

So far as is known, the flatback nests only in Australian waters and even the adults do not appear to move away from Australia. Part of our work in Queensland is directed towards finding out more about the biology of this species and also seeing that important breeding rookeries are set aside in perpetuity as National Parks.

The flatback has never been subject to any substantial level of exploitation in Australian waters. Its flesh does not have the appeal of the green turtle to Europeans nor indeed to most aborigines, but its large eggs are eagerly sought by aborigines, as are those of all species of sea turtles. However, at present this does not constitute a threat to the species since much of its nesting occurs in uninhabited areas which are rarely or never visited by aborigines.

The flatback also occurs in the Northern Territory and possibly also in Western Australia but I know of no positive records. Now, while the species is not subject to any commercial exploitation whatsoever, would be the ideal time for Queensland, the Northern Territory and Western Australia to agree to a convention. In Queensland, as with all sea turtles, the flatback and its eggs are totally protected throughout the whole State at all times (aborigines are not subject to the Fauna Acts). Nevertheless, this does not ensure that exploitation could not take place at some future date if a commercial use was found for the species.

Undoubtedly the main threat to the flatback turtle will come from land alienation which is why we are hoping to obtain National Parks as soon as possible.

THE LOGGERHEAD TURTLE

The loggerhead is not an important commercial species, but like all sea turtles suffers as a result of the human population explosion and associated seaside development projects. Much of the nesting of the Atlantic race of the loggerhead occurs in the United States and until recently these populations appeared to be in no serious immediate danger. However, the situation has recently changed for the worse as a result of two factors. Professor Archie Carr in his book *The Turtle* wrote: 'These are the rapid development of coastlines as real estate and recreational areas, and the marked expansion of racoon populations. Because the racoon is able to live well with man the two factors often operate together against the loggerhead (racoons eat turtle eggs), and in spite of the laws on the books (to protect the turtles), the hold of *Caretta* on shores of the United States is slipping fast. Many of the best of the old loggerhead beaches have become cluttered with people and the constant traffic of cars. Even where the beach itself is not invaded, lights along coastal highways confuse the turtles when they come ashore to nest, or draw the emerging hatchlings away from the sea to be mashed by the thousands on the highways. Even in places in which good will towards sea turtles is highest, the nesting females are interfered with by well-wishing posses who walk the shores at night, and arrange themselves in rings around every turtle that comes out.'

I have quoted Professor Carr as there is a lesson here. Perhaps it can be learned by the rest of the world which has not yet 'developed' to the extent of the United States? It is most encouraging to discover just how much the effects of urban sprawl and industry can be ameliorated at no extra cost by a little foresight. Coastal highways are a case in point. Surely it is possible for conservationists and planners to get together so that development goes ahead while minimising the impact on the natural resources of the country. This is equally important in a developed country with a high standard of living, or in a developing country, where unspoiled beaches cluttered at night by stars and turtles rather than motor cars, are an important ingredient in tourism.

The racoon situation is an example of human interference with the balance of nature having wide repercussions. Professor Carr continued, 'At most of the loggerhead beaches in the United States the racoon has become an important obstacle to protective measures. In primitive times racoons were no doubt kept in check by natural predators. Certainly, for instance, they are a favoured game of the few remaining pumas . . . racoons are more abundant than anybody ever heard of in the old days.

'To racoons, turtle eggs are manna from heaven. Being bright animals, they harvest them with deadly efficiency. On one stretch of Hutchinson's Island in St Lucie County, Florida, that I traveled not long ago, eight loggerheads nested before midnight and every nest was destroyed by racoons before daylight . . . The magnificent Cape Sable beaches lie within the Everglades National Park. The cape is almost completely free of human interference of all sorts. In a recent study, however, Ranger Max Holden found that of 199 loggerhead nests on a five-mile extent of the east cape beach, 140 were destroyed by racoons.'

In Australia substitute 'pig' for 'racoon' and you have a description of the situation on huge areas of mainland north Queensland. The pigs, feral descendants of escaped animals brought to Australia by British settlers, patrol the beaches and detect fresh turtle nests by sight and locate the actual position of the eggs by smell. During aerial survey work in north Queensland in 1969 and again in 1970 we commonly saw bands of pigs on the beaches, numbering up to fifteen individuals in a single group, and evidence of nest destruction was very extensive. Certainly pig tracks were much more numerous than turtle tracks even at the height of the turtle nesting season!

The abundance of pigs in north Queensland makes the creation of mainland National Parks for turtles of doubtful value. For this reason we are concentrating most of our effort on islands which, fortunately are usually much more important rookeries in Queensland and, unless very large, usually lack introduced predators. In the south of the State, foxes, likewise introduced from Britain, destroy many nests. Dingoes, probably introduced to Australia by Australoid man, may also be an important predator in parts of Australia.

Large monitor lizards have always been a deterrent to mainland nesting in Australia and may be a reason why most important rookeries occur on islands. However, in recent times as a result of human introductions, the odds have been biased much more heavily against successful incubation of eggs deposited on mainland beaches. I am sure there are many other similar examples in different parts of the world. In any consideration of the influence of man, his effect on the species' balance by introductions (as in the case of pigs and foxes to Australia) or by destroying natural predators as has happened with the racoons in the United States, must be considered together with other factors such as land alienation.

To summarise, the loggerhead has no problems which are peculiar to its species. The Red Data Book lists the loggerhead as status category 3 like the green turtle.

KEMP'S RIDLEY

This species, like the flatback, is particularly vulnerable as a result of its very restricted distribution. The best solution to a situation such as this is for I.U.C.N. to arrange by a Convention that the Government of Mexico accept full responsibility for the species and guarantee that exploitation of a commercial nature will be totally prohibited at all times.

This species has a remarkably aggregated nesting behaviour in that virtually the entire breeding population of the species nests in the one locality, and furthermore, at the one time (see Chapter 7). The turtles almost all come ashore to nest on the same day.

The nesting locality is in the Mexican state of Tamaulipas. As pointed out by Professor Carr, this concentrated reproductive activity, which makes Kemp's ridley an extremely vulnerable species, also makes it the most susceptible to protective supervision.

'All that would be required would be systematic patrols of some sixty miles of shore during the months from March through June. The failing colony now gets no protection at all. . . . Only a consistent, careful vigil along the shore will save the species; and obviously, only Mexico can patrol a Mexican beach. It is very seldom that the fate of a species has so clearly depended upon the prompt and wholehearted application of a simple enforcement operation.' (Carr, 1968). The Red Data Book lists Kemp's ridley as category 1, which reads as follows: 'Endangered. Actively threatened with extinction. Continued survival unlikely without the implementation of special protective measures.'

PACIFIC RIDLEY

The conservation of this species is complicated by the fact that it has been consistently confused with the loggerhead so that many literature references are of doubtful validity.

To some extent its wide distribution reduces its vulnerability. However, the species is subjected to a great deal of uncontrolled exploitation, for the turtles themselves, for the eggs, or for both turtles and eggs.

The Pacific ridley is known to lay in northern Australian waters; however, no information on its numbers is currently available. The species is totally protected, along with all other sea turtles, in Queensland, and there would appear to be little difficulty in ensuring that any important rookeries which may be discovered in Queensland, the Northern Territory, or Western Australia are safeguarded. Undoubtedly action of this kind is needed and efforts should perhaps be concentrated in areas of stable government where important conservation can result from sound scientific advice.

The Pacific ridley is protected at Bigi Santi in Surinam but not farther east where there are important breeding aggregations. Although there is protective legislation in West Africa, Burma and India, legal harvesting occurs and it is extremely difficult to police the exploitation.

The Red Data Book lists the Pacific ridley as species category 2. This reads as follows: 'Rare. Not under immediate threat of extinction, but occurring in such small numbers and/or in such a restricted or specialised habitat that it could quickly disappear. Requires careful watching.'

THE HAWKSBILL TURTLE

The situation facing the hawksbill is typical of many animals whose fate has depended on the vagaries of fashion. From earliest times the species was hunted for its shell (tortoiseshell) but the development of plastics took the hunting pressure off the species and for a time it appeared less threatened than many other sea turtles. This is because the adult turtles are not eaten by most people although the eggs are used for food as with all species. Furthermore, the hawksbill nests very rapidly, and nesting is more diffuse than in most other species both seasonally and geographically with the result that a substantial proportion of the natural egg production is not molested.

Unfortunately the demand for tortoiseshell has returned. Calipee from the hawksbill turtle is also in demand now to augment decreasing quantities of green turtle calipee, and the skin from the soft parts can be sold to leather manufacturers. Professor Archie Carr is highly doubtful that the presumably small world populations of hawksbill turtles can long survive the spread of this new commerce. Writing in the Bulletin of the International Union for the Conservation of Nature and Natural Resources in January 1969 he said, 'This drain (imposed by the growing demand for tortoiseshell), stimulated also by the calipee and leather trade and combined with the constant raiding by egg hunters, makes *Eretmochelys* seem *one of the most clearly endangered genera of reptile in the entire world.*' (My italics).

What can be done to save this, the most decidedly tropical of the world's marine turtles? Apart from trying to bring about an improved conservation situation worldwide, by encouraging rationalised exploitation based on sound scientific advice, and backed up by effective legislation to control the level of exploitation, there are two main lines of action in my view. Firstly one should ensure that hawksbill rookeries in 'safe' areas are mapped and brought to the attention of governments so that they can be protected. This would appear to be obvious but requires to be stated as it has not been done. Australia provides an excellent example of this. We are just becoming aware of all the most important green turtle rookeries in Queensland. As yet no important Australian rookery for the hawksbill has been reported in the literature. Work has not yet begun to delineate the main turtle rookeries in Western Australia and the Northern Territory, yet Australia as a Continent is rich in sea turtle resources, as they have been little exploited.

This situation is particularly topical at present regarding the hawksbill as we have only this year got clear evidence of the first important rookery areas in Australia. These are on islands of the Torres Strait, northern Queensland. We will carry out work on these islands later in the year.

The other situation which requires investigation is the possibility of farming hawksbills to provide tortoiseshell etc. without slaughtering wild individuals. The hawksbill is very easy to rear in captivity and if farming proved to be a commercial undertaking wild populations would soon return to the situation they enjoyed following the advent of plastics. The aim would be to satisfy the commercial demand for tortoiseshell from the farms. This would result in depressing the price for tortoiseshell, which is high as a direct reflection of short supply, and falling prices would surely result in reduced hunting effort. Conservation must at all times try to take a positive stand.

The Red Data Book lists the status of the hawksbill as species category 1 (the highest priority category) which reads as follows: 'Endangered. Actively threatened with extinction. Continued survival unlikely without the implementation of special protective measures.'

THE LEATHERY TURTLE

For some considerable time I have been particularly worried about the future of this species of turtle, which is the only member of its family. Its problems have been overlooked in recent years as a result of the fact that it is not being actively worked upon by anyone in a position to loudly pronounce upon its status, and because the most famous rookery (that at Trengganu in East Malaya) is the subject of intensive, but apparently well organised, exploitation.

My own view is that the situation at Trengganu is unsatisfactory. Virtually every clutch of eggs laid on the beach is taken by licensed egg collectors for sale for human consumption. Against this a small conservation scheme operates in which eggs are protected until they hatch and the hatchlings are then liberated. There is no evidence that this scheme is protecting sufficient eggs to offset the very efficient egg collection. Indeed a few simple calculations with pencil and paper will lead any competent ecologist to believe the reverse to be the case. The conservation programme there released 26,581 hatchlings in the five year period 1961–65, and about 48,000 in the three years 1966–68. Pritchard (1971) points out that 16,000 hatchlings would represent the production of only two or three good nesting nights and, of course, the turtles nest for many months. It is essential, therefore, that the conservation effort be greatly increased. I have visited the Trengganu rookery and prepared a plan for its future (Bustard, 1971a).

The leathery turtle, like the hawksbill, is listed in the I.U.C.N. Red Data Book as category 1. However, it is also given what is called 'star listing' (the data are listed on a pink page) together with Kemp's ridley which means that the species is critically endangered. Yet little appears to be being done to improve its status!

Part of the confusion surrounding the status of the leathery turtle stems from a reappraisal of Anon's (1961) estimate of possible world stocks. At that time the evidence available suggested there might be as few as 1000 mature females in the world. Recent information has permitted this figure to be revised upwards. However, in the absence of tagging work, population estimates must remain extremely tentative. It seems that world populations of mature females may number of the order of 20,000. This estimate could be too high, it could also prove to be slightly conservative. However, for a species with a world-wide distribution, this is certainly not large. Indeed it is disturbingly small when one recalls that at one of the two major world nesting beaches for the species (Trengganu) it is subject to virtually 100 percent egg collection.

In a world survey of the status of leathery turtles' nesting beaches Pritchard (1971) makes the following comments: 'Egg collectors are probably still a serious problem in Costa Rica . . . In Trinidad the present situation is not very hopeful . . . The main hope is for parties of sightseers and tourists to gather round each nesting turtle in such numbers that no poacher would dare

23. (a) One-year-old Heron Island green turtle, reared in captivity by the Tanis's.

(b) Katie Pau meets a five-year-old green turtle reared by the Tanis's.

24. (a) One-year-old loggerhead raised by the Tanis's. Note the prickly posterior edges of the carapace shields, particularly the centrals, at this age.
(b) Close-up of an Australian hawksbill turtle showing the pronounced 'beak' of this species.

attempt to kill the turtle. In Guyana the situation is probably hopeless, and many – possibly most – nesting turtles are killed quite legally ... In Surinam the leatherback enjoys complete (effective) protection. In French Guiana (where there is an extremely large rookery) sea turtles and their eggs are now protected by law; there are no enforcement personnel, but the beach where most of the leatherbacks nest is so remote that egg collectors are very rare ... Nothing is known of the survival situation or prospects of the eastern Atlantic leatherback colonies, though it is very likely that human predation is intensive.' Pritchard notes that the small rookeries in Tongaland (Natal) and Mexico are probably safe with little poaching. Finally he states, 'Koford's discovery in September 1969 of remains of at least 28 slaughtered leatherbacks on one kilometre of beach ... in Peru may indicate that a nesting colony there is being decimated.'

The above is not pleasant reading. In addition to confirming a very high level of predation on the species it demonstrates how little is yet known about its rookeries. Without this information it is totally impossible to plan concerted world-wide action to save the species. In view of the above statement by Pritchard it is extremely curious that he writes elsewhere of the leathery turtle, 'In fact it may be the least seriously threatened of the sea turtles' (Pritchard, 1969), and that Professor Archie Carr stated that the leathery turtle 'may have the least dreary outlook' (Carr, 1968). In my opinion, we have a larger population of green turtles in Queensland than *the total world population of the leathery turtle*. Since the green turtle is totally and effectively protected throughout Queensland at all times and the leathery turtle, as Pritchard has shown, is subject to intensive depredation by man almost everywhere, these figures are even misleading.

There is an urgent need to awaken informed interest among conservationists and people interested in nature world-wide to the real situation facing the various species of sea turtles. If the turtle experts themselves cannot agree on the basis of the available data then hope for a wider dissemination of information is indeed grim.

Carr (1968) after stating that eggs not adults form about the entire harvest of the leathery turtle commented as follows:

'The mild optimism I expressed over the survival outlook of the leatherback is based on the belief that cutting off the egg traffic could be done without great effort or expense. At the big Malayan rookery, for example, the whole operation could probably be bought out for a few thousand dollars.'

In my view optimism should be curtailed until this has been achieved. The fact remains that this has not yet been done. If, as Professor Carr believes, it could be done 'without great effort or expense' then it would appear that conservationists are not very active in trying to save the leathery turtle!

Professor Carr continues his statement as follows: 'At the African and Surinam colonies the problem appears to be arranging effective patrol of the beaches. In Costa Rica the situation is somewhere between those of Malaya and Tongaland. Taking any turtle eggs is against the law in Costa Rica; but the Matina beach remains wholly unguarded and the *veladores* – the egg hunters – do as they please. Eggs are bootlegged out on mule cars and in canoes and sold with only moderate surreption in the coastal towns, and clandestinely, even in the capital.'

In view of this statement the reader may be excused if he is somewhat dubious that the egg traffic could be cut off quite simply.

The reader will appreciate that there are many different ways in which particular problems can be tackled. In the above chapter I have merely stated what in my view would seem to be priorities for action and how best the problems can be overcome or at least greatly reduced. I do not think for a moment that my ideas are the only possible solutions. They are put forward as a plan for positive action.

Identification Key for the World's Sea Turtles

Shell covered with horny scutes (tortoiseshell), a claw present
on each forelimb   I
Shell without horny scutes, forelimbs lack claws   II

I. A. Four costal scutes on either side of carapace (Fig. 14a, C_1–C_4);
nuchal (N) separated from the first costal (C_1) by first vertebra
(V_1).

    1. One pair of elongated prefrontals (Fig. 15a, pf), scutes of the
shell do not overlap.

        a. Scales on upper surfaces of distal half of front flippers
large (Fig. 16a). Areas of much smaller scales between the
phalanges lacking. Postocular count usually four. Shell
coloration usually light to dark brown with darker markings giving a mottled effect.

green turtle (Chelonia mydas) Plate 2/3

        b. Distal half of front flippers with single rows of large scales
extending along phalanges. Many minute scales or
wrinkled skin present on intervening areas (Fig. 16b).
Three postoculars. Shell greatly depressed, marginals
(M) curve upwards. Shell coloration olive-grey.

flatback (Chelonia depressa) Plate 2/3

    2. Two pairs of prefrontals (Fig. 15b, pf); scales of the shell over-
lapping like the tiles on a roof. Shell coloration amber with
streak-like markings of red-brown, black and yellow.

hawksbill (Eretmochelys imbricata) Plate 2/3

B. Five or more costal shields on either side of carapace (Fig. 14b–c,
C_1–C_5); nuchal (N) in contact with first costal (C_1) (Fig. 14b–c);
two pairs of prefrontals or a group of five or more shields and
scales on the prefrontal region (Fig. 15c).

    1. Five (rarely six) costal shields on either side of carapace
(Fig. 14b, C_1–C_5).

        a. Shell always considerably longer than wide. Inframarginal
scutes lack pores. Shell coloration reddish brown to
brown.

loggerhead (Caretta caretta) Plate 2/3

b. Carapace extremely broad in relation to its length; may be even broader than long. Inframarginals with a pore (minute opening) at hind border. Carapace grey-brown to blackish or olive-green.

Kemp's ridley (*Lepidochelys kempi*) Plate 2/3

2. Six to nine costal shields on either side of carapace (Fig. 14c). Shell relatively broad. Shell coloration grey-green to dark brown. olive ridley (*Lepidochelys olivaceas*) Plate 2/3

II. Shell covered with a thick leathery skin and strongly tapering towards rear (Fig. 14d). Forelimbs lack claws. Coloration of upper parts blackish. Small irregular white or pinkish spots often present.

leathery turtle (*Dermochelys coriacea*) Plate 2/3

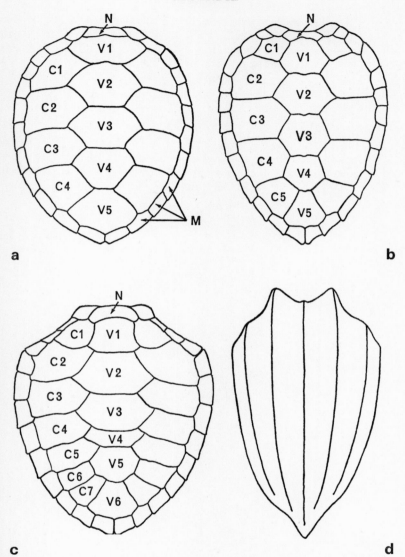

FIG. 14 Appearance of carapace and arrangement of shields, (a) in *Chelonia* and *Eretmochelys*, (b) in *Caretta* (*Lepidochelys kempi* has similar shield arrangement but carapace is much broader), (c) in *Lepidochelys olivacea*, and (d) in *Dermochelys coriacea*. N – nuchal, C – costal, V – vertebral, M – marginal.

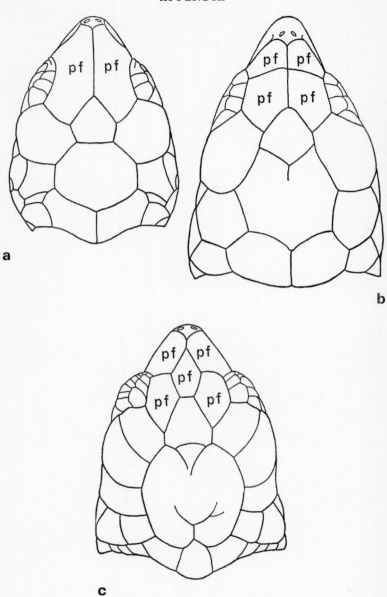

FIG. 15 Arrangement and appearance of head shields, (a) in *Chelonia*, (b) in *Eremochelys*, and (c) in *Caretta* and *Lepidochelys*. Pf – prefrontals.

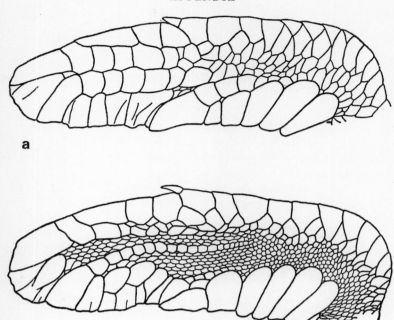

a

b

FIG. 16 Left front flipper of (a) *Chelonia mydas* and (b) *Chelonia depressa* to show difference in scalation.

References

In these references the author's name is followed by the date of publication and the title of the book or article. In the case of books the name of the publisher and place of publication are then listed. For papers, as scientific articles are called, the name of the periodical is given together with the volume number (italicised) and the pagination so that the paper can be located readily.

ANON, (1961) 'The leathery turtle or luth.' *Oryx 6*: 116–25.

BARBOUR, T. (1914) 'On some Australian Reptiles.' *Proc. Biol. Soc. Wash. 27*: 201-6.

BAUR, G. (1890) 'The genera of the Cheloniidae.' *Am. Nat. 24*: 486–7.

BEEBE, C. W. (1938) *Zara Venture*. Harcourt, Brace and Co. New York.

BOULENGER, G. A. (1889) 'Catalogue of the chelonians, rhynchocephalians and crocodiles in the British Museum (Natural History).' Second edn. London.

BRANDRETH, H. R. (1835) 'Communications on the island of Ascension. I. Notes communicated by Captain H. R. Brandreth, R.E.' *Journ. Geog. Soc.* London. *5*: 243–56.

BRONGERSMA, L. D. (1969) 'Miscellaneous notes on Turtles. II.' *Proc. K. Ned. Acad. Wet. Sci. C. 72*: 76–102.

BUSTARD, H. R. (1967) 'Mechanism of nocturnal emergence from the nest in green turtle hatchlings.' *Nature 214*: 317.

BUSTARD, H. R. (1969) 'Marine turtles in Queensland, Australia.' pp. 80–7 in *Marine Turtles I.U.C.N. Publs. N.S. Supp. Paper* No. 20 Morges, Switzerland.

BUSTARD, H. R. (1970a) 'The adaptive significance of coloration in hatchling green sea turtles.' *Herpetologica, 26*: 224–7.

BUSTARD, H. R. (1970b) 'Turtles and an iguana in Fiji.' *Oryx 10*: 317–22.

BUSTARD, H. R. (1970c) *Australian Lizards*. Collins. Sydney.

BUSTARD, H. R. (1971a) 'Conservation and rational exploitation of the leathery turtle, *Dermochelys coriacea*.' *Oryx*.

BUSTARD, H. R. (1971b) 'Temperature and water tolerances of incubating sea turtle eggs.' *Brit. J. Herpetol. 4*: 196–8.

BUSTARD, H. R. (1972) 'Turtles of coral reefs and coral islands' in *Coral Reefs* Vol. 1 edited by O. A. Jones and R. E. Endean, Academic Press, New York.

BUSTARD, H. R. and GREENHAM, P. M. (1968) 'Physical and Chemical factors affecting hatching in the green sea turtle, *Chelonia mydas* (L.).' *Ecology 49*: 269–76.

BUSTARD, H. R. and GREENHAM, P. M. (1969) 'Nesting behavior of the green sea turtle on a Great Barrier Reef island.' *Herpetologica 25*: 93–102.

BUSTARD, H. R., GREENHAM, P. M. and LIMPUS, C. (1971) 'Nesting behavior of loggerhead and flatback turtles in Queensland, Australia.' *Proc. K. Ned. Acad. Sci. C.*

BUSTARD, H. R. and LIMPUS, C. (1969) 'Observations on the flatback turtle *Chelonia depressa* Garman.' *Herpetologica 25*: 29–34.

BUSTARD, H. R. and LIMPUS, C. (1970) 'First international recapture of an Australian tagged loggerhead.' *Herpetologica 26*: 358–9.

BUSTARD, H. R. and LIMPUS, C. (1971) 'Loggerhead turtle movements.' *Brit. J. Herpetol. 4*: 228–30.

BUSTARD, H. R., SIMKISS, K. and JENKINS, N. K. (1969) 'Some analysis of artificially incubated eggs and hatchlings of green and loggerhead sea turtles.' *J. Zool. London 158*: 311–5.

BUSTARD, H. R. and TOGNETTI, K. P. (1969) 'Green sea turtles: a discrete simulation of density-dependent population regulation.' *Science 163*: 939–41.

CALDWELL, D. K. and CALDWELL, M. C. (1969) 'Addition of the leatherback sea turtle to the known prey of the killer whale, *Orcinus orca.' J. Mammal. 50*: 636.

CARR, A. (1952) *Handbook of Turtles*. Comstock. New York.

CARR, A. (1954) 'The passing of the fleet.' *A.I.B.S. Bull.* Oct. 1954: 17–19.

CARR, A. (1962) 'Orientation problems in the high seas travel and terrestrial movements of marine turtles.' Paper read at Inter-disciplinary Conference on the use of Telemetry in Animal Behavior and Physiology. *Amer. Scient. 50*: 359–74.

CARR, A. (1968) *The turtle: a natural history*. Cassell. London. (Published in the United States 1967 as '*So excellent a Fishe. A natural history of Sea Turtles*' Natural History Press. New York).

REFERENCES

CARR, A. (1969) 'Sea turtle resources of the Caribbean and Gulf of Mexico.' *I.U.C.N. Bull 2*: 74–5.

CARR, A. and CARR, M. H. (1970) 'Modulated reproductive periodicity in *Chelonia*.' *Ecology 51*: 335–7.

CARR, A. and GIOVANNOLI, L. (1957) 'The ecology and migrations of sea turtles (2) Results of field work in Costa Rica, 1955.' *Amer. Mus. Novit.* No. 1835: 1–32.

CARR, A. and HIRTH, H. (1961) 'Social facilitation in green turtle siblings.' *Anim. Behav. 9*: 68–70.

CARR, A., HIRTH, H. and OGREN, L. (1966) 'The ecology and migrations of sea turtles, 6. The Hawksbill Turtle in the Caribbean Sea.' *Amer. Mus. Novit.* No. 2248: 1–29.

CARR, A. and OGREN, L. (1960) 'The ecological migrations of sea turtles. 4. The Green Turtle in the Caribbean Sea.' *Bull. Amer. Mus. Nat. Hist. 121*: article 1, 1–48.

COLBERT, E. H. (1962) *Dinosaurs: Their discovery and their world*. Hutchinson. London.

COGGER, H. G. and LINDNER, D. (1969) 'Marine turtles in northern Australia.' *Australian Zoologist 15*: 150–9.

DAMPIER, C. W. (1697) *A new voyage round the world*. James Knapton. London. (A 1906 edn. of Dampier's Voyages in 2 vols., edited by John Masefield, was published by Grant Richards, London.)

DRESDEN, D. and GOUDRIAAN, J. (1948) 'Het Welvaartsplan Nederlandsche Antillen 1946.' Van Stockum and Zn. 'S-Gravenhage.

DUNCAN, D. D. (1943) 'Capturing giant turtles in the Caribbean.' *Nat. Geogr. Mag. 84*: 177–90.

FLINDERS, M. (1814) *A voyage to Terra Australis*. 2 vols. G. and W. Nicol. London. (Available in Austral. Facsimile Edns. no. 37, Libr. Bd. S.A. Adelaide, 1966.)

FLOWER, S. S. (1925) 'Contributions to our knowledge of the duration of life in vertebrate animals. III. Reptiles.' *Proc. zool. Soc. London* 1925(3): 911–81.

FLOWER, S. S. (1938) 'Further notes on the duration of life in Animals. III. Reptiles. *Proc. zool. Soc. Lond. 107*: 1–39.

FRY, D. B. (1913) 'On the status of *Chelonia depressa* Garman.' *Rec. Aust. Mus. 10*: 150–85.

FRYKE, C. and SCHWEITZER, C. (1929) *Voyages to the East Indies*. Cassell & Co. London. (Reprint of original published in 1700).

GARMAN, S. (1880) 'On certain species of the Chelonioidea.' *Bull. Mus. Comp. Zool.* Harvard 6: 123–6.

GREGORY, W. K. (1946) 'Pareiasaurs versus placodonts as near ancestors to the turtles.' *Bull. Amer. Mus. Nat. Hist.* 86: 279–326.

GREGORY, W. K. (1951) *Evolution emerging.* 2 vols. Macmillan and Co. New York.

HARRISSON, T. (1951) 'The edible turtle in Borneo. 1. Breeding season.' *Sarawak Mus. J.* 5: 593–6.

HARRISSON, T. (1954) 'The edible turtle (*Chelonia mydas*) in Borneo. 2. Copulation.' *Sarawak Mus. J.* 6: 126–8.

HARRISSON, T. (1956) 'The edible turtle (*Chelonia mydas*) in Borneo. 4. Growing turtles and growing problems.' *Sarawak Mus. J.* 7: 233–9.

HARRISSON, T. (1962) 'Notes on the green turtle. 11. West Borneo numbers, the downward trend.' *Sarawak Mus. J.* N.S. 10: 614–23.

HENDRICKSON, J. R. (1958) 'The green sea turtle, *Chelonia mydas* (Linn.) in Malaya and Sarawak.' *Proc. zool. Soc. London* 130: 455–535.

HILDEBRAND, H. H. (1963) 'Hallazgo del area de anidación de la tortuga marina "lora" *Lepidochelys kempi* (Garman) en la costa occidental de Golfo do Mexico.' (Rept. Chel.) *Ciencia Mex.* 22: 105–12.

HIRTH, H. and CARR, A. (1970) 'The green turtle in the gulf of Aden and the Seychelles Islands.' *Verk. K. acad. Wet.* (*Kon Wetensch*) 58: 1–44.

HORNELL, J. (1927) 'The turtle fisheries of the Seychelle Islands,' H.M.S.O. London.

HUGHES, G. R., BASS, A. J. and MENTIS, M. T. (1967) 'Further studies on marine turtles in Tongaland, I and II.' *Lammergeyer* 7: 8–72.

INGLE, R. M. and WALTON SMITH, F. G. (1949) *Sea turtles and the turtle industry of the West Indies, Florida and the Gulf of Mexico*, with annotated bibliography. Univ. of Miami Press. Miami.

KENYON, K. W. and RICE, D. W. (1959) 'Life history of the Hawaiian monk seal.' *Pacific Sci.* 23: 215–52.

LOVERIDGE, A. (1934) 'Australian Reptiles in the Museum of Comparative Zoology, Cambridge, Massachusetts.' *Bull. Mus. Comp. Zool.* Harvard 77: 243–383.

LYNN, W. G. and ULLRICH, M. C. (1950) 'Experimental production of shell abnormalities in turtles.' *Copeia 1950*: 253–62.

MOORHOUSE, F. W. (1933) 'Notes on the green turtle (*Chelonia mydas*).' *Reports Great Barrier Reef Committee 4* (1): 1–22.

MUSGRAVE, A. and WHITLEY, G. P. (1926) 'From sea to soup, an account of the turtles of North-West Islet.' *Austral. Mus. Mag. 2*: 331–6.

McCULLOCH, A. R. (1908) 'A new genus and species of turtle from North Australia.' *Rec. Aust. Mus. 7*: 126–8.

McNEILL, F. (1955) 'Saving the green turtle of the Great Barrier Reef.' *Austral. Mus. Mag. 11*: 278–82.

OLIVER, J. A. (1955) *The Natural history of North American Amphibians and Reptiles*. Van Nostrand. Princeton.

OLSON, E. C. (1947) 'The family Diadectidae and its bearing on the classification of reptiles.' *Fieldiana, Geol.* Chicago *11*: No. 1: 1–53.

PARSONS, J. J. (1962) *The green turtle and man*. University of Florida Press. Gainesville.

POWER, C. (1835) 'Communications on the island of Ascension. 2. Extract from a private letter by Mrs Colonel Power.' *Journ. Geog. Soc. Lond. 5*: 256–62.

PRITCHARD, P. (1969) 'Sea turtles of the Guianas.' *Bull. Fla. State Mus. Biol. Sci. 13*: 85–140.

PRITCHARD, P. *editor* (1971) 'Leathery Turtle (*Dermochelys coriacea*).' I.U.C.N. Publs. Morges, Switzerland.

ROMER, A. S. (1956) *Osteology of the Reptiles*. University of Chicago Press. Chicago.

SIEBENROCK, F. (1909) 'Synopsis der rezenten Schildkröten.' *Zool. Jahb. Jena* Suppl. 10: 427–618.

SMITH, M. A. (1931) *The Fauna of British India, including Ceylon and Burma. Reptilia and Amphibia*. Vol. 1 Loricata, Testudines. Francis and Taylor. London.

WERMUTH, H. and MERTENS, R. (1961) *Schildkröten, Krokodile, Bruckenechsen*. Gustav Fischer. Jena.

WILLIAMS, E. E., GRANDISON, A. G. C. and CARR, A. F. (1957) '*Chelonia depressa* Garman re-investigated.' *Breviora* No. 271: 1–15.

YONGE, C. M. (1930) *A year on the Great Barrier Reef*. Putnam. London.

Index

Numbers given in **bold** type refer to the plates

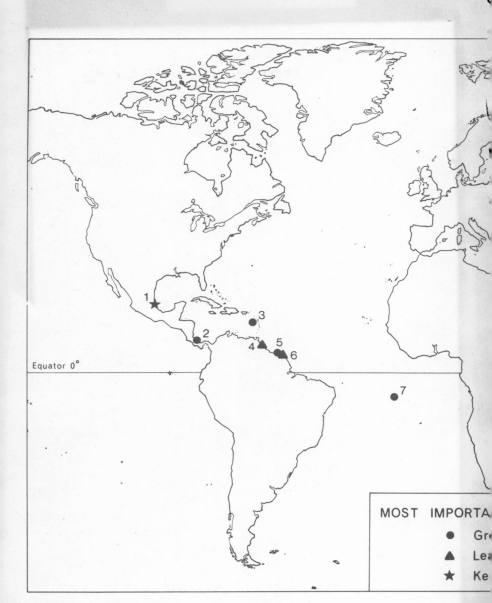

Equator 0°

MOST IMPORTA

● Gr

▲ Le

★ Ke

1. TAMAULIPAS, MEXICO	5. SURINAM	9. EUROPA
2. COSTA RICA	6. FRENCH GUIANA	10. SHARMA
3. AVES ISLAND	7. ASCENSION ISLAND	11. TRENGA
4. GUYANA	8. TURKEY	12. SARAWA